THE MESMERIZING - ALLURING OF HUMANS

VOLUME II

AKASH

AKASH

THE MESMERIZING

Alluring of Humans

VOLUME II

Contents

Contents

Foreword

Contents

Part V: Unknown World Resources

1. African Resource

a. Black Panther
b. Exploitation of Africa

2. Crude oil Resources

Part VI: Extra for You

1. Tea Politics
2. India was divided by White
3. Black Gold

Summary
Reference

Preface

Evolution is not just about living things; it's about things that humans need. The more we know our history, the more we can know what is happening in real-time. Do not think that this is of any use to us. Everything that happens here is just a matter of money. Why can't we make money like them? In the eyes of the laity, money is a piece of paper that satisfies their hunger and meets the needs of everyday life. But there is a lot of psychology behind that. This one book is not enough to know how to become rich. The only difference between a rich person and a poor person is how they use their money. But I can give you some tips. We must first understand the beauty of money and its workings. Warren Buffett owns $ 85 billion at the age of 65. Before that, his net worth was just 10 percent compared with the previous one. Patience and self-control are first and foremost important for making money. Money, whether it is high or low, will not make us happy if it is not under our control. Life is like sitting in the driver's seat, there is nothing we can do if the car is not under our control even though we are moving towards the desired goal.

A good investment is not always to make the right decisions, but also to know how to be without loss. How to make money is one thing and how to keep money is another thing. We can only say the word money in one word, like Survival. Capitalism is just going on in a lot of places. Even it is a very difficult thing. But the main reason capitalism happens is the individual's ability to make money and the know-how to use it. You have to take a lot of risks you have to do a lot of things; you have to cross a lot of paths to make money. But at the same time, if we want to know how to keep money, we should not take too much risk, we should have a little bit of fear and a little bit of humility. This is why money has to end in a single word, Survival. Time is more important for making money. Start knowing how to earn money as soon as possible. Some will only succeed in their last attempt. For example, we know the biggest company, Walt Disney. But comparing the starting point of the company with the current situation is not even a little relevant. The company was on the verge of closing. They ended up doing more than 400 cartoon characters. A lot of people liked those cartoons but the cost of them was very high, as well as their loss was very high. The last cartoon that they made was Snow White and the Seven Dwarfs in 1937. In 1938, The Snow White and the Seven Dwarfs alone grossed $ 8 million. All of Disney's debts were settled. But that last tip is not what people see. The great things that exist, the great profits that exist, the great lives that exist, all things happen at that end. That's why people can't see anyone. The end of one thing is the beginning of another. It does not matter if you are wrong or right, it is important how much you lost when you are wrong and how much you earn when you are right. There are billions of planets in our galaxy, but we are the ones who built the vast empire in this galaxy. The birth of the earth came from a great end.

Are these rich countries fooling the common people who are like us? Why?

Here are some cash crocodiles just for the addiction of wanting to earn more and for the pleasure of being a man of status among others. Thus, we are their victim.

Money is the worst discovery of human life.

But it is the most trusted material to test human nature.

Is it any wonder that a miniature paper rules this whole world?

Let us see what is going on in modern politics...!

Acknowledgements

OVERVIEW

Why do we call it world politics? If one thing vibrates all over this world it is world politics. Money is not the only reason for world politics. After that, some money crocodiles do some things to show their status and power and this world vibrates for its selfishness. Politics is nothing but a psychological game. Some capitalists or managers play games with us for their owners to earn money. For example, Marketing is also a part of Politics. It's like a **"Cognitive ease"** Which means "Our brain wants to make easy decisions" For example "Select a price which has the smallest number of letters Fewer syllables in the price market more instantly recognizable and will make your customers feel subconsciously more comfortable and in control of their buying situation. When you have a lot of information to consider it's hard to make a good purchasing decision, right? It's pretty obvious yet *so* many companies and adverts overwhelm their audience with information in the hope that *something*will help convince them to buy.

They have failed to consider **cognitive ease** in marketing and the way our brains work, but by understanding a few simple aspects of the brain you can make your marketing campaigns far more effective.

The human brain is a creation of nature that is so wonderful. World politics is something very difficult to understand. Because we first need to understand the function of our brain. If we say that the beautiful things, we have seen so far are wrong then our brain will not accept them. Because in our corner we only remember the things we are used to seeing and it reminds us when we needed. Our brain will only show us the easy way out. It can take some time for our brain to adapt to a sudden change in thinking. It is by using it that these rich people keep us like a toy.

> Money has no motherland; Financiers
> Are without Patriotism and without
> Decency; their sole object is gain.
>
> - Napoleon Bonaparte

When we think of world politics, we must remember that it affects our lives because of this world politics. The beginnings of world politics that are takings place now are all in the first volume of the book and a short look at it. The first book covers the beginnings of world politics only begins with wars and controversy. The capital of everything starts with the name of religions. It includes Christianity, which is now the ruling religion of the world, and Islam, which follows it. Not only religion but also their selfishness and many efforts made for the development of their own country. In modern politics, it has evolved from its origin and along with its tricks and strengths has evolved.

I know it is tough to understand. Even professors can't understand what is going on here. Because it's our function of the brain. We need to think out of the box. This is not a human world except for some good people. I just find it too hard to say that this world is selfish. But there are some exemptions although they will lesser than one percent.

Let's start to read about the real world...!

CHAPTER ONE

ILLUMANITI - EXTRA ADDED FAMILIES

THE MEROVINGIAN BLOODLINE

This page has been arranged to give some kind of list of chapters to the different things which 'will be remembered for this part "The Thirteenth Satanic Bloodline". In my compositions this bloodline has been intertwined into the text of many articles, however, it hasn't been singled out without a doubt. Albeit an incredible arrangement has been gloving by this writer on this last family, to take out articles that focus on it exclusively is troublesome. After collecting a few pages on it, a couple of expressions of clarification were as yet required. Permit me to momentarily clarify those things which were chosen:

An addendum to the Be Wise as Serpents book about the British Royalty. The British Royalty is connected to the thirteenth Bloodline.

Large numbers of the American political pioneers have been connected with the British Royalty incl. George Bush and Dan Quayle. A flier from a Christian gathering is Included the appearance of who the speakers are.

At long last, a tad bit of the genealogical data I collected on the Mormon heavy is given. This was remembered for the Be Wise as Serpents book to provide individuals with a thought of how the Mormon initiative connects back to the main mysterious bloodlines of the Merovingian administration. The graph for LDS President Albert Smith is around 1/3 composed. The rest of Albert Smith's (as well as other Mormon-heavy) genealogical work is in a record in some obscure box at my home.

This bloodline is more diligently to follow because it zigzags all around the other 12 bloodlines. Numerous last names are essential for this bloodline (Including the Smith family), but I can give one exceptionally conspicuous one, the Sinclair family. We realize that Satan is the dad, all things considered, and Christ told the religious heavy who went out to annihilate him that they were from the seed of Satan.

SECOND FEATURE

This bloodline is so broad in its many branches that its participation takes in large numbers of the Presidents of the United States, including George Bush and George Washington. The explanation that I gave the lineages of a portion of the Mormon Presidents to individuals back in 1991 in my Be Wise as Serpents book is that every one of the Mormon Presidents ever, regardless of whether RLDS or LDS, followed their blood back to this thirteenth bloodline. Inside the Illuminati ceremonies, the accentuation of the thirteenth bloodline is that they are the seed of Satan. As their mysterious story goes, they are the immediate relatives of Jesus' profound sibling Lucifer. Since the Freeman family and the Rothschild family have individuals who are likewise in the thirteenth bloodline, it is hazy to me how entwined the "seed of Satan" is.

The absolute earliest endeavors to follow the seed of Satan were a few books that did broad exploration on the Tribe of Dan and the decedents of Cain.

"The Curse of Canaan" is an intriguing book alongside its mate World Order by Eustice Mullins. One of the books which I looked with trouble for before tracking down it, was Gerald Massey's A Book of the Beginning. The book goes in and shows exhaustively how the occupants of the British Isles came initially from Egypt. This is Important because (as this bulletin has consistently fought) the Druidism of the British Isles was just a subordinate from the Egyptian Satanic black magic/wizardry of Ancient Egypt.

The Egyptian word Makhaut (tribe or family) turned into the Irish Macca and the Macca of the Donalds (clan of Donalds) presently reflected in the name MacDonald. The holy guardians of the Clan-Stone in Arran, were additionally known by the family name of Clan-Chattons. One more word for family is Mack and the Clan-Chattons were otherwise called Mack-Intosh. Ptah-rekh the name of the Egyptian god Ptah was passed down to us by the Druids embracing the name Patrick, which sounded comparative. St. Patrick's Day then, at that point, is a Christianized type of a druidic occasion that initially had its beginnings in Egypt. The All-Seeing Eye can be found on old structures in antiquated Chaldea, in old Greece, and in ancient Egypt.

The MI-seeing eye addresses Osiris. Osiris had debased parties (saturnalias) celebrated in his honor. The sanctuaries in Arabia clear back in the time that Moses had his dark dad in-regulation Jethro utilized the infinitely knowledgeable eye to address the misleading evil trinity of Osiris, Isis, and Horus of Egypt. This MI-Seeing Eye springs up wherever the Illuminati has been. In the Winter Palace Square in St. Petersburg, Russia is that Illuminati omnipresent eye on top of a pyramid. You will likewise see it in the old Mexican Senate Building which is currently a historical center in Mexico City. You will view this as on the rear of our one-dollar note, and you will observe the omniscient eye was put on Ethiopian stamps when they got a socialist government in power.

The Illuminati is the continuation of the Mystery Religions of Babylon and Egypt. Also, the bloodlines of the Illuminati return to individuals who at one-time lived-in Babylon and Egypt. Exactly how the House of David (the Satanic one) and the Holy Blood of the thirteenth family found a place with all the other things in history I can't say. I'm certain It would be an issue on everyone's mind to let Know if I knew. However, I truly do feel that in some way the thirteenth Illuminati family returns to old times. Is this using the Tribe of Dan or through some Druidic bloodline or is it using the Merovingian's or alternately is it through every one of the three' And where do the Guelphs and Black Nobility squeeze into this?

Regardless, the thirteenth bloodline has amassed a lot of influence and abundance on this planet. The thirteenth bloodline doesn't need anything to deliver their Anti-Christ who will seem to have every one of the right certifications. I would not be astonished if their Anti-Christ to show up genuine will uncover another Anti-Christ. The thirteenth bloodline has kept quiet. I would invite additional Input from informed people concerning this bloodline. The clan of Dan was forecasted to be the black sheep of the country of Israel which would chomp different clans of Israel. The clan of Dan had the snake and the hawk as its two logos. The clan of Dan left its bringing card all over Europe as it relocated west in the names of many spots. The clan of Dan managed the Greeks, the Roman Empire, the Austro-Hungarian domain, and numerous others which involved the falcon as its logo.

Extraordinary Britain is the motherland of Satanism. Scotland has for some time been a mysterious focus. The public image of Scotland is the winged serpent (the snake), and for a really long time, the head of Scotland was known as the mythical beast. The Gaelic language is a significant language for Satanism, albeit English and French are additionally used broadly by the Illuminati. The arranging meetings for the world takeover that a few ex-Satanists experienced were held in French.

The British Royal Family have for some time been engaged with the mysterious. For more data on this, there is an itemized assessment of the Royal family and the mysterious in the book The Prince and the Paranormal - the Psychic Bloodline of the Royal Family by John Dale (1987).They have additionally been effectively associated with Freemasonry. (See the graph.) British MI6 has been a significant vehicle for the Satanic progressive system working behind the mysterious cloak of Freemasonry to control world events. British MI6 is the most mysterious knowledge association in the world.(It is appropriately known as British Secret Service not to be mistaken for the U.S. office by that name however filling an alternate role altogether.)

The British Royalty has filled in as significant nonentities to British Freemasonry loaning validity and decency. English Freemasonry has figured out how to keep itself liberated from a large part of the analysis that the other public Masonic gatherings have welcomed on themselves. Notwithstanding, a significant part of the validity of British Freemasonry is inappropriate. Valid, British Freemasonry is what it depicts itself to general society for the lower levels. Yet, the lower-level Masons by their contribution and exercises are accidentally supporting an association that is driven by Satanists at the top. An illustration of the ploy continually practiced on general society by Freemasonry is a book purportedly composed by a non-Mason entitled The Unlocked Secret Freemasonry

Examined. The book depicts itself as an impartial and complete uncover of Freemasonry. The book states unequivocally that the Masonic request called Societal Rosicrucian in Anglia is simply open to Christians and is a "Christian Order." However, Edith Star Miller reprints duplicates of various letters from the head of the Societal Rosicrucian in Anglia which show that the English Grand Masonic Lodge, the SRIA, the OTO, and the German Illuminati are largely working together. She momentarily clarifies how she acquired the letters.

CHAPTER TWO

THE KRUPP'S BLOODLINE

One of the large examples from history is that humanity doesn't gain from history.

The historical backdrop of the Krupp family which is in the Illuminati would give the world a boisterous and clear admonition for now. The principal illustration that could be learned is how a tactical development and military aims can be completely covered for quite a long time. Today, the New World Order has gotten countless unfamiliar soldiers into the United States, they have acquired thousands, if not a huge number of guillotines for executions, they have assembled an organization of unused inhumane imprisonments across the U.S., they have constructed crematoriums close to these death camps, but then most Americans seem to accept the lies of President Clinton and others very much like they trusted the lies of Krupp, and the German Chancellors BEFORE Hitler, and the German military pioneers who were generally very much aware of the mysterious German development that started following W.W. I finished!

We are going to go into a New World Order that will be more terrible than Hitler's New World Order, yet the power in the background is something very similar, the Illuminati getting their power from their extremely old generational sinister practices. One ex-Illuminati feels that the Krupp family turned out to be important for the Illuminati in 1836. The Halbach and Bohlen families had joined in marriage before the Civil War. The Halbach family had enormous possessions of coal around Scranton, PA. I accept the Halbach family was important for the Illuminati, and the Halbach family was wedded to the Krupps in 1906. Apparently, the 1836 date can't be far away, because the record shows that the Krupp family started getting a wide range of favors from states starting late during the 1830s. Preceding this time frame, such a large number of things went the incorrect way for the Krupp family for them to play any unmistakable part in the Illuminati authority. In the mid-year of 1838, Alfred Krupp, top of the Krupp Factories left his business and went to Paris and afterward on to Liverpool. He quit venturing to every part of the Midlands of England that colder time of year and lived in Liverpool, England for a considerable length of time with an English family named Light body. By the late spring of 1839, he was back in Essen, Germany. After that excursion to England, the Krupp fortunes started to turn.

The Alchemists were soothsayers who worked with synthetic substances and metals. The chemists connect to the Rosicrucian's and the early renaissance specialists in science. The Krupp's since they were engaged with metallurgy likewise have been engaged with synthetics. The primary Krupp known about was Arndt Krupp who showed up all of a sudden (it is hypothesized he came from Holland) and showed up at Essen in 1587 a tycoon and turned into a shipper nearby. His child Anton became one of the tactical arms vendors of the times. Anton's dad in-regulation ran a gunsmith exchange where he made weapons. By around 1650, the Krupp's were Essen Germany's uncrowned rulers" (as per the German book Die KRUPP'S composed by Norbert Muehlen. Frankfurt am Main: 1960, p. 13). They controlled the regional government. In 1800, the Krupp's went into steel and coal, and delivered guns. During the period of revelation when the New World was being investigated the strong mysterious governments of Europe set up exchanging organizations to cut up control of the world. The East India Company was one of the more striking of these first-class controlled exchanging organizations. These exchanging organizations connect to the mysterious world's initiative and the arrangement of medication cartels during the time of disclosure. The 13 Illuminati families were members in the opiates cartel that was set up clear back before the United States turned into a country. The foundations of the cartels, return to Knights Templar's, the Knights of Malta, and a portion of the Italian theocracies who had been associated with opiates exchange for a really long time. That drug cartel has gone on as the centuries progressed. I.G. Farben has been a twentieth century part of the German component of the cartel. Clear back during frontier days, every one of the different mysteries administering mysterious families from England, Germany, France, and the Netherlands were given a piece of the opiates/substance exchange. The full story of the Krupp family would incorporate how they connect to I.G. Farben and the overall compound syndication that the Illuminati families have. Obviously, Gustav Krupp was educated regarding I.G. Farben's mystery examination into engineered nitrates before W.W.I, on the grounds that Gustav told the incomparable German physicist Emil Fischer not to stress over the guncotton issue brought about by low nitrate supplies.

The Krupp's dealt with a more pressing issue during W.W.II in getting sufficient high grade creature fat for holding the cotton set up for explosives. This was addressed by utilizing the fat of individuals killed in the death camps. Since the Illuminati's Chemical cartel and I.G. Farben and Krupp were associated with the utilization of human items, the inhumane imprisonments were freed by the Illuminati's men, and the utilization of human fat, and so on concealed.

In our advanced times, two men of Illuminati from the Krupp family stick out, Alfred Krupp von Bohlen und Halsbach (1907-1967) and Charles "Chip" Bohlen (1904-1974). Chip Bohlen's granddad and Alfred Krupp's incredible granddad were siblings. Alfred Krupp was the most impressive and most extravagant man in the normal market or Europe during the 1960s, and Chip Bohlen was quite possibly the most remarkable political figures of the United State filling in as the U.S. diplomat to the USSR for a long time. New World Order pioneer and Chip's colleague George F. Kennen depicted Chip Bohlen with the accompanying: "No single individual was available at a greater amount of the great level political experiences of the wartime [WW II] and quick after war periods than Charles Bohlen."

And yet how frequently are Americans informed that while Charles Bohlen was encouraging Roosevelt to give the Soviets eastern Europe at Yalta in 1943. His family members Gustav and Alfred Krupp were coordinating the assembling of Hitler's best weapons? The world really isn't such a big place at the top.

On Jan.21. '33, Papen told Hugenberg, 'We've recruited Hitler." Although Hitler was his very own lot individual, individuals who put him into power knew what they were doing. The Illuminati, as they so frequently do, put their kin in as Hitler's guide and his protector. Dietrich Stepp, Hitler's own protector, was in the Illuminati. They have done likewise with various others, for example, the encompassed Howard Hughes. Hitler was encircled by Satanists who took orders from the Illuminati first and Hitler second. In the event that you don't completely accept that that Hitler submitted to his Illuminati counsellors, check out a portion of the progressions that he made in Nazi tenets over the course of the years in his discourses to ensure that the world class of Germany was safeguarded. Hitler backtracked on a portion of his stands.

Four significant Illuminati counsels to Hitler were Rudolf Hess, Martin L. Bormann, Gustav Krupp, and Alfred Krupp. Rudolf Hess was concealed by the Illuminati during W.W. II. There is a book out which shows the tactical clinical records of the genuine Rudolf Hess who was injured in W.W. I, and the clinical records of the phony "Hess" who was detained in Spandau jail after W.W. II. For this reason, the Nazis being investigated at Nuremberg giggled when they saw "Hess" without precedent for care, they snickered because they realized he wasn't the real Hess. Bormann came from a generational mysterious family. Bormann's granddad was Johann Friedrich Bormann (b. 1830) and his dad was Theodora Bormann and his mom Louise Grobler. Bormann before joining the Nazis had worked for Hermann von Treuenlels as a foreman on a ranch. He was noted for his cruelty, ruthlessness, and ruling character. He likewise provided the orders for hooligans to pummel a man named Walter Kadow, who passed on while being beaten. Bormann served some jail time for his inclusion in Kadow's demise. Bormann later as Hitler's no. 2 man utilized his situation to institute a few horrible measures on Europeans constrained by the Germans. Every one of the main Nazis concurred among themselves that Bormann was "Hitler's Lucifer." Goring expressed at Nuremberg, "The conclusive effect on the Fuehrer himself during the conflict, and especially from 1942 on...was practiced by Herr Bormann. It was a grievous impact "Bormann held the most noteworthy Nazi position, Reich Leiter, and was Hitler's shadow all over, but most Germans didn't have any idea what his identity was. Whenever Hess vanished from the get-go in W.W.II, Bormann took his position. Gustav Krupp saved the Nazi party in 1932.

On the off chance that it had not been for Gustav Krupp, Hitler couldn't have ever come to drive. During 1932, the Nazi Party had irritated many individuals and had lost significantly in the races. A large number of their enormous monetary allies had stepped back and it appeared as though the party planned to wilt up and pass on. Dr. Goebbels, of the Nazi Party composed now in 1932, "...We are generally exceptionally deterred. especially despite the current peril that the whole party might implode and all our work be to no end. We are presently confronting the unequivocal test." Soon after he stated, "The monetary circumstance in Berlin is sad. Only obligations and commitments." At this point. Gustav Krupp tossed his groundbreaking impact and large cash (100,000,000 German Marks) into saving the Nazi party from their dubious position. Gustav Krupp was maybe the most impressive industrialist in Germany with maybe the best steel manufacturing plants on the planet, and the heaviness of his assistance pulled the Nazi party up onits feet and to triumph that year. Whenever Krupp made his huge monetary commitment, Hitler appointed Bormann to monitor all the cash. From that point on, Hitler's individual budgets and a portion of the party's funds were completely controlled and directed by Martin Bormann, an individual from the Illuminati. I say Gustav Krupp was "maybe the most impressive industrialist"- - simply because I don't know any individual who knows how large Gustav Krupp was monetary.

Gustav Krupp was the sole proprietor, that is the sole owner of every one of his organizations - there were no investors. Gustav Krupp possessed a huge swath of partnerships and organizations and properties from one side of the planet to the other. Nobody realizes the amount he possessed, yet he claimed sufficient that his child who was the sole inheritor of all the Krupp fortune had the option to have his processing plants completely annihilated by the partners in W.W. II, and afterward rapidly modify by utilizing cash got from unfamiliar (non-German) property everywhere.

In any case, was Hitler the individual who drove Germany to rearm and go into W.W.II? Gustav Krupp started covertly rearming Germany following W.W.I, in anticipation of the following universal conflict. The documentation that Krupp started arranging and furtively remaking German deadly implements in anticipation of W.W. II IMMEDIATELY

AFTER W.W. I IS INCONTROVERTIBLE.

I propose that sceptics read William Manchester's gigantic book The Arms of KRUPP. 1587-1968. The German government collaborated. Arrangements were reached with the Soviets not long after W. W. l finished to help the Germans covertly get around the severe necessities of the Versailles Treaty which enormously confined Germany in numerous ways to keep it from turning into a tactical power. On May 11, 1921, (German **Chancellor Wirth**, the head of the German government marked the Versailles Treaty promising demilitarization. At exactly the same time he was completely helping out the Krupps and the military to rearm Germany furtively. Wirth was exceptionally proficient at interest, and he and Krupp did global interest all around the world to pull off their mysterious military development. Today, the Illuminati are doing exactly the same thing. (More with regards to this in the blink of an eye.)

Whenever Hitler came to drive, Gustav Krupp charged the Nazi government 300 million for having subtly developed the German conflict machine during the 1920s, and the Nazis paid it to Krupp. Later in 1943, during W.W. II when Gustav and Bertha needed to hand their whole realm over to their first child Alfred, Alfred actually went to Hitler's mysterious underground safe-house in East Prussia to get Hitler to buy and by causing an exemption for the German regulation that to preclude passing everything in a legacy to only one youngster. Hitler welcomed Alfred with an extraordinary greeting and afterward let him converse with Martin Bormann. Keep in mind, Bormann, an exceptionally ruthless man, was essential for the Illuminati.

Alfred and Bormaun talked, and afterward, Bormann coordinated Hans Lammers, the Nazi-protected prophet to furtively declare: "The firm of Fried. Krupp, a family venture for quite a long time, merits the most noteworthy acknowledgment for its exceptional exhibitions in helping the tactical force of Germany. Along these lines, I desire that the venture is protected as a family property."

At the Nuremberg preliminaries, Gustav was one of the Nazis at the first spot on the list of crooks to be attempted, and Alfred was erroneously not placed on it until some other time. Gustav was proclaimed unsuitable wellbeing savvy for preliminary, and Alfred was given extremely indulgent treatment. For Nazis set being investigated were condemned to death with less proof and fewer violations than Alfred. At the point when the conflict finished, elderly person Gustav was at Bluembach Castle which is situated at a remote site in the Austrian Alps. The American official who caught the palace was Chip Bohlen's brother by marriage Col. **Charles W. Thayer** (at the end of the day a comparative with Gustav Krupp), who ensured the American soldiers did not plunder the palace. This is an extremely odd occurrence, that of the large numbers of partnered troops, a relative of the Krupps is the one to catch Gustav Krupp's palace. Col. Thayer knew what was genuinely going on with Bluenbach Castle before he took off with his men to track down it. The four-celebrated ivy-shrouded palace has a pink stone carport, and an excellent and rich inside. Regardless of whether a guest gets to the principle entryway which is far adequately off, there is as yet a long excursion to the palace. One of the snow-shrouded mountains encompassing the postcard wonderful palace has the incredible cavern of Barbarosa, who is supposed to be sleeping ready to be woken by dark ravens to return to life and save Germany. The Illuminati's controlled media depicted Gustav's child Alfred as a casualty ofthe Nuremberg preliminary, even though heaps of archives demonstrate that he was, even more, a conflicted criminal rather than Adolf Hitler.

The gigantic preliminary records of the Nuremberg preliminary of Alfred Krupp were never imprinted in Germany, and surprisingly today reality with regards to Krupp is obscure. History was changed by the controlled presses to portray Alfred Krupp as the casualty of Nazism, rather than to come clean with regards to how he ran the Krupp realm starting in 1943, and was effectively associated with the assault and plunder of numerous countries, and effects associated with the torment of innumerable slave workers who came from countries everywhere (anyone the Nazis found to capture.) The slaves who worked for Krupp were not slaves. Hitler had made a regulation that slaves were to be taken care of so much each day as indicated by how hard the work was that they needed to do. Krupp's slaves were famished to death while being compelled to do difficult work. There was an intense deficiency of captives to work and radical requirements for tanks, ships, mounted guns, subs and other Krupp delivered weapons, so there was not a really obvious explanation for Krupp's own production line watchmen to starve and pound the life out of slaves on a customary way. The appalling maltreatment that the slaves got quite kept the Krupp industrial facilities from being effective in their creation objectives. Slaves are by and large taken care of and dealt with so they can work, however, Krupp's slaves were not given the nuts and bolts that a slave gets- - they were not as much as slaves, or as one slave who worked for Krupp said that as Krupp's slaves, they didn't have the situation with "slave" yet were like bits of sandpaper to be utilized and disposed of. Krupp's slaves were the most obviously awful treated in Germany and every now and again neglected to accomplish the creation that was needed because of the complete dehumanization and horrendous maltreatment methodically loaded upon them. Slaves were tormented in the storm cellar of Krupp's (the chief enterprise place of business in Essen).

Irreproachable observers announced that probably the most incredibly revolting torment of slaves happened inside the earshot of Alfred Krupp's office. The secretaries who worked with Krupp could hear the shouts of individuals being tormented, and there is no question assuming that they could hear them, Alfred could as well, however he generally disregarded the shouts with a stone-like face, as he did later in Satanic customs. One Illuminati survivor recalls Alfred's particular face. Later **John J. McCloy**, top of the Council of Foreign Relations, and an individual from the Illuminati was given the occupation of High Commissioner over Occupied Germany. He toppled the Nuremberg Trial choices, misbehaving with legalities and liberated Alfred Krupp from jail, and excused himof "war responsibility". The preliminary of Alfred Krupp's W.W.II atrocities had required 5 years and took 330,000 pages of court records. With or without that work was cleared by John J. McCloy- - a generational Satanist himself like Alfred. Alfred had 37 of the best attorneys who had given more than a decent battle for Alfred. They pulled each stunt in the book for their client- - including killing observers, smothering proof, and so on (The foundation papers in Europe and the U.S. depicted Alfred as having not been permitted sufficient legitimate assistance! Nothing could be further from reality - he was the best-protected Nuremberg criminal.)

However, the proof against Krupp was overpowering and the 5 Nuremberg judges had condemned him to jail. The appointed authorities additionally condemned that every one of his assets is taken from him. This was more than fair thinking about all the plunder and stealing from Krupp had by and by coordinated all through Europe. The British and American states never completed these judges' requests to remove Alfred's property, and in the wake of serving for some time (having a get-away from his responsibility) in jail, the Illuminati set him liberated from jail. Alfred was portrayed as a saint in the press, they asserted he was the main Nazi who had property seized (which was clearly false by the press), so it appeared as though he'd been singled out for unique exploitation by the Nuremberg court. While looking to the public like a casualty for losing his property- - none of it was ever taken away!

Today, the interest of the Illuminati to subtly get ready for their takeover is stupendous in extent. Nonetheless, it is following a considerable lot of the attempted and tried strategies of the Krupp's. Before W.W.I, the Krupp's made a Dutch organization in Hague with the English name **Blessing and Company**. Favoring and Co. was used just sometimes by the Krupps. After W.W.I, it was sold with every one of its resources for the Hollands CheIndustrieen Handel Maatschappij (another Dutch front), and afterward its name was changed to Siderius A.G. It was then utilized as a holding organization for 3 Dutch shipyards, their names being Piet Smit in Rotterdam, Maschinenen Apparaten Fabrik in Utrecht, and Ingenieur-Kantoorvoor Scheepsbouw in the Hague. Around then two Krupp chiefs unobtrusively held every one of the offers in Siderius. Thusly, a front organization was created that nobody even associated with being a Krupp organization. Afterward, select Dutchmen were sold the portions of the organization that the Krupp chiefs had. This finished the deception. When partnered insight in 1926 got on and requested that the Dutch government intercede, Queen Wilhelmina of Holland briefly educated associated knowledge that her govt. would not the slightest bit disrupt a private Dutch enterprise?

At the point when one examination the maneuvers George Bush and Bill and Hillary Clinton, they also have worked with front organizations. The CIA is incredible at making front organizations that are offered to different fronts, and whose control, in the long run, gets covered up and clouded. Three instances of Illuminati families with a lot of force however who have their broad monetary possessions darkened are the Payseur's, the Springs, and the Vanduyns. The public media of America have ceaselessly run master harm control for George Bush and Bill and Hillary Clinton. The White water outrage, Vincent Foster, and the Waco occurrence ought to have sunk the Clinton's nevertheless the media has run incredible purposeful publicity crusades that have stood reality on its head. Under the pre tense of doing unprejudiced examinations, the New World Order's media has truly caused refined harm control.

Assuming we check out the historical backdrop of the Krupp's, we can see that humanity hasn't gained from history. The Kingpins of the Illuminati were exempt from the laws that apply to everyone else nevertheless are. Friedrich Alfred Krupp (1854-1902) was the top of the Fried. Krupp

Industrial Empire. He was a pedophile who preferred young men for sex. Whenever he headed out to different huge urban communities, he would get young men. Conrad Uh I, owner of the Hotel Bristol in Berlin learned with regards to Friedrich (Fritz) Krupp's desire for young men when he was constrained by Krupp to supply him with youngsters at the Hotel. Conrad Uh I, would rather avoid being constrained into his job as a pimp and went to the Berlin police. Whopromptly advised him to stay silent? Krupp was exempt from the laws that apply to everyone else, nobody would contact Krupp particularly not even the King of Germany Wilhelm, who was best of companions with the krupps.

The police magistrate Meerscheidt-Huellessem who ran harm control for the Krupps and others kicked the bucket before political rivals of Krupp could get police records out to general society. In Capri, Italy a cave was changed into Krupp's private sex club where an endless quantity of youthful Italian young men routinely physically overhauled Krupp. This was at the Quisisana Hotel. The proprietor was likewise a noticeable legislator who could safeguard Krupp's exercises. Strong gold pins molded like mounted guns shells or two crossed forks (both planned by Krupp) were given to the youngsters assuming they performed well. Krupp would have skyrockets shot off when he had his climax, and pornography photographs taken of his exercises. The pornography pictures got out into the public area and this and every one of the observers to Krupp's criminal sexual exercises, made the Italian government request Krupp to leave Italy. Any normal individual would have been captured and the way into their cell discarded - yet Krupp was basically approached to leave. Notwithstanding, the press in Italy had snagged the succulent story for their Italian perusers and soon all of Europe knew about Krupp's pedophilia besides in Germany where the public authority and the controlled media kept quiet. A couple of German newsmen attempted to get the story out in Germany however were captured. Whenever Krupp's significant other scholarly of the embarrassment she was disturbed and went to specialists who then through the System utilizing actual power tossed Krupp's better half in a psychological emergency clinic in Jena. Nonetheless, tossing Krupp's better half Margaretha into a psychological clinic wasn't going to place a cap on the embarrassment, and suing the newsmen wasn't going to work, and attempting to run a concealment as large and brutal as the JFK death conceal was begun however clearly it would need to be such a huge and savage concealment that it would be challenging to pull off.

In the perspective on this large number of hardships, on November 21 or 22, 1902 Friedrich (Fritz) Krupp ended it all. The self-destruction was concealed, and his body was placed in a disguised coffin and indirect insubordination, to the law, there was no post-mortem examination –even though the law required it. No one, even Friedrich Krupp's direct relations were permitted to see the body. Following 3 days, Germany had an incredible function including the King, extraordinary words were said with regards to Krupp, and afterward, Krupp was let go in a protected burial ground. Since it is presently not significant, current realities of what happened can be contemplated, yet the situation of Friedrich A. Krupp's mistakes and the subsequent outrage show plainly that influential men are exempt from the laws that apply to everyone else, any openness of their exercises can be concealed, and even suicides can be concealed.

Presently antiquarians will come clean, when it is as of now not very sensitive to lie. What amount of time will it require for reality to emerge about George Bush being a pedophile, or about Bill and Hillary's cocaine running, or a thousand and another crime these Illuminati men have occupied with? The Supreme Council of the 330 of Southern Rite of Freemasonry had pictures of George Bush in their New Age magazine holding kids in his lap. For those of us who realize that he is a pedophile the image showing him as a protective Jesus-type figure who youngsters love is nauseating. Will we gain from an earlier time, or will we keep on rehashing it and its outrages? Indeed, even today, in Germany the Krupp name is unquestionably sound. The fact of the matter isn't being told. The Krupp's have had an excess of control over the German media for the German broad communications to at any point say the veritable negative truth regarding the Krupp's.

During W.W. II, the Krupps took a huge number of Jews and others and involved them as slave labor. Inhumane imprisonment at Buchmannof, Germany was made for the children of Krupp's slave work. The infants who were shipped off this death camp would then pass on from starvation and illness. The captives of the Krupps during W.W. II were tormented in little boxes, whipped and so forth, and so on in any case, the socially sensitive line today in Germany is that the Krupps were made to do this by the Nazis. What's more that very sensitive line is a created lie, because various reports show that the Krupp's went to the Nazi government and asked for captives to work in their industrial facilities, and that the Krupp's purposefully set. up very unforgiving working circumstances for their slaves. Indeed, letters exist that show the Krupps couldn't get sufficient stock of torment weapons to use on their slaves.

However, at that point, the laborers for Krupp have consistently worked under serf conditions. A guest to a Krupp plant said, "For all useful purposes individuals of Essen are body and soul the property of the Krupp's." At times the Krupps have been seen as God figures by a portion of their laborers. Is it true that we will gain from history?

Today, the general population is purchasing the System's publicity to make prisoners work under training camp conditions. The stage is being set in the United States to see detainees as not exactly human. The unfamiliar slaves in Germany were regularly viewed as not exactly human by quite a few people of the German public. That is the force of control and publicity. The media can take somebody like Tim McVeigh who every individual who knew him during his life says was a great person who could never have set the bomb(s) and make him look to the public as a mean beast. I accept Tim McVeigh is a patsy for the public authority's own vile besieging of the Oklahoma City Federal structure very much like Hitler firebombed his own Reichstag. Discussing fires set by the Illuminati, the Krupps attempted to copy piles of records before the Allies caught their production lines. A ton was scorched yet many still delicate records actually made due. These delicate records showed their atrocities, Krupp's own secret activities organization, and other touchy things. Krupp needed to cover a portion of the archives at an unused Bohien palace that he had.

The Krupp's have coordinated with all the world-class. The Krupp's representative was an influential man while alive, he could recruit or fire corporate forerunners in a significant number of Germany's companies, since his different banks held the handbag strings in Germany. He additionally had worldwide clout, for example, Banco Aleman Transatlantic (Deutsche Oberseeishe Bank) which works in South America, and Spain is controlled by Deutsche Bank. In July, 1944, the Illuminati's financial masterminds discreetly settled the World Bank at Bretton Woods, New Hampshire.

Illuminatus John J. McCloy, the one who set Krupp free, turned into the leader of the **World Bank**. The U.S., Japan, and Germany are the most remarkable democratic individuals from the World Bank as indicated by the new yearly reports which I have.

At the point when a suitable Krupp couldn't be found in 1967, the Illuminati gave Krupp's Industrial Empire to its worldwide financiers.

Charles Eustis Bohlen (1904-1974) was brought into the world to Celestine Eustis and Charles Bohlen. His dad Charles Bohien was a rich man and his mom's family had additionally been unmistakable. His mom Celestine's dad was the American Ambassador to France in 1893. Since Chip Bohlen had associations, it was commonly settled by a few groups that he should turn into a negotiator. The state division at the time he got had discoloredit's standing together with general society with a few embarrassments. One ambassador had obscenely uncovered himself; one more had been captured for attacking 2 young men and one more had shot himself. Chip Bohlen appears to have been way above embarrassments. Chip was exceptionally shrewd and extremely attentive. As well as being exceptionally attentive and quiet, the world class press and the System overall over the years have stayed quiet about Chip Bohlen's life from the general population. Most men of Chip Bohien's height would show up in the' s Who in America. Not Chip Bohlen. He has figured out how to stay under the radar because of the Illuminati's command over a wide range of data, while staying one of the most influential men in the twentieth century. **Sen. McCarthy**, who was getting on to the Illuminati's scheme attempted to keep Bohlen from being supported as the U. S. "Diplomat unprecedented and emissary to the U.S.S.R." yet on Mar. 2 and 18, 1953, the Senate gave him the significant position.

Nonetheless, Chip's brother by marriage quit his political vocation after being uncovered by Sen. McCarthy. (I had accepted the lie of the press that McCarthy was after socialists, however, I read something the Senator composed which showed that he was out to uncover an overall mysterious scheme - not just socialism. The work the Senator did is consistently alluded to as a "witch chase", yet sometimes the witches he attempted to safeguard America from may very much put this country through another Holocaust, and afterward, the "witch chase" of the Senator will appear to be gentle.) Chip Bohlen likewise filled in as the no. 1 guide for three Secretaries of State - James F. Byrnes, George C. Marshall, and Christian Herter. After moving on from Harvard in the last part of the 1920s, Chip worked for Frank B. Kellogg and Henry L. Stimson. The U.S. State Department prepared Chip to communicate in Russian quite a long while before the U.S. had political binds with Russia. Whenever the U.S. put in a consulate in Moscow in 1934, Chip helped open the main American government office in socialist Russia. The American negotiators remained at the Savoy Hotel in Moscow. The Savoy Hotel in London has been utilized as a significant Illuminati building.

Chip remained in the socialist USSR until 1940, when the U.S. government moved him to Tokyo to help in Japan. As per Chip, he and others were not shocked that Pearl Harbor occurred because there were solid signs that it planned to occur. (See Chip's Book Witness To History, pp. 110-112. His book was altered by an individual Illuminatus Phelps.) After the assault on Pearl Harbor, Chip was set nabbed by the Japanese. Then, at that point, on June 20, 1942, Chip, Keith Meyers head of Standard Oil in Tokyo, and a few different Americans were placed on board the Asama Maru and got back to the United States through Portuguese East Africa. Chip Bohlen deciphered for Averell Harriman, when Harriman met the Russians for talks. Chip Bohlen did the deciphering and some educating concerning the President when Roosevelt had his gatherings with Stalin. **Averell Harriman**, an individual from the Illuminati, preferred Chip and the work he did. Assuming one gander at photos of the Yalta and the Tehran gatherings between Stalin, Churchill, and Roosevelt you will see Chip Bohlen behind the scenes. Chip was likewise at the Potsdam Conference among Truman and Stalin. He was likewise in San Francisco as a member who made the United Nations in 1945. It was Bohlen and other people who really worked out the Marshall plan and afterward mentioned that Sec. of State George Marshall explain it in a discourse at Harvard. It would take a long article to cover every one of the enormous gatherings that Bohlen took part in.

He went to more enormous gatherings including worldwide governmental issues than some other Americans.

At the point when Chip turned into the American Ambassador to the USSR, the Russians confided in Chip to the point of halting their act of having specialists generally follow the American Ambassador. Chip's ancestors as ministers had been George F. Kennen and Llewellyn E. Thompson. They had been followed all the time by Russian specialists. However, things changed for Chip. Incidentally, both Kennen and Dean Acheson both were dear companions with Chip.

Chip was noted for his insight and sincerity by his partners, yet the Establishment has stayed quiet about the full tale about him without question. Maybe just individuals like the CIA and knowledge staff know the full story. For however strong as Chip Bohlen might have been, he has been consigned to being in the shadows. Whenever we take a gander at the photographs of the incredible culmination gatherings, Chip should be visible behind Stalin, Churchill, and the American Presidents. Francis

Hermana Bohlen (1808-1942) was a well-known legal counselor, legislator, and an instructor at Harvard from 1925-28. This is only one a greater amount of the well-known Bohlen's. This creator delayed until there was a check from autonomous ex-Illuminati sources that Alfred Krupp (his complete name incorporates the title "von Bohlen und Halbach") had been an individual from the Illuminati. There is no question that Chip Bohlen was important for the Illuminati. As recently referenced, one of the Illuminati survivors I have worked with was alive during W.W.II and his recollections of how the Russians, Germans, and Americans in the Illuminati held cooperating in any event, during W.W. II.

An extremely close assessment of what truly continued in the background, particularly at the top shows that the pieces of the Illuminati have kept on working together in any event, during wars. They are numerous family members of Krupp in Europe, South America, and the United States. Arndt Krupp, Alfred's child who picked to turn into an expert playboy, purchased a bequest in the inside of Brazil. The bequest covered 43 square miles, had residences for 180 workers (harking back to the 1960's- what's occurred lately I don't have the foggiest idea), had a recreation area displayed after Versailles, and the biggest pony pens in Brazil. His personal luxury plane could convey his uniquely assembled Rolls-Royce.

Significant Illuminati ceremonies have occurred in Argentina and other South American places where Illuminati individuals from the U.S. furthermore different European countries have flown in to take part in. As more data comes in, this creator will actually want to decide if Arndt Krupp partook in any of those South American Illuminati functions. There are relatives of Hitler in a few states in the U.S. (Since individuals move around, there is no reason in giving their areas as of now.) obviously, the controlled media would have us accept that Adolf Hitler, who was exceptionally famous with ladies during his life, and an extremely influential man at the tallness of his power, didn't have any relatives. Numerous German ladies might have asked to have a youngster by him, and there was a number who did.

There is almost certainly in this present creator's psyche that the Krupp has a hold of the Illuminati equation for making various characters who are modified into Systems of Alters. The Krupp family members have various palaces and different bits of property all over Germany, and all around the world indeed. I keep on getting reports of Illuminati mind-control programming happening in palaces, and Illuminati customs occurring in

German palaces. It is a particular chance that palaces attached to the Krupp tribe are being utilized for programming. A portion of their palaces and homes have been remote and some have been left unused to the extent that the general population was toldOutline. What we have discovered is that the Krupp's have taken part in the Illuminati, and were essentially answerable for both Hitler coming to drive and for Germany rearming itself furtively disregarding the Versailles' Treaty. We have discovered that Illuminati Kingpins like the Krupp's are exempt from the laws that apply to everyone else, and are as a rule above getting themselves truly uncovered in the controlled media. The Krupps give an astounding illustration of how a tactical development can be covered up, and how shameful conduct of the tip-top can go unpublicized and unpunished. The same things are as yet happening today.

We have found out around two Krupps who used tremendous power during the 20th century, Alfred Krupp and Chip Bohlen. Alfred Krupp was the most influential man in European financial undertakings during his lifetime, and Chip Bohlen, who was maybe the most compelling American negotiator of the 20th century. We have gotten a brief look at how the excess Krupp's today is dissipated and are not out of the ordinary to keep on assuming a functioning part in the custom life/and brain control programming of the Illuminati. Later articles: The German association with the Illuminati is broad; the Order of the Skull and Bones is a significant component.

Instances of **German world-class soothsayers** who might be uncovered in later articles include: a. "Lord" Adolphus Busch, who obtained Ulysses Grant's (predecessor of a few in the present Illuminati) St. Louis property and fabricated a superb palace on it called Grant's Farm. b. Bleich Roeder, who was a significant Satanist and high-positioning Mason and a significant mysterious pioneer. Berlin was one of the significant Masonic base camps for quite a long time. c. The Johnson-Wilson families. One evil German bloodline which came from the area Tristie in Germany has been working with the Rockefeller and Johnson sinister families. They are dynamic on the west coast-incl. have a house furnished with a torment prison in Tacoma. The Johnson and Johnson tribe have family members in Satanism in Germany. d. The Committee for the Care of European Children brought kids from the inhumane imprisonments into the U.S. At minimum, a portion of these youngsters had as of now gotten Nazitrauma-based brain control, and were set into mysterious families. The German association with the

Illuminati needs further inclusion in thisnewsletter.

CHAPTER THREE

THE DISNEY BLOODLINE

The Illuminati have refined the specialty of duplicity a long way past what the everyday person has envisioned. The very life and freedom of mankind require the exposing of their double-dealings. That is what's going on with this book.

Genuineness is an important element for any general public to work effectively. Trickery has turned into a public side interest, beginning with our business and political pioneers and falling down to the grassroots. The double-dealings of the Illuminati's psyche control might be covered up, however afterward; they are leaving tsunamis of doubt that are obliterating

America. While the CIA claim to have our country's wellbeing on the most fundamental level, any individual who has truly concentrated on the outcomes of trickiness on a general public will let you know that trickery will truly harm any general public until it breakdowns. Lies truly harm a local area, since trust and genuineness are crucial for correspondence and usefulness.

Trust in some structure is an establishment whereupon people fabricate connections. Whenever trust is broken human organizations break down. Assuming individual questions the expressions of someone else, he will experience issues additionally believing that the individual will treat him reasonably, have his wellbeing on the most fundamental level, and abstain from hurting him. With such feelings of dread, an environment of death is made that will ultimately attempt to annihilate or wear out the participation that individuals need. The large numbers of casualties of all-out mind-control are deprived of all trust, and they discreetly spread their apprehensions and doubt on a psyche level all through society. One issue about lies is that one falsehood will require another and afterward another. It's difficult to keep lies single. They appear to need to raise a greater amount of their sort to safeguard themselves. Before long the liar turns into his very own survivor lies, caught in an exploitative web that requests bunches of energy to safeguard his misleading fronts. This is the pitiful destiny that the insight offices have painted themselves into. They should keep up with bunches that manage their twofold specialists deceives guarantee that the falsehoods that they have spread don't go against themselves. At last, they have put out such a lot of disinformation, they forget about reality themselves. A long way from saving this country, the knowledge organizations have spread the malignant growth of double-dealing into varying backgrounds, with the goal that this disease is sullying and killing anything of significant worth in the United States.

The soon-to-come demise of this present country's sway, as well as the obliteration of this present country's ethics, are the after effects of this malignant growth. Individuals who have gone to undeniable level Illuminati gatherings were told in how the Illuminati plan to get the NWO Anti-Christ rule by causing everything to show up as though it has happened normally. The Illuminati have chosen to disguise their activities with the formation of business as usual to turn away any doubts. An instance of something which seems to have happened normally is the O.J. Simpson case, which was arranged in light of past homicide situations which had been effectively concealed. **O.J. Simpson** was a CIA mind-controlled slave, and the whole Simpson case was devised as an intricate work to cause racial pressures. The Mishpucka, the CIA, the Mob, and the Illuminati have all had their grimy hands associated with the whole undertaking.

The whole issue stinks of control and arranging. It isn't the objective of this passage to go into the case, yet to several subtleties. Joey Ippolito, Jr. is both CIA and Mob. Ippolito at one-time lived-in Hallandale, FL, a crowd lodging region that was safeguarded by a police power run by the horde. He has helped run medications and wet operations for "the Combination" which interconnects with the Illuminati. O.J. Simpson's companion Cowlings worked for Joey Ippolito, as well as O.J. Simpson. Simpson conveyed cocaine for Joey Ippolito and the Combination. Simpson's legal counselor additionally is attached to the Illuminati, the CIA, and the crowd. One of his legal counselors on TV said the preliminary smelled of government debasement. Nicole Simpson lived nearby to Carl Colby (previous CIA chief Bill Colbys child). Colby's significant other and children have been exposed to mind-control. Colby's significant other affirmed in O.J. Simpson's preliminary, yet was tended to as "Miss Boe" rather than by her name. O.J. Simpson's mom worked for a California State Mental Hospital in San Francisco for a very long time. The many States Mental Hospital laborers have youngsters who have been customized. Whenever one of the attendants for Simpson's situation, Tracy Hampton, had her brain control programming go haywire, she started gazing for significant stretches at a clear TV and hearing voices. She must be excused. During the Simpson preliminary, Judge Ito gave Joe McGinniss all that fantastic view that a writer could have. Joe McGinniss was the coverup writer who composed a book concealing with regards to the McDonald-Fort Bragg Drug Smuggling Case.

The McDonald-Fort Bragg Drug Smuggling Case included the Illuminati drug-carrying activity inside the U.S. military during the Vietnam War. Endlessly the smell goes. The control of history by people with great influence has been very much covered over. An illustration of how mind-control and its job in control of occasions have been concealed by the culprits is an article written in the Journal of the American Medical Association (JAMA) in the Sept. 11, 1967, Vol. 201, No. 11 issue. The article, which was submitted to the magazine by three CIA specialists (Mark, Sweet, and Ervin), claims that mobs are brought about by mental sickness. While the article is right in the subpoint that main a little level of oppressed metropolitan tenants takes an interest in a considerable lot of the mobs, the article's proposal is clearly a slide to keep individuals from getting on that the modest number of freaks who make mobs may be under mind-control or could have another inspiration past essentially being cerebrum ailing. Any trickery, regardless of whether it is an embellishment or a misrepresentation of the reality of the NWO's abilities is viewed as a helpful trickiness for the Illuminati's twofold specialists to spread. The German warship the Bismarck has sunk because of a little falsehood shipped off Germany by a twofold specialist which misjudged the scope of British radar. The Germans, thinking they were out of British radar range, settled on a few awful choices that cost them the warship.

THICKNESS DIMINISHES POWER

Information is power, and lies decrease the information on beguiled tricks, and in this manner lessens the force of the bamboozled. Misdirection darkens the options that individuals have. It additionally mists up different goals individuals would run after. Certain individuals surrender specific goals because of their mis-discernments that the goal is bothersome or impossible.

PROGRAMMING DECEPTIONS

In the programming, tones and headings are utilized. Be ready to discover. that at some point developers utilize their innovative minds like utilizing the shading "doctrine," or the heading "TURNWISE" or maybe "WIDDERSHINS". During the most fundament programming which is done through LSD trips in tangible hardship tank to establish in frameworks of the Alpha, Beta, Delta, Ome, and Theta programs, each programming memory will be given a code. Where one well-known programming duplicity happens that the developer knows early h to arrange his memory codes so that case, the fifth memory is coded as an outing, and exhausting strategies are utilized to up the recollections of the initial four excursions. casualty's s psyche will be told to fail to remember the four outings. The memory codes are beguilingly intended to trick the deprogrammer and the casualty the same. Part of the explanation the software engineer does this, is that they realize that IF an advisor should stagger onto these first recollections, the reinforcement programming to safeguard these recollections is extreme to the point that the specialist will break the casualty's psyche. Reinforcement projects, for example, Atom bombs and vegetable programming are locked into a pot to safeguard the fundamental programs.

BE WISE AS A SERPENT

The Holy Spirit moved a messenger to express, "We are not uninformed about Satan's gadgets." Christ cautioned his devotees to "be savvy as snakes and innocuous as pigeons." The Israelites conveyed spies before entering the guaranteed land. Inside the text of The Art of War by Sun-Tzu (a book concentrated on today by men in insight), he talks about "stowed away incitement specialists" in Book 13. Sun-Tzu was brought into the world in 534 B.C., what's more, lived undoubtedly until after the year 453 B.C. In 500 B.C., a few men were ranchers, and some were specialist provocateurs. Today, the two occupations actually exist. The cutting-edge American rancher is tremendously better than the old rancher of 500 B.C., so how does the advanced troublemaker analyze? He is tremendously predominant moreover. It seems the Word of God is exact, for it cautions that God's kin will be annihilated for the absence of information. The trouble in getting legit data in the present Big Brother world is appropriately portrayed by a knowledge resource over the Internet, "If you are fortunate and really buckle down, you will discover a portion of reality. On the off chance that you are fortunate and buckle down, you could find the WHOLE truth...as somebody needs you to know it. Assuming you are PHENOMENALLY fortunate and truly work extremely hard, you could even proceed to track down the REAL truth. In any case, no outsiders...and truth be told, not very many insiders ever become familiar with the WHOLE REAL truth."

This book and our two past books on mind-control are the after effects of incredibly difficult work and various supernatural occurrences of God, and what non-Christians would call " loads of karma". The story behind the books is astonishing.

This current book's two writers have needed to "swim upstream" for quite a long time in looking for the genuine truth. One thing is extremely obvious to this creator, during the most recent seven years of uncovering the NWO pretty much every individual who is accepted to be a pioneer against the NWO has attempted to obstruct the work this creator has been doing. Individuals should know that the New World Order made their own resistance sometime before a few of us started earnestly attempting to uncover it. This present creator's educated assessment is that basically around (98% of individuals driving the resistance to the NWO are twofold specialists), and something like half of the advisors is twofold specialists. In this express, this creator knows as a reality that half of the authorized advisors working with customized DID patients have modified DID (MPD) slaves themselves. As of late, one of the advisors around here, who the False Memory "Twist"- drome and the Illuminati brought down, was a specialist who had additionally been on a nearby T.V. syndicated program uncovering that she was a numerous and an SRA casualty.

DISINFORMATION TO MAKE THEIR DOUBLE-AGENTS LOOK GOOD

"A Force" was MI-6's gathering that did misdirection. They would have their twofold specialists pass out CHICKEN FEED (which is what they call arranged data that can be tossed out to general society) to lay out their twofold specialists' certifications (BONA FIDES) as specialists against the British. Today, there are the various enemies of NWO individuals who are really twofold specialists. They are dispersing chicken feed to make individuals think they are genuine. Incidentally, it is fascinating to note for the individuals who acknowledge how significant merry go rounds are to programming that MI-6 (HO in Vauxhall Cross, Eng., with a preparation ctr. at Ft. Monckton, close to Gosport, so. Eng.) is nicknamed (really its cryptonym) "Merry go round" by its girl association Mossad (authoritatively also known as Central Intelligence Collection Agency).

An illustration of a twofold specialist who is famous among Christians is an Illuminati which named Gretchen Passantino, who visits around to Christian meetings deprecating brain control. Dr. Loreda Fox reports in The Spiritual and Clinical Dimensions of MPD that 74% of ladies mishandled by SRA come from "Christian homes." The Christian temples are vigorously penetrated.

SLEEPER AGENTS

Setting somebody someplace in the public arena and allowing them to have an ordinary existence for quite a long time while never being utilized is intended to give an authentic distraction concerning what they are about. Mind-controlled slaves make brilliant sleepers. The idea of making sleeper specialists is not confidential. The CIA has freely conceded that they attempted to find long-range sleeper specialists in the Los Niñios offspring of Republican Spain who was the relatives of socialist Spaniards who got back to Spain in the 1950s. They likewise have confessed to having attempted to get rid of long-reach sleepers in the Trebizond Greeks who lived close to the USSR in Turkey and returned in the 1950s to Greece. As the CIA and KGB reflect imaged each other in their fabricated Hegelian Dialectic false double (which was genuine for the "little" individual) you can well envision that the CIA sent sleeper specialists against the KGB.

DECEIVING SUSPECTS

One stunt (or varieties of it) that has been utilized with suspects is to capture them, place what is happening where the police are in two gatherings - one gathering resembles police, the other gathering looks like thegroup the suspect has come from. After the suspect shows up, the gathering professing to be captured bunch individuals, overwhelms the police unexpected and breaks to some other setting where another police bunch claiming to be significantly a greater amount of the speculate's gathering ask him what his identity is and to clarify his accreditations. Letting his gatekeeper down, the first suspect clarifies what's genuinely going on with him, subsequently giving them the data, they required in any case. Varieties of this content can be run. English insight calls this essential content CACKLEBLADDER because chicken blood is utilized on the police entertainers that are overwhelmed to make them look injured.

THE NAMES OF DECEPTION TRICKS

FOUR FACES alludes to guises utilized by specialists to get interviews. Hang is the specialty word for attracting a casualty into an incitement. A hang activity would be an activity to incite a gathering or individual into a specific activity. This was finished with Elohim City and numerous different gatherings that the NWO is attempting to set up as patsies.

VEILS

The utilization of veils in the mysterious world is old. For a really long time, the vagabonds have involved them for their mesmerizing abilities. Unique mending covers for their kin are kept mysterious and never displayed to people in general. Covers have a shock esteem and interest esteem. Wanderer and other mysterious gatherings have extraordinary customs to make the covers, including utilizing hair clippings from the individual who will wear the veil. Vagabond recuperating covers are obliterated after the patient recovers. Illuminati programming veils could conceivably be obliterated after their utilization. The Illuminati's veil-making capacities (as indicated by deprogrammed survivors of their psyche control) are exceptionally great. Once in a while the developers essentially wear Halloween animation character covers that anybody can get, to satisfy their part in the programming script that they are associated with during the time.

COVERS

A few novices who have recently begun concentrating on the World Order question why the Illuminati would utilize authentic strict covers.

How could the Illuminati need to make a slave who is an evangelist? Why?

Since those new believers will go to some foundation church where other customized products in administrative roles will request submission (and afterward support those requests by citing sacred texts that cause them to appear as though they are God's power over that new proselyte). Since the evangelist or teacher and the cleric or minister are controlled manikins, the believer won't ever get the full truth, barely enough truth to keep him really buckling down for their association. Even though the believer "got God in my life", the Illuminati never let completely go over him.

The Christians have as much personal stake in forestalling the openness of the Illuminati modified products who are large name Christian clergymen running Christendom, as the Illuminati has. Envision what might occur assuming the world discovered that the vast majority of Christianity was controlled by the human-forfeiting, slave-production Illuminati? This is one of the miserable impacts of the penetration. Maybe the subject of covers can be clarified from another point. The peruser realizes that the first-classlikes imposing business models. They play imposing business model for real- - for us it's just a pre packaged game! To layout an imposing business model, you observe a decent item that everybody needs or needs, and afterward, you dispose of all the opposition by either obliterating them, or claiming the opposition yourself. In the U.S., the Illuminati can't have a one-religion imposing business model. In Russia, they had socialism with Marx, and Lenin as the Father God and Gon the child figure. Socialism had a restraining infrastructure on worship.In the U.S., they have laid out a syndication by controlling all the different religiousgroups.

(This writer composed an 800 page vigorously recorded book Be Wise as Serpents to show the subtleties of how this is done.) It's not an issue of what they educate, it's a question of control, with the goal that the tip-top has a syndication. Also, when you, as a mover and shaker on the planet, control this multitude of different religions using cash, shakedown, and modified products under your administration, and so on which religion could you pick to underline the most?

You will pick the one that sells the best, i.e., the best item. Also, which brand of Christianity will sell the best? The broadcast magnetic brand will sell the best. Covers that slaves use to clarify how they treat life are quite often "genuine". A minister, a tactical official, a salesman, and so on will typically really do their cover work more often than not. Their cover is their occupation, their administration as a psyche-controlled slave is just about an accidental hobby. Associations are utilized as covers. The Illuminati utilize military, social, knowledge, schooling, banking, and different associations as covers. (See my Be Wise as Serpents book for a significant number of these.) Moriah's front associations, like the CIA, thus utilize different associations. Here is only an examination of **CIA fronts**, to show the assortment of fronts utilized:

Asia Foundation was a scholarly association made by theCIA.

Palace Bank and Trust Co. have been a bank in the Caribbean that is a CIAfront.

Gathering World Features has been a front made for CIA publicity purposes and situated in London,UK.

Geschicter Foundation for Medical Research (as well as the Josiah Macy Foundation) was utilized asa knowledge front to launder cash utilized forming-control.

Air-Sea Forwarders, Inc. was the legitimate company's name of a CIA front in North Hollywood, CA. The organization was associated with moving cargo. Over the most recent couple of years, this partnership sued E-Systems, the organization which constructs the CIA and the NWO's electronic frameworks, for example, their interchanges satellites. In court, the organization demonstrated that it was a CIA front, notwithstanding CIA disavowals. As this section gives data about a portion of the Illuminati/ insight associations with Hollywood, remember that this CIA front was demonstrated in court to be a CIA front in Hollywood. An accomplishment that rarely occurs.

PROBABLY THE BEST TRICKERY OF ALL TIME - DISNEY PRESENTATION

For a really long time, I have heard numerous Americans say that something is horribly off-base in this nation and that thingsare "going to the dogs", but Americans can't place their finger on what precisely isn't right. Whenever I initially started to get reports from survivors of Illuminati mind-control about Disney's association in their brain control, I kept an open ear, however, I needed some substantial evidence. In the wake of exploring for myself, there is currently no doubt as far as I can tell that Disney (the man, the motion pictures, and the diversion parks) has been a significant supporter of the downfall of America, while keeping an all-around built front of healthiness. In this section, you will realize the reason why Disney is probably the best duplicity of the Illuminati. This writer has perused a decent part of what is accessible to general society concerning

Disney.

This report is without a doubt the most profound on Disney that has at any point been finished. Maybe some portion of my inspiration is that I've worn out on Christians talking and behaving like Disney represents sainthood. Christians, who ought to have known better, are a portion of the ones who have accepted "with barely a second thought" the huge trickiness that involves Disney. They feed their youngsters a consistent eating routine of mystery and black magic since they have been customized to consider Disney's healthiness and all that is great with regards to America. Numerous authors throughout the years have attempted to uncover Disney, most have been halted before they could get their books distributed. A couple of creators who have overseen have confronted awful assaults on their personality and respectability, and have confronted tremendous battles against advertising efforts paid for by the Disney's.

The Disney's power, and the power behind them, has terrified the vast majority away from testing them. In any case, somebody needs to talk to the people in question. Whether or not anybody tunes in, the casualties will realize that someone minded to the point of standing up and composing reality. Disney has not just left-brain control casualties afterward, however they have hassled land-proprietors, taken representative thought's and left a wide range of harming casualties in their way. Disney has ascended to turn into the certain biggest media-diversion aggregate on the planet, and was positioned organization no. 48 in the best 500 organizations by Forbes 500.

Perceptions concerning HOW THE ILLUMINATI LIKE TO HIDE BEHIND PERFECT FRONTS

There are various Illuminati homes, cafés, wineries, and different organizations that are today doing the very kind of severe norms upon their representatives that Walt Disney Studios kept up with. While Hollywood was inundated in moral foulness from the beginning, Walt Disney Studios had severe guidelines. In the 1930's, Disney had a clothing regulation that expected men in ties, and ladies in calm shaded skirts. If a man checked out a lady at Walt Disney Studios, he gambled with being in a flash terminated. Walt was a brilliant illustration of the strictest legalism. In any event, during the '50's, assuming a representative was found saying anything considered a cussword, for example, "damnation" they were right away terminated regardless of what their identity was. Walt would not permit his male representatives to have any beard, despite the fact that he, at the end of the day, donned a mustache. He never permitted representatives to have liquor at the studios, (which probably won't be an essential norm aside from that Walt himself drank weighty measures of liquor in his private office at work for quite a long time). At first, Walt was exceptionally hesitant to have his young craftsmen, who were being prepared by Don Graham, draw live bare models, however hesitantly gave endorsement.

Once more, the intention was not to serve God, but rather to ensure the Disney notoriety stayed clean. With the force of the foundation media behind Disney, Walt didn't have anything to stress over, news about the bare drawing classes and their nitty gritty drawings never arrived at the illumination of day. Behind such severe fronts of legalistic ethics, neatness, and soberness, you will frequently track down bunches of culpability and undeniable level evil ceremony. For example, Hitler (who was by the way additionally a bombed craftsman and who preferred mechanical things more than individuals) fanatically cleaned up frequently (out of culpability), thus did Walt Disney. Walt fanatically cleaned up a few times 60 minutes, consistently. Walt loved creatures and his trains more than individuals. This creator has seen some modifies who had to take another human's existence, and when they remembered the memory, the changes then, at that point, attempted to truly wash the blood responsibility off of their mind. Another model is that throughout the long term this creator has found that a significant number of the selective eateries that are careful in everything about connected to the psyche control and crimes of the tip top. Filthy cash is keeping the spots looking shimmering clean.

Walt Disney took a stab at keeping an extraordinary picture for him as well as his organization. An illustration of this, is the way he detonated in rage and composed a furious reminder when a Disney character was set in a larger promotion. (Update referenced in Thomas, Bob. Walt Disney An American Original. Hyperion, 1994, p. 7.) He had an individual picture manufacturer, Joe Reddy, who worked all day to construct Walt's picture. Joe Reddy was a stooge smoking Irishman who cherished the catholic school Notre Dame's football crew. He likewise was an exposure specialist for Shirley Temple. Yet, the Disney trickery involves undeniably more than Joe Reddy's times of picture making, and Walt's own capacities to make great pictures of himself.

Similarly, likewise with Billy Graham (see Vol. 2 with regards to Billy Graham), the whole Illuminati tossed their weight behind advancing Walt Disney. Ronald Reagan and Walt Disney were old buddies and both cut from the similar pass on in numerous ways. The two men were high positioning

Freemasons, both came from communist foundations (Ronald's mom was Eleanor Roosevelt's dearest companion, and Walt's Dad was a communist chief), both were paid FBI sources, and both were involved vigorously in the maltreatment of psyche-controlled slaves. Walt in every case liberally upheld Reagan's political mission, and thus Reagan offered political courtesies to Walt as Gov. of California. For example, Disney's Mineral King Mountain resort required an entrance course through the Sequoia Nat. Park when there were loads of legislative strain to protect the final turning points of redwoods.

Government Reagan helped his companion Disney his street through the recreation area.

Reagan filled in as the emcee for the first day of the season of Disneyland on July 17, 1990. He got back with Illuminati TV has Art Link letter for the 35th commemoration. Ronald Reagan and Art Link letter both siphoned Disney openly.

One more slave victimizer that invested energy with Disney was Bob Hope, who might invest time on the fairway with Walt. On the first day of the season's broadcast, cameras showed Sammy Davis, Jr. (an individual from the Church of Satan) and Frank Sinatra (a brain control slave controller) driving the diminutive Disney ears at the Autopia ride. At the point when Disney commended its fifty yr-commemoration with a two-hour exceptional on May 20, 1991, the program included individuals like medium Bill Campbell and was named "Best of Disney, 50 Years of Magic." For the silver commemoration of Disney World in Oct. '96, the Clinton's were welcome to assist with opening 15 months of festivities. The topic of the commemoration festivities was "Recall the Magic". A Boys & Girls Club sang 'When you send up a little prayer to heaven' (a famous programming melody). Hillary Rodham Clinton (herself an Illuminati Grand Dame and a psyche control software engineer) imparted to the crowd that she and Bill "first carried girl Chelsea to the Magic Kingdom when she was four." Roy E. Disney, nephew of Walt, told the public that Disney World "is the account of people who grabbed hold of a fantasy and never given up." There is a two-sided connotation to that. Numerous survivors of injury-based psyche control have grabbed hold of the deceptions that were customized into their brain covertly at Disney, and never given up.

Among the guests to Disneyland have been every one of the American Presidents from Eisenhower to Clinton, north of twelve lords and sovereigns, as well as Emperor Akihito of Japan, Anwar Sadat, and Robert

Kennedy (who rode the Matterhorn with space explorer John Glenn.) Both Denmark's and Belgium's rulers who are in the Illuminati visited, as well as the despots of Indonesia, the Shah of Iran, and Ceausescu of Romania. (As a side-note Roy E. Disney was cautioned by Arab pioneer that the Shah was to be ousted.)

Associations that have been effectively working for a New World Order for a long time gave enormous honors to Walt in his initial years like the B'nai B'rith (Man of the Year Award to Walt) and the Chamber of Commerce. In 1936, Walt was given the Chamber of Commerce's yearly, Outstanding Young Man" grant. The foundation's Yale and Harvard University's gave him privileged degrees. Walt Disney biographer Leonard Mosley, who explored Walt Disney for a really long time (as well as composing books on the Dupont's, the Dulles siblings, and Hirohito) wrote in his book on Walt Disney, "The studio exposure machines in the film province had, not surprisingly, made a special effort to attempt to convince me, as an essayist for an effectively persuasive British paper, that this was a city of rebellious divine beings and goddesses, loaded with clean-living, disinfected stars.

"It was considerably to a greater extent an aerated world at the Walt Disney Studio where the exposure men demanded their supervisor was flawless - never drank excessively, never utilized a swearword, never blown his top, never fought with his better half or family, never let down a companion. Also, burden betide any individual who attempted to recommend in any case. Individuals from the inhabitant unfamiliar and neighborhood press took a chance with their positions assuming they set out to compose stories inducing that Walt Disney could be overbearing, unyielding, and unforgiving (just like the case, for example, previously, during, and after the 1941 studio strike). The Disney flacks were equipped for applying weighty tension on editors and owners or, through the promoting pages, against any individual who gathered Walt Disney was not the embodiment of very much cleaned and considerate flawlessness." (Mosley, Leonard. Disney's World. New York: Stein and Day, p. 10.) Disney is maybe the exemplification of Illuminati capacities to make pictures. They have made incredible pictures for things Disney, incl. Walt Disney, Disney films, and Disney's Amusement parks. Sometimes, these things have been exaggerated, in different cases, the vile side to them has been painstakingly covered up. To cause motion pictures that to contain the ordinary filth of Hollywood, sex, and brutality, Disney did a skilful deception and made auxiliaries which Disney runs, which has permitted them to keep their great picture. They additionally never showed the public the in-your-face pornography that was made for quite a long time in mystery for the tip top.

Behind Disney's great front lies hard pornography, snuff movies, white servitude, Illuminati mind-control, and the enchantment of a few ages into black magic. Disney's contribution to these sorts of things will be clarified in this part. No one has sold America black magic as well as the Disney siblings. A large number of films has shrewdly carried the mysterious into the twist and woof of the American idea, all under the camouflage of amusement. For example, it was Disney that brought us savagery and let us know that it was a "win of the human soul" (an immediate statement from Disney's Touchtone Producer Robert Watts concerning Disney's film "Alive" including overcomes of a plane accident who went to barbarianism). Under the mask of diversion and showing us how "victorious" the human soul was they inconspicuously advanced barbarianism.

Mickey Mouse assumes the main part in "The Sorcerer's Apprentice." And yet when this creator has proposed that Disney films aren't healthy, numerous Christian guardians come disturbed and have become irate with this creator. The misleading picture that Disney films are healthy is a victory in Illuminati trickiness. Guardians wouldn't believe what is slipped into kid's shows.

In Disney's "The Little Mermaid" the palaces are male sexual organs. In one animation Mighty Mouse is displayed without remark plainly grunting cocaine. Walt Disney Studios Chairman Joe Roth is responsible for Walt Disney as well as auxiliaries Touchtone, Miramax, and Hollywood Pictures, which were completely made to cover the Disney creation of pornos. Disney works in a covert way in regards to the advancement, dissemination, and rating of the movies created by their auxiliaries.

DISNEY MAKES MALE PHALLUSES INTO CASTLES

Roth regulated Disney's auxiliary Hollywood Pictures' Evita film. Evita has as its fundamental beginning "Material Girl" Madonna. Madonna is actually a brain-controlled slave who has showed up in various underground pornography/&ritual pornography films. (This creator has an underground inventory from a pornography business, that has as of late changed its area of business. The inventory offered a film of Madonna playing out a real blood penance.) She additionally was the primary entertainer in Disney's Dick Tracy film which is accounted for to be utilized for mind-control. During an Arsenio Hall show, Madonna, who as a visitor acted dissociative, was gotten by the cameras during the show kissing her Baphomet ring. Disney controls the items that are related to the motion pictures of their auxiliaries. For Evita's situation, they are promoting caps and different things, as only one a greater amount of Disney's innumerable misleadingly produced commercialization crusades. In Ruth Stein's meeting with Madonna, Madonna seemed exhausted with stopping Disney's buyer items. At the point when gotten some information about the tango dresses and caps enlivened by Evita that sprung up in stores after the film, Madonna said, "Accept me, I don't have anything to do with it. Disney is pushing the entire thing." (San Francisco Chronicle, 12/29/96, Datebook area). In one meeting Madonna states she needs her little girl to grow up knowing Catholicism, however, she doesn't completely accept that that it might work out great for her girl assuming Madonna wedded the dad of her youngster from Lourdes, Carlos Leon. In another meeting, Madonna says, "Really, I'm an awesome good example, since I say, 'Look, these are my standards'..." She then, at that point, proceeds to plug homosexuality, same sex marriage, and single families in the meeting. Walt Disney expressed that it intends to deliver a collection by DANZIG, a weighty metal band whose songs contain "dull subjects". The Disney official statement reports on its by-line "Mickey Mouse is going weighty metal." Disney's collection, BLACK ACID DEVIL" was because of hitting the music stores on Oct. 30, 1996, during Halloween time. As per Disney this music has no evil references, yet has "dull, Gothic and sexual" suggestions. Glenn Danzig rejects that he is a satanist.

OUTLINE

Disneyland and Disneyworld are incredibly popular and the pride of America. They are likewise critical programming communities for the Illuminati to make absolute brain-controlled slaves. Disneyland is likewise associated with giving a spot to ceremonies, pornography, and other sinister exercises. As far as trickiness, Disney films and Disney Amusement Parks rate as perhaps the best misdirection. As indicated by deprogrammed ex-Illuminati slaves, the Illuminati in the 1960's expected to move their programming away from the army installations, because a lot of exposure (heat) was radiated on the army installations. Their objective was to have somewhere that individuals from everywhere the world could come to without raising any doubts, and a spot that would be the ideal cover for a large number of their crimes.

As indicated by an observer, the Illuminati Programmers got a major giggle out of involving Disneyland as a significant Illuminati base for the crime. Under the camouflage of engaging the world, they did illegal tax avoidance, kid bondage washing, and brain control. For scratch named Disneyland was "the little organization of psyche control." When an offspring of 3 or 4 was grabbed, they could torment the youngster and afterward set him on a ride, for example, a Ferris wheel or merry go round that a. made separation from the aggravation, while additionally b. obliging some fantasy programming script. A snatched youngster while ready to be gotten from one Illuminati non-parent overseer by another, could be kept blissful and occupied while hanging tight for the pickup. For a really long time, Disneyland was an Illuminati place for a significant number of their overall exercises. Presently Disney has made different destinations all over the planet like EuroDisneyland 20 miles east of Paris and Tokyo Disneyland. Tokyo Disneyland in 1991 had 16 million individuals join in. With such Hugh swarms, it doesn't take a lot of creative minds how the Illuminati have had the option to do subtle crimes directly before individuals, and general society never sees it, in all the action. Euro Disney has been a cash losing an illicit relationship, however, the Saudis who benefit from its brain control, gave Disney the cash to keep it monetarily in business. Walt Disney Records is the biggest kids' record mark on the planet. Disney through its films, books, toys, records, and so forth hugely affects the offspring of the world. Their film Return from Witches Mountain was perhaps the most remarkable black magic advancement made. Ducktails, which has pondered Monarch mind-control triggers composed into the content, is likewise communicated in Poland and the previous USSR.

From the hour of the Roman Empire (at any rate, while perhaps not previously) the oligarchical initiative, who has been in charge of both the Mystery Religions and European nobility, have had some significant awareness of BREAD and CIRCUS. Bread and Circus allude to the idea that IF the majority of individuals are given amusement and food staples, THEN they are not difficult to control. Walt Disney films play had a critical impact in giving diversion to the majority to protect Illuminati control. Walt Disney's companion the Masonic prophet H.G. Wells in his book A Modem Utopia that there would be heaps of shows in the New World Order. The World Future Society in a book audit in their distribution Future Survey Annual, 1993, depicts Disney: "Control of items [such as entertainment] and admittance to products converts into command over individuals. 'The postmodern US is a gigantic surge of detached items, each looking for a snapshot of our consideration." The universe of wares is our soma, and diversion is the current type of public talk. Walt Disney World, spread north of 27,400 sections of land of central Florida bog and clean backwoods, 'is the most philosophically significant real estate parcel in the U.S.' What continues here is the quintessence of the American way. It is visited by north of 30 million individuals every year- - not just the significant working-class journey place in the US, however by a long shot the main diversion community on the planet. It is plainly Oz, perfect world as an advertising gadget."

Two Disney siblings Walt (Walter Elias) and Roy O. Disney have been at the focal point of the production of event congregations and well-known Disney films. In later times, two different men, Eisner and Katzenberg have been striking at Disney. Eisner and Katzenberg, as well as others, will be examined later. One of Disney's chiefs, Victor Salva, was sentenced for attacking a kid and recording one of the sexual attacks.

As of late Disney Director Salva delivered the Disney film "Powder". (Victor Salva's sexual attack conviction was covered by paper articles like Robert W. Welkos of the LA Times, in papers like The Oregonian, Weds. Oct. 25, 1995, An order.) The effect of the Disney siblings is amazing. Mickey Mouse tee-shirts should be visible being worn by locals from one side of the planet to the other. Disney World and Disneyland are the journey for an enormous portion of mankind, who frequently regard these event congregations as the feature of their life. What is exceptionally regarded among men, is a horrifying presence to God as per the Word of God. The Bible randomly makes this case, however tragically, research by this creator over the course of the years demonstrates that a nearby assessment of Disney and humanity's regard for "Disney" things justifies the Biblical assumption. As such, as perusers of this article will discover, behind the presence of healthiness of the Disney siblings and their manifestations lays cursed things - probably the most peculiar parts of generational mystery the world has at any point seen. Disney's Magic Kingdom has turned into an American Institution that affects individuals all around the world from the support to the grave.

WHO WAS WALT DISNEY?

In the enormous book The Art of Walt Disney from Mickey Mouse to the Magic Kingdom by Christopher Finch (N.Y.: Harry N. Abrams, 1975) on page 11 a fascinating and uncovering proclamation is made: "By definition, people of note are known to everybody; yet, even subsequent to conversing with a portion of Disney's nearest relates, it is difficult to get away from the end that no one truly knew him. Continuously there was some part of his character that was barely unattainable."

The people who got to realize Walt also intently submit questions, for example, he was "smug, unmanageable, and pompous." He could carry his specialists to tears or outrage very quickly. Finch isn't the main writer who has attempted to caution his perusers that the public's picture of Walt Disney was only that- - just a misleading picture. Mosley additionally writes in his account of Walt Disney, "Since Disney is respected by a large number of individuals, especially in the United States, as maybe this present century's most splendidly effective maker of screen movement, I figure I should make one thing gather straight up. I share the overall adoration of a man who's true to life accomplishments were generally so joyfully motivated and exciting. In any case, - and this is the place where I vary from careless worshipers of another god - I need to know the real factors, regardless of how unpalatable, as well as the heartfelt fantasies about any extraordinary man or lady I respect. Large numbers of the legends that have been made by his marketing experts about Walt Disney are unpalatable, mind boggling, and unacceptable because such a great deal of the genuine Walt Disney has been purposely hidden. Walt Disney...had grave defects in his personality." (Mosley. Disney's World, pg. 9) Year's prior, an Illuminati Grand Master and software engineer expressed, "If the world just had the eyes to see the filaments which lay underneath Walt Disney's picture, they'd publicly shame him, and drag him through the roads. If by some stroke of good luck, they realized what Disney's essential objective s."

INDIVIDUAL DETAILS

Walt had dark hair with a dark mustache, and splendid fast eyes and was around 6' tall. He utilized his own facial highlights to piece of information craftsmen on the best way to draw Mickey Mouse's elements. He enjoyed extraordinarily moved earthy colored cigarettes which he smoked up to 70 per day. He got the smoking propensity in the military. He adored costly Scotch Whiskey, red night falls, and ponies. He had a getaway home in Palm Springs, CA called the Smoke Tree Ranch. He regularly wore the Ranch's letter STR decorated on his bowtie. He played heaps of golf with Bob Hope and Ed Sullivan at the ST Ranch. His fundamental home was a bequest in Holmby Hills. The Holmby Hills bequest was situated in an extravagant region where heaps of rich the big-time families resided. It was situated between Bel-Air (a mysterious word for Satan) and Beverly Hills.

Walt spent a significant number of his evenings at the Disney Studios and later he had his own private quarters at the focal point of Disneyland. He had repeating episodes of a sleeping disorder. (For his nerves and a sleeping disorder, he'd take liquor and sedatives.) He'd go a long time on end without venturing foot on the Holmby Hills bequest and seeing his family.

The primary theme at the studio by the staff during various time-frames was Walt's peculiar conduct - he would not be accessible until late evening, when he would rise out of the studio's underground labyrinth of passages, where apparently, he was "talking with the upkeep designs" consistently. The worth of his bequest when he kicked the bucket was 35 million dollars of which Lillian his significant other acquired half. In his later years, when Disney got away, he went to Paris for quite a long time, and 3 weeks at the Hotel du Cap, in Antibes, and afterward traveled on Fritz Loew's yacht with Ron and Diane Disney. In England, Walt invested energy with the British Royal family and met secretly with masonic prophet H.G. Wells. In Rome, Walt visited secretly with the Pope and the tyrant Mussolini. In 1966, Walt Disney kicked the bucket. Before his death, he had researched cytogenesis being frozen, and it is accepted by some that his body is frozen someplace in California, while others guarantee he was incinerated.

MICKEY MOUSE

As per one source, the motivation for Walt to make Mickey Mouse came when he was jobless and saw a mouse in the drain. There are many stories available for use with regards to where the thought came from. Ub I werks asserted he thought Mickey up at an illustrator's gathering in Hollywood. Walt once said, "There is a ton of the Mouse in me." (Biographical article composed by Elting E. Morison,) indeed, Ub I werks told Walt that Mickey Mouse "appears as though you- - the same nose, same face, same bristles, same motions, and looks. All he really wants presently is your voice." Walt frequently filled in as Mickey's voice. A book put out by Walt Disney Co. in 1988 uncovers that Walt Disney told Ward Kimball "In all honesty, I favor creatures to individuals." Walt generally was the voice behind Mickey Mouse, (despite the fact that he wasn't the craftsman.) His mom was crisp for quite a long time about the work Walt did. Around 1940, after much arguing, he, at last, got her to watch Mickey Mouse. His unsupportive mother (which he would inside a couple of years learning was not really his natural mother) let him know she tried to avoid Mickey Mouse's voice, to which he told her it was his, and afterward she reacted by saying he had a horrendous voice. The "chilly towel" she tossed on Mickey Mouse persuaded Walt to stop making Mickey Mouse kid's shows. Not very many emerged from Disney from that point onward, and the exceptionally next Mickey Mouse full-length include animation, Fantasia, had Mickey generally quiet.

Walt's thought for The Sorcerer's Apprentice depended on his very own portion thoughts. Walt had the fantasy which was utilized for Mickey Mouse in The Sorcerer's Apprentice of having "full oversight of the earth and the components." Disneyland and Disneyworld were incomplete achievements of that fantasy for control. Walt's last pet undertaking only before his passing was the fastidiously re-established rendition of the black magic film "Bedknobs and Broomsticks." As a programming gadget, Mickey Mouse functions admirably because it plays on the inner mind hereditarily communicated anxiety toward mice that ladies have. Mickey's picture can assist with making an affection disdain relationship, which is so esteemed during the injury and programming of brain-controlled slaves.

A few sources express that Walt's affection for animals came from the time his family had a ranch close to Marceline, Missouri. Walt started his tutoring at Marceline, yet proceeded with it after the age of eight at Benton School in Kansas City, MO. Walt's Dad had a genuine betting issue and passed the soul of betting to his child Walt. Walt never moved on from secondary school. He had a characteristic love and an energy for work of art, albeit (as opposed to his public picture) he never became capable at it. He enlisted in the military in W.W. I as a rescue vehicle driven by lying about his age. During the conflict, he additionally chauffeured dignitaries. He additionally did a few different things that are exceptionally uncovering. He delighted in drinking and betting while in the help, and he ran a trick where he doctored German relics got on the combat zone to offer to individuals. War relics were messed with to get them in shape to get the most cash from them conceivable. Walt took the fight keepsakes - and dressed them up, for example, covering the internal parts of protective caps with oil, hair, and blood and placing openings in them to make them into costly gifts. This shows that Walt was ready to assemble deceptions assuming it paid.

He could be underhanded assuming he saw a benefit to it. From gleanings from things Walt said to individuals, apparently as a kid, he'd seen the hazier side of life (for example, his dad had a propensity for beating him in the storm cellar) and had some interest or openness to enchantment as a youngster. Sway Thomas expresses, "Walt took an innocent take pleasure in pulling pranks on his folks. He was entranced with sorcery tricks..."

After the military, Walt wanted to have a profession as a craftsman. He applied to the publicizing organization of Pesman-Rubin. Roy, his sibling, asserted that Pesman-Rubin recruited Walt as an individual blessing to Roy who dealt with the office's record at the bank Roy worked at. Walter endured a month until the promoting organization let him go because of Walt's "particular absence of drawing capacity." According to Current Biography 1952, in 1923, Walt and Roy had together $290. They acquired $500 from another Disney, one of their uncles named Robert Disney, and started to attempt to make kid's shows. Robert Disney had resigned in the L.A. region in Edendale, CA after an effective mining vocation. Robert had been close all the time to Walt's dad Elias, and aided Walt and Roy out when they came to California. Walt wanted to concentrate on Charlie Chaplin (an individual from the Collins family). He scribbled notes about his non-verbal communication, facial elements, and his gag techniques. He likewise read all that he could about activity and cartooning. They worked out of their uncle's carport in Hollywood, CA. They were at long last ready to make a decent animation Steamboat Willie in 1928, which turned into a moment hit. Likewise, with numerous things throughout everyday life, the animation was great, yet Walt at long last had the right, associations." On Nov. 18, '28, Steamboat Willie was displayed in a little, autonomous performance center with no development advancement or promotion. Yet, incredibly the New York Times, Variety, and Exhibitor's Herald all ran rave audits of the animation the following day. Was this a mishap? did columnists from this large number of esteemed periodicals simply end up going to this little free theater? No, it was associations.

MICKEY MOUSE

As per one source, the motivation for Walt to make Mickey Mouse came when he was jobless and saw a mouse in the drain. There are many stories available for use with respect to where the thought came from. UbIwerks guaranteed he thought Mickey up at an artist's gathering in Hollywood. Walt once said, "There is a ton of the Mouse in me." (Biographical article composed by Elting E. Morison, p. 131) indeed, Ub I werks told Walt that Mickey Mouse "seems as though you- - the same nose, same face, same bristles, same signals, and demeanours. All he really wants presently is your voice." Walt frequently filled in as Mickey's voice. A book put out by Walt Disney Co. in 1988 uncovers that Walt Disney told Ward Kimball "Without a doubt, I lean toward creatures to individuals." Walt normally was the voice behind Mickey Mouse, (despite the fact that he wasn't the craftsman.) His mom was crisp for a really long time about the work Walt did. Around 1940, after much arguing, he at long last got her to watch Mickey Mouse. His unsupportive mother (which he would inside a couple of years learning was not really his natural mother) let him know she tried to avoid Mickey Mouse's voice, to which he told her it was his, and afterward she reacted by saying he had an awful voice. The "cool towel" she tossed on Mickey Mouse persuaded Walt to stop making Mickey Mouse kid's shows. Not many emerged from Disney from that point onward, and the exceptionally next Mickey Mouse full-length highlight animation, Fantasia, had Mickey for the most part quiet.

Walt's thought for The Sorcerer's Apprentice depended on his very own portion thoughts. Walt had the fantasy which was utilized for Mickey Mouse in The Sorcerer's Apprentice of having "unlimited authority of the earth and the components." Disneyland and Disneyworld were incomplete achievements of that fantasy for control. Walt's last pet venture only preceding his passing was the fastidiously re-established rendition of the black magic film "Bedknobs and Broomsticks." (Disney Magazine, Winter 96-97, bar. by Disney, p. 96 notices this.) As a programming gadget, Mickey Mouse functions admirably because it plays on the inner mind hereditarily sent anxiety toward mice that ladies have. Mickey's picture can assist with making an affection disdain relationship, which is so esteemed during the injury and programming of brain-controlled slaves.

A few sources express that Walt's affection for animals came from the time his family had a ranch close to Marceline, Missouri. Walt started his tutoring at Marceline, yet proceeded with it after the age of eight at Benton School in Kansas City, MO. Walt's Dad had a genuine betting issue and passed the soul of betting to his child Walt. Walt never moved on from secondary school. He had a characteristic love and a style for fine art, albeit (in spite of his public picture) he never became capable at it. He enlisted in the military in W.W. I as a rescue vehicle driver by lying about his age. During the conflict, he additionally chauffeured dignitaries. He additionally did a few different things that are extremely uncovering. He delighted in drinking and betting while in the assistance, and he ran a trick where he doctored German antiquities got on the war zone to offer to individuals. War relics were altered to get them in shape to get the most cash from them conceivable. Walt took the fight trinkets - and dressed them up, for example, covering the inner parts of protective caps with oil, hair, and blood and placing openings in them to make them into costly gifts. This shows that Walt was ready to construct deceptions assuming it paid.

He could be underhanded assuming he saw a benefit to it. From gleanings from things Walt said to individuals, apparently as a kid, he'd seen the hazier side of life (for example, his dad had a propensity for beating him in the storm cellar) and had some interest or openness to sorcery as a youngster. Weave Thomas states, "Walt took an innocent get a kick out of pulling pranks on his folks. He was interested in enchantment tricks..."

After the military, Walt expected to have a profession as a craftsman. He applied to the promoting office of Pesman-Rubin. Roy, his sibling, guaranteed that Pesman-Rubin employed Walt as an individual blessing to Roy who took care of the organization's record at the bank Roy worked at. Walter endured a month until the publicizing organization let him go because of Walt's "particular absence of drawing capacity." According to Current Biography 1952, in 1923, Walt and Roy had together $290. They acquired $500 from another Disney, one of their uncles named Robert Disney, and started to attempt to make kid's shows. Robert Disney had resigned in the L.A. region in Edendale, CA after a fruitful mining profession. Robert had been close all of the time to Walt's dad Elias, and aided Walt and Roy out when they came to California. Walt wanted to concentrate on Charlie Chaplin (an individual from the Collins family). He scribbled notes about his non-verbal communication, facial elements, and his gag strategies. He likewise read all that he could about movement and cartooning. They worked out of their uncle's carport in Hollywood, CA. They were at last ready to make a decent animation Steamboat Willie in 1928, which turned into a moment hit. Likewise, with numerous things throughout everyday life, the animation was great, yet Walt at long last had the right, associations." On Nov. 18, '28, Steamboat Willie was displayed in a little, free performance center with no development advancement or promotion. Be that as it may, incredibly the New York Times, Variety, and Exhibitor's Herald all ran rave surveys of the animation the following day. Was this a mishap? did writers from this multitude of esteemed periodicals simply end up going to this little autonomous theatre? No, it was associations.

The explanation the world class chose to advance Walt Disney after Steamboat Willie emerged as Hollywood's most current "kid wonder" was to divert gigantic harshness that had been created by the Stock Market breakdown toward Jewish agents. Hollywood, even in its initial twenty years, was known as "Babylon" and "Sin City". The film business was not able to be controlled by Jews, and many individuals accused the Stock Market Crash of the ethical corruption that Hollywood had acquainted with this country. There were calls for government administrative gatherings to stop the filthy Hollywood movies. Edgar Magnin, the otherworldly head of the significant film creators who were important for the Los Angeles B'nai B'rith purportedly energized those in the Mispack and other people who were B'nai B'rith film producers that Hollywood expected to safeguard itself by placing Walt Disney at the center of attention as a Christian "white knight with family esteems". (Incidentally, Edgar Magnin was nicknamed "Rabbi to the Stars", since he was "the Hollywood rabbi".) E. Magnin's granddad's retail chain was one of the primary significant records of the Bank of Italy, and Edgar Magnin had proceeded with his family's nearby relationship with the Bank of Italy. The closeness likewise came from the Bank of Italy's nearby connections to the B'nai B'rith and ADL. In 1930, the film business made a creation code that expressed that the business should put forth a unique attempt to make motion pictures fitting for kids. Hollywood straightforwardly lauded Disney in that code as a commendable model of what the film business needed to do.

With the force of the B'nai B'rith and ADL behind him, Walt started cruising to notoriety. Film studios that had been turning out the filth, with loads of sex and savagery all, got on board with that temporary fad to show Walt's spotless healthy kid's shows. Walt was the facelift Hollywood required after the Depression made Americans contemplate America's ethics. Large numbers of the normal film producers were so bad they were withdrawn from moral issues, yet Walt Disney knew dark from white. The Jewish film creators "pushed the man [Walt] they thought about their best desire to the front of the pack" who was charged as a fundamentalist Christian Strangely, the accounts show that Walt quit doing the real attracting 1927, and Walt committed himself altogether to the improvement of the animation business, like fund-raising. At the end of the day, the picture of Walt Disney being the craftsman who has made the Disney animation's is erroneous. The Disney siblings really recruited numerous different specialists to accomplish the craftsmanship. Assuming Walt quit attracting 1927, and their first attractive animation was in 1928, that plainly shows that Walt didn't do the genuine cartooning. He kept on supervising the work, strolling in and unbendingly examining how was being fit his own instinctive preferences. All things considered, the virtuoso animation craftsman (illustrator) who made Walt Disney a triumph was Ub I werks, regarding whom Walt on various events said was "the best artist on the planet". Without Ub I werks to take Walt's thoughts and transform them into the real world, Walt couldn't have ever become popular.

Up was a fantastic virtuoso who had a feeling of line, an awareness of what's actually funny, persistence, association, and an incredible feeling of what Walt needed. Walt treated him mercilessly on occasion, intruding on him, pulling pranks on him, and not being absolutely genuine with paying him, however, he remained with Walt throughout the long term and made Walt the achievement Walt became. (The books Disney's World and Disney Animation: The Illusion of Life have data on the unheralded virtuoso Ub I werks.) Another obscure incredible craftsman was Floyd Gottfredson. Floyd Gottfredson drew all the Mickey Mouse kid's shows from 1932 until October, 1975- - which is a time of 45 1/2 years. Floyd Gottfredson was a Mormon brought into the world in a rail route station in 1905, and brought up in a small Mormon town, Sigurd, 180 miles so. of Salt Lake City. In 1931, preceding Floyd completely assumed control over the Mickey Mouse drawings, he would take ideas from Walt on what to draw. For example, Walt perplexed him by demanding he does an animation series of Mickey Mouse ending it all. Floyd had said, "Walt, you're joking!" But Walt believed that a series on self-destruction would be entertaining. Throughout the long term, the Walt Disney items never referenced Floyd's name. The heft of the fans was persuaded to think Walt did the cartooning of Mickey Mouse himself. (See the book Walt Disney's Mickey Mouse in Color. Ed. Bruce Hamilton, bar. The Walt Disney Co., 1988.)

Fred Moore was associated with the formation of Pluto and some other animation characters. The thought for Pluto was Walt's and it was Norm Ferguson's virtuoso at drawing that took the thought and made the genuine pictures. Walt Disney was granted 32 individual foundation grants for the work that was finished by his studios. Walt Disney's popular mark was really planned by another person, and was instructed to Walt. Walt could make an unrefined Disney signature, so he assigned the composition of the mark to a few craftsmen including Bob Moore, Disney's exposure craftsman. Afterward, after much practice, he figured out how to make it alright to accomplish for exposure. Many individuals who composed letters requesting his real signature, and who really did his mark, imagined that they had gotten imitations by his staff, because the popular Disney mark was so unrefined. The more pleasant looking ones were the imitations. One animation artist who joined Disney in 1940 reviewed that Walt let him know the principal day, "You're new here, and I need you to see only a certain something. What we're selling here is the name, Walt Disney. Assuming you can swallow that and consistently recollect it, you'll be blissful here. Yet, on the off chance that you have any thoughts regarding seeing the name Ken Anderson [his name] up there, its best for you to leave immediately."

MYSTERIOUS PORN KING

Walt grew up entranced with the mysterious and in an oppressive home circumstance. He was captivated with kid's shows, nature, and youngsters. He had a natural sense for quality kid's shows that would interest kids. Sooner or later, the organization got him obligated to them. By then he was their man. He owed them an obligation that they held over him. Covertly, Walt turned into a pornography ruler. A casualty recollects that he was cruel and appreciated snuff pornography films. His advantage in kids was a long way from charitable.

The Hapsburgs of the thirteenth Illuminati bloodline had a sex salon in Vienna, where a pornography photographic artist named Felix Salten worked. Felix Salten composed a book Bambi, which was then converted into English by the notorious socialist Whittaker Chambers. The world class was simply starting to frame the roots for the present ecological development. The book engaged Disney, since Disney loved creatures better than individuals. In the book, tame creatures view people as divine beings, while the wild and free creatures consider people to be devils who they just called "Him." The book starts with both free and manageable creatures seeing people as appropriately having domain over them. Eventually, the creatures view all people as essentially being on a similar level as creatures, a horrendous creature simply fit to be killed.

Disney taught his artists to make the creatures "to be human. I need individuals to fail to remember they are watching creatures." Bambi was to get a Christ-like trough birth, with the creatures hailing him as a "ruler." Due to his sexual issues, Walt at one guide allowed himself toward being exposed to the pressing of his private parts in ice for quite a long time at a time. (Elliot, Walt Disney Hollywood's Dark Prince, p. 83.) Children were told to refer to Walt as "Uncle Walt." An illustration of this was the Musketeers. For the people who realize how mind-control software engineers have generally preferred to be classified "uncle" by their kid casualties, the demand by

Walt to be known as "uncle" is disagreeable. From what this creator has gained from certain sources about Walt's non-public life as a secret savage pornography lord, it brings up issues about different pieces of his life. "A few artists expressed that the supervisor [Walt Disney] appeared to have fallen head over heels for the kid. There might be a trace of validity in this..." The kid, who Walt experienced passionate feelings for, was a little youthful alluring kid entertainer named Bobby Driscoll who joined in 1946 with Disney. He acted in Song of the South, Treasure Island and Bobby's voice was utilized in Peter Pan. Bobby Driscoll was extremely wise and appealing. Did Disney help or misuse him? Assuming Disney was such an up building healthy climate, and this kid entertainer had everything going for him, for what reason did Bobby turn into a methamphetamine someone who is addicted at 17 and kick the bucket inside only a couple of years? For what reason didn't his ability and early profession prompt something positive in his life?

From the people who knew Walt by and by one discovers that he had a fixation on the butt cheek part of living systems. He delighted in kids concerning this piece of the life structures, which he told to his staff often. The staff altered out a significant number of his unrefined back jokes from animation scripts. Two models that got by the editors are a Christmas exceptional where a young man can't fasten the drop seat of his night wear. The young man's concern in keeping up with his unobtrusiveness is the running gag of the animation. Eventually, Santa gives him a bedpan. The second model is the rowing machine utilized on the wolf in The Three Little Pigs. Various Disney kid's shows include the rear end of characters provocatively jerking.

AS A WITNESS BEFORE CONGRESS

After W.W. II, Walt Disney was called upon by Hollywood to affirm with all due respect at the Un-American hearings which were being done by representatives who were worried about the weighty socialist impact inside Hollywood. Walt minimized any socialist impact in Hollywood toCongress. Curiously, Walt's dad was a straightforward Socialist Party pioneer in the United States who pushed a communist New World Order. He routinely decided in favor of communist official competitor Eugene Debs. One of the principal drawings Walt did as a kid was to copy the communist political kid's shows, he found in a communist periodical Appeal to Reason that his dad bought into. At the point when Walt asked in the 1930's the way his dad had an outlook on communism's victories, his dad Elias said, "Today, all that I battled for in those early days has been ingested into the foundation of both the significant gatherings. Presently I have a very decent outlook on that." Walt's film Alice's Egg Plant (1925) was an unadulterated socialist tenet where the red hen (socialist) drives the functioning chickens on a negative mark against Julius the ranch administrator (addressing industrialists.)

The strike at Disney and unionization of Disney in 1940, soured Walt toward socialism. The specialists at Disney freely made individual obnoxious ambushes on Walt and he never pardoned the embarrassment. Disregarding his public aversion for socialism, his Magic Empire (his palace where he was the best) was run like a communist tyranny, like what the NWO plans. Workers at Disney didn't have titles; it was nondescript libertarianism with an almighty despot Disney at the top. It was racially elitist as well. The main full-time African-American during Walt's lifetime at Disney was a dark shoe sparkle man. Was Walt a communist of the National Socialist (Nazi) assortment? Arthur Babbitt claims, "time and again I noticed Walt Disney and Gunther Lessing there [at Nazi meetings], alongside a great deal of other unmistakable Nazi-distressed Hollywood characters. Disney was going to gatherings constantly." Lessing was mobster Willie Bioff's sidekick. Bioff had gone through his prior days running a whorehouse, prior to coming to Hollywood for the crowd. In the last board of the Mickey Mouse funny cartoon of 6/19/40, an insignia showed up.

Certain individuals have considered what this and other "secret signs" in Disney's work implied. Disney was not Illuminati. The strong tip top is exceptionally talented at controlling individuals that hobnob with them, the people who are starting to turn out to be freely well off. For example, they obliterated Robert Morris, the incredible lender of the American Revolution. They just utilized Hegelian Dialectics on Walt Disney. Their Unions and the Mob made Disney's studio one of their ideal objectives. For Walt to shield himself from the associations, which he saw as socialist, Walt found support from the FBI and the horde. Walt was defenceless against the associations, since he treated his laborers awful, with extended periods of time, low compensation, notwithstanding rehashed maltreatments to their nobility. Walt's enormous number of representatives basically never got any credit or acknowledgment for their long stretches of inventiveness and difficult work, which was generally basically taken and attributed to Walt by the foundation to assemble his picture. (I express "basically", because somebody could discover some dark exemption, yet no matter how you look at it, Walt got all the credit for what his innovative specialists created.) Perhaps Walt required the injection of self-confidence from all the purloined public applause which he took from his staff to be viewed as an incredible artist, since he had needed to be a craftsman/visual artist and fizzled. The acclaim helped soothe the injuries.

One specialist reviews that Walt "had no information on craftsmanship, no information on music, no information on writing, no information on anything truly, with the exception of he was an extraordinary proof-reader." This may not be a lot of an embellishment, because Walt was a secondary school nonconformist, who experienced childhood in neediness on a Missouri ranch.

Walt's first authority endeavor to coordinate a film (and last) was the film The Golden Touch in 1935. The film was a humiliation. Walt needed to pull it from appropriation. Assuming Walt needed capacities to enliven, and direct, what was Walt's ability? Walt was the main impetus, the soul so-to-talk behind Disney. He was the tyrant who was dreaded to the point of requesting more from his laborers than they realized they could give- - and he could get it. He was the main thrust that took a horde of craftsmen, and gag makers, and so on and formed them into a strong power to make kid's shows and later films. He was the hard-driving virtuoso who knew what he needed and got others to make it for him. He was the main impetus that kept a multitude of costumed disinfection men fastidiously cleaning Disneyland. In an ordinary year, Walt would have 800,000 plants supplanted at Disneyland, and Walt wouldn't set up signs asking the "visitors" (guests) not to stomp on them. How strong was Walt? Here is a man who during his lifetime and surprisingly up into the 1990's had a standard in the studio and Disneyland that no male representatives could have any beard, yet he personally wore a mustache for a large portion of his life.

A Possible CHRONOLOGY OF EVENTS Surrounding WALT DISNEY'S ILLEGITIMATE BIRTH

It is certain that Walt Disney was an ill-conceived youngster, yet that reality brought about a not insignificant rundown of secretive happenings. It additionally gave power hungry men, something to coerce Walt Disney with. Since this section 5 on Deception is zeroing in on Disney, and the huge young men utilized coercion to keep Disney in line, this data is appropriate. The accompanying sequence of occasions is the thing this present creators accepts doubtlessly occurred. With next to no hereditary tests, it is hard to decide for certain who Walt's organic guardians were, and what the genuine history of Walt Disney was. A few groups have gone through numerous years examining the genuine realities encompassing his introduction to the world. Many fascinating and enticing hints have been found. This creator accepts that the accompanying sequence is recommended by the proof. (This current creator's sequence is presented without many pages of proof, on the grounds that the secrets around Walt Disney's introduction to the world are digging in for the long haul, regardless of reasons individuals think of, and this creator would rather not stray from the expected motivation behind the section. This is to show that Walt Disney had a mysterious jerk birth which gave J. Edgar Hoover and his bosses - shakedown influence over Walt Disney.

1890- An appealing Spanish lady Isabelle Zamora Ascenslo of Mojacar passes on Spain and goes to California to a Franciscan cloister.

Around the same time, yet later on, In 1890-Walt's future dad Elias, who likes himself a women man, passes on his family to look for his fortune in the goldfields. In California, he meets one more rookie to the state, Isabella Ascensio, and the two newbies in California share a lot of practice speaking, have a sexy illicit relationship, and become hopelessly enamored.

1891- Elias neglects to make a fortune and gets back to Chicago, however, he doesn't fail to remember Isabelle.

1893- Isabelle and Elias have a child, and Elias persuades his better half to acknowledge the child as theirs instead of having the family's standing, their marriage, and their family destroyed. The child doesn't resemble the initial two young men by any means.

1901- Isabelle and Elias have another knave child, who Elias brings back and names Walter after the priest of the congregation he joins in. The two knave children don't resemble the more seasoned children of Elias, and they never have a lot to do with them, however stick to one another as siblings.

1903- The priest of the congregation Elias goes to learn about the unwanted youngsters and Elias rapidly moves out of state so the outrage will stay mysterious. Elias has likewise added to betting obligations.

1905- After moving to Marceline, Missouri, Isabelle is recruited as the Disney's servant, so she has a reason to move in with them without making doubts. She likely does a large part of the raising and care of the two young men.

1918- J. Edgar Hoover is occupied engaged with the arraignment of draft dodgers in WW I, and it crosses his work area about the instance of Walt Disney carrying out the wrongdoing of manufacturing his parent's mark to enlist in the military. Cases like Walt's were watched because individuals who could be extorted could be assets in the future for Hoover. That year, Walt found that he had no birth declaration. Drift notices his parent's odd responses concerning his introduction to the world endorsement and different inquiries, and starts to profoundly doubt his dad.

November, 1938- Walt's mom bites the dust by gas, and the Disney's servant pulls Elias to somewhere safe from the vapor, however, Walt's mom passes on.

1939-40- Hoover offers Walt Disney to assist Walt with finding his genuine guardians assuming that Walt will work for the FBI. Either Hoover definitely realizes that he is an illegitimate youngster or he before long gains reality from an examination. This gives Hoover shakedown control over Walt Disney, and guarantees Hoover that Waft will be steadfast. Hoover educates Walt Disney regarding the reality, and afterward moves to liberally safeguard Disney and his dad's standing. Two FBI men plant baptismal data of a youngster brought into the world to Isabelle in 1890 named Jose Guirao in Mojacar, Spain. This date is 10 years off of Walt's birth date, and is planned to lose an individual's track. They can't establish a phony birth endorsement for Waft in the records for 1901, on the grounds that everybody knows from WW I that none exists. Consequently, they plant a phony birth endorsement for Walt in the Illinois State records in the year 1890. They trust individuals will believe that in some way a recording mistake happened. Thusly assuming anything holes, and most horrendously terrible came to most exceedingly awful, Waft could no less than imagine he was embraced and is certifiably not an ill-conceived knave. They take care of residents in Mojacar to recount a specific story. Residents likely get progressing instalments.

1941- Walt defies his dad with reality, and his dad ends it all, and his genuine mother comes to live with him as his house cleaner.

1954- In a request to build up the legend that Walt was brought into the world in Spain, a gathering of Franciscan priests goes to Mojacar and apparently requests about the birth records of Jose Guirao and additionally Walt Disney. They invest energy with the city hall leader and ensure that everybody associates Waft Disney with Jose, who is a made up (ostensible) character that the FBI has made records of.

1967- A year after Walt's passing, a huge gathering of Americans (an enormous gathering was required because they are not talented like the 2 FBI men in 1940) profess to be on "true" business for the American government. They go to Mojacar Spain to obliterate every one of the records of Jose Guirao to guarantee that there will be no Spanish inquirers to Walt Disney's fortune. Later to guarantee that the made-up story is firmly set up to delude the rare sorts of people who could get by the haze of mystery over Walt Disney, the Spanish government helps out to specific influential individuals and pays an examiner to explore the Spanish beginnings of Walt Disney. Individuals of the town readily tell individuals with next to no dread or with next to no display that Walt Disney was brought into the world at their town.

Except if they have as of late done as such, the town has sat idle - no landmarks, no markers, or anything about the birth site of Disney. They most likely didn't do this for a really long time, since a portion of the town presumably realized it was completely false. With the more seasoned individuals gone, the untruth has presumably become all around dug in as truth and there is doubtlessly some kind of commemoration to Walt Disney.

WALT DISNEY'S CHARACTER

Since the Disney trickiness is a particularly major Illuminati duplicity around the world, and because Walt Disney was the significant impetus behind all the Disney amusement parks, motion pictures, knickknacks, and so forth it is of significance to inspect his personality. In concentrating on chronicled figures, this creator has attempted to get to the absolute bottom truth. One might ask, how could this be finished? - particularly since there have been many years of legends spread by the foundation and their media? The accompanying technique which has worked with other chronicled figures was additionally finished by this creator with Walt Disney. The initial segment of this present creator's own system is to concentrate on all that one can find on the man, really focusing on what predisposition and vantage point another creator comes from. Unique consideration is additionally paid to biographers who attempt to give every bit of relevant information as they have tracked down it, rather than supported life stories that recurrent legends, axioms, and honeyed words. The specialist must be cautious since there are writers who misleading say in their presentations that they are "segregated examiners" who are "going to be horrendously genuine in their announcing" when they really are capable of cover up craftsmen for the individual they expound on. At the point when your writer, Fritz Spring Meier, completed the process of researching composed material with regards to Walt Disney, then, at that point, I mentally placed what I knew on the rack briefly, and did a penmanship examination in light of the logical standards of Graph investigation as well as the more extensive area of Graphology. This writer is a Certified Graph examiner who has done penmanship examination expertly. Utilizing Graph investigation/graphology is a great method for getting a fair-minded exceptionally profound glance at a chronicled figure. It is an approach to bypass all the purposeful publicity and fantasies. Be that as it may, a nearby recorded look and the penmanship examination (of different verifiable figures) have matched each other all the time, as they did for this situation as well. Here is the thing that was found. The accompanying passages are the means by which Walt was in the 1920's. The character profile you will peruse didn't persevere. Under the strain of continuously fussing over Disney Productions as well as living with monetary anxieties, by the 1940's, Walt could be found in seethes giving unpleasant treatment to his significant other, and harsh spankings to his two youngsters. He went to mental advising to adapt to the pressure. What's more tragically, with the movement of time, by the 1960's Walt had turned into a vicious vain drunkard. One biographer portrayed him as, a domineering jerk and a smarty pants" (Disney's World, p. 220) Even then, at that point, Walt had men working for him, like Bill Walsh (who had been a vagrant as a kid) who revered Walt. In any case, this is the way he was in the 1920's:

Walt was a self-spurred person with loads of energy who was continually looking for some outlet. (Individuals have expounded much on this quality of his.) He was more the provider than the taker seeing someone. (In the initial not many years, when he was liable for making business contracts, he frequently offered his work without setting costs for benefits. He even composed letters to his supervisor such that his primary goal was great kid's shows, not benefits, and that he'd work without benefits, however, he needed some appreciation for his work. That was his delicate nature appearing.) Walt wouldn't trust that others will concoct a thought or another person to take action - he was there first. He could discuss his thoughts without breaking a sweat and move effectively from one thought to another. (He would burst into Disney Productions and heave an endless series of thoughts into his laborers' ears.) He delighted in the contest. He had a speedy brain and sharp insight. He much of the time followed up on instinct and motivation, taking risks and jeopardizing his own security.

(He oftentimes bet for his entire life reserve funds and all that he could figure out on an undertaking.) Long activities exhausted him. (Luckily, the genuine monotonous work of cartooning was finished by a huge staff of specialists.) House tasks and dull errands exhausted him and he kept away from them. (He was totally an absolute lazy pig around the house as a single guy.) He was eager with dubious ways of thinking, he preferred substantial real factors. He was challenging to coexist with in the light of the fact that he had both a fun-loving side (even to the mark of brutal viable jokes) to his character and a forceful prejudiced restless side that needed to accomplish. Normally, individuals around him were bothered because on an inner mind level they never realized which side of him they would manage. He was designed for activity. He was continuously designing ways of getting what he wanted. He could be unstable when incited. (The bygone era partners of Walt recollect his hazardous attitude.) He was an individual of dynamic energy, arousing quality, and sharp reasoning, and a devotee of the delight standard.

Since his dad was so oppressive and abused his, influential place, Walt came to be profoundly imbued with resistance toward power. (The topics of his movies over and over identify with the people who oppose authority, and the police and other power figures are reliably displayed as silly. One way he communicated flippancy was with exuberant dance scenes, which has been a corridor sign of adolescent resistance during the twentieth century. "Comic turmoil arrives at its fullest articulation in Alice Rattled by Rats, which shows how the rodents treat the felines disappear!) He felt that rules were for others to keep. (That is one explanation he would venture outside of the law and submit illicit demonstrations. This is one characteristic that might be liable for a portion of the crimes Walt wound up taking part in.) Walt additionally preferred not to be firmly regulated. (He needed to deal with his Disney Magic Kingdom as though it were his own realm. He needed to be a powerful figure, and for sure turned into the tyrant of his Magic Kingdom. Whenever his laborers varied with his own perspectives, he felt that they were encroaching upon his own natural freedoms as an individual.) He was to some degree a melancholic demeanor, that kind of stickler who actually appreciates life. He wanted to safeguard himself against closeness with others. He was most home in a setting which he made for himself. Walt had the characteristics of a leader.

He was delayed to uncover his deepest sentiments, and certainly put forth his own objectives. Walt was one of those people that while the going got intense, he held tight. Moreover, he would stick to his thoughts, plans, and assets. (His difficult refusal to permit his sibling Roy to stop the making of Disneyland prompted occasions that split the siblings. His assurance to succeed was exploited by the criminal organizations to extort him with a few obligations. To get his fantasies, he was ready to give them what they needed.) A piece of information to Walt's horrifying funny bone, on occasion right around a burial ground comical inclination, and his high resilience of seeing agony in others, is that Walt was genuinely considering chipping in again as a surgeon after the W.W. I battling in France was finished, when volunteers were required for the Balkan battling.

Walt cherished creatures more than individuals. The main individual that he had an affinity with while experiencing childhood with the ranch was his Uncle Ed (who he called Uncle Elf), who resembled a hybrid of a leprechaun and a prune. Uncle Elf could make creatures sounds and bird whistles to Walt's enjoyment. Walt adored the appeal of the homestead and nature and he cherished sovereignty, display and a severe social order, for example, Freemasonry gives. He frequently wove a blend of the farm in with illustrious motorcades and different features of eminence. For example, in Alice the Piper, the King Hamlin is a rancher who dozes in a farmhouse. In Puss in Boots, the nearby ruler lives in a real castle indiscernibly positioned in a town. His initial film Alice's Day at Sea incorporates both the elements of a regal court and an American carnival. On average Disney scorn for power, he makes fun of criminal brotherly gatherings with their ceremonies and passwords in Alice and the Dog Catcher, Alice Foils the Pirates, and Alice's Mysterious Mystery. And keeping in mind that he was a mysterious FBI specialist, he conflicted with Hoover's desires and made fun of the FBI's position. Walt was faithful to what he accepted and could be faithful to those people who he considered deserving of his dependability, yet he didn't need anybody to have authority over him. (Walt was a 320 Freemason and a medium, he was faithful to that way of thinking and steadfast in his initial a very long time to his more established sibling Roy O. Disney, who was a mentor to him.) If anybody at the studios concurred with him when he resented his sibling Roy, the person in question gambled losing their employment. The two siblings were defensive of each other, and felt they were the ones in particular who could censure the other one.

WHO WAS ROY O. DISNEY?

Roy O. Disney was brought into the world in 1893, and his sibling Walt in 1901. They had three different siblings; however, Roy and Walt (1901-1966) were simply near one another and not to their different siblings, who didn't look like them. Walt was named Walter Elias, his center name got from his dad's first name. The Disney family had moved from Ireland to Canada and afterward to the U.S. The dad of the siblings as expressed was Elias, and their mom of Scottish plummet, who might not have been the organic mother, had the birth name Flora Call. Roy kicked the bucket in 1971, not long after the initial services for Walt Disney World. He stayed faithful to his obligations to his sibling to assemble Walt Disney World. He reneged on his guarantees concerning the city of Epcot (which was wrecked into becoming EPCOT). Roy O. during the 1930's lived in North

Hollywood. Roy's family was later situated in Napa Valley, CA, and was related with the Illuminati top dogs nearby. Napa Valley has been nicknamed the Valley of Kings.

This "Valley of Kings" assumes a significant part in the messy exercises uncovered in this section. Roy 0. Disney assumed a greater part at Disney Studios than individuals understand. For instance, it was Roy O. who settled on the choice to cut 45 min. out of Fantasia, so that Walt's pet task could be conveyed to cinemas. Roy O., considered by certain insiders as the eviller of the two siblings, saved the monetary books for the Disney's as the years progressed. It is realized that Disney kept two books during the 1950's, so it is difficult to trust anything with the exception of that Roy 0. was completely mindful of how Disney got their cash. The huge young men generally kept the monetary screws to Walt and Roy. The enormous young men regularly sorted out tricks to take their cash. Whenever the Disneybrothers had a game plan with Columbia Studio (run by Harry Cohn) they were progressed $7,500 for each animation which cost them an unrewarding $13,500 to make. Further, Cohn got a kick out of the chance to swindle them by not sending them their cash, and investing in some opportunity to pay them what he owed them. The income issues of the Disney siblings additionally came from Walt's longing to continue improving and overhauling the innovation they utilized. Whenever Walt went to shading over Roy's complaints, Disney's net revenue was harmed and the studio was left with deficiencies of money. In 1937, Walt's rehashed bets with animation creation thoughts caused Roy O. to say, "We've purchased the entire condemned sweepstakes." From 1940 through1946,

Disney lost cash consistently. In '46, he lost $23,000. At last, in 1947, things turned around and the Disney studio created a gain of $265,000. Kid's shows and motion pictures were not actually huge money makers for the Disney siblings, until it was understood that old movies could be replayed on TV. Generally speaking, from the 20's through the 50's, the Disney's might have made back the initial investment with liveliness. For this reason, Disney Studios at Christmas, 1931 couldn't pay its finance. Pinocchio cost $2.6 million to make in the last part of the '30's, a sum hard to recover around then from the movies, and Fantasia's unique delivery in the '40's was a horrid monetary disappointment. While Sleeping Beauty was delivered in 1960, it was a failure, film attendees were aloof towards it. The genuine cash made by the Disney siblings in the 1930-1950's came from the marketing of Disney items, the creation of underground hard pornography, and the payoffs from different gatherings which involved Disney for mind-control programming, and illegal tax avoidance. Whenever Walt kicked the bucket, his portions in Disney were valued at $18 million. His family with everything taken into account held 34% of the stock in Walt Disney Productions. Roy o. Disney's little girl Dorothy Disney Puder& spouse Episcopalian Rev. Glen Puder bought the property at 1677 Sage Canyon Rd., Napa Valley east of Rutherford. (This is near the Rothschild's Opus One Temple referenced in VoL 1.) O.J. Simpson's attorney Johnnie Cochran Jr. was in the Rothschild's difficult to-enter Opus 1 when the jury showed up at a choice in O.J. Simpson's case.) It is extremely common for Mafia families in south Boston to have one relative in the church and one full-time in coordinated wrongdoing. (See creator's Be Wise as Serpents for an uncover on the Episcopalian Church, which is just a part of Freemasonry.) All sorts of intriguing Mafia figures, Illuminati, and Bohemian Grovers live up the Sage Canyon Rd. This is a region that has a huge all-around saved graveyard for pets. Candid Well's sister and Rich Frank, who will be in every way talked about later in this section, likewise, live on Sage Canyon Rd.

WHO WAS ROY B. DISNEY?

Roy Edward Disney (nephew of Walt) is the child of Roy Oliver Disney (sibling of Walt). Now and again, he has been called Junior. The 9/5/94 Newsweek story on Disney's Magic Kingdom referred to him as "Attendant of the Flame." Roy is a chief with Walt Disney Co. at 500 5. Buena Vista St., Burbank, CA 91521. He has functioned as an asst. maker at Walt Disney Co. from 1954 to 1977. He has additionally been the bad habit pres. of Walt Disney Co. He is the leader of Roy E. Disney Prods. in Burbank. He is director of the board for Shamrock Broadcasting Co. As though that weren't sufficient, he is on the governing body for St. Joseph Med. Ctr., fellowU.

Ky. Beneficiary of the Academy grant selection for Mysteries of the Deep. He is an overseer of the Guild American West, the Writers Guild, which is significant. He has a place with the 100 Club, the Confrerie des Chevaliers du Tastevin, and St. Francis Yacht Club. He loves speed boat hustling. Roy E. Disney was thecocky child of Roy O. He wedded a lady named Patricia. He was just endured by his uncle Walt, particularly after Roy E. offered a few mean comments about Walt's arrangements for Disneyland, which he and his dad went against until Walt Disney by and by got the task moving. Walt's child in-regulation Ronald Miller is one of the Disney groups who can't stand Roy E. The two never preferred one another, and in the battle for control between them after Walt's demise, Roy E. won and wound up with Disney. Even though individuals called Roy E. "Walt's numbskull nephew", he at last (with the assistance of his dad and pariahs) won the different fights for control at Disney after Walt kicked the bucket, and is presently a strong figure. Roy E. Disney and Stanley P. Gold work together in different ways, and are both on the current Disney Bd. of Dir. They are companions and attempted to forestall antagonistic takeovers of Disney in 1984. Gold is responsible for Shamrock Holdings, Inc.

THE BETWEEN THE TWO DISNEY FACTIONS

In 1953, the two siblings and their particular sides of the family parted when Walt made RETHAW organization. The different sides have battled from that point onward. At the point when Walt Disney made RETLAW (his name Walter spelled in reverse), this estranged his sibling Roy O. and Roy's side of the family. Without delving into every one of the subtleties, how RETLAW treated cut Roy O's. side out of the cash that should have been made. Yet, Roy's side didn't hold on and inactively let their portion of the pie be lost, they retaliated and stood their ground. Their enormous break came when Michael Milken and his band of garbage bond specialists did a "greenmail" on the Disney Corp. A couple of insiders know how greenmail functions. It is an authoritative document of a shakedown. Milken would work with his companions Saul Steinberg, Sir James Goldsmith, and Carl Icahn. Milken would give them the monetary clout, to make them look monetarily able to do monetarily buying an organization that they had chosen as an objective.

As per insiders, Milken got 40% of the potential gain of any "greenmail" that went right. The designated company would discover that somebody like Saul Steinberg planned to get them out. To forestall the buyout, and to keep their positions, the officials of the designated company would become hysterical, and either does self-destructive renegotiation's, or purchase the supply of the expected acquirer at a lot more noteworthy costs than the Milken bunch paid for them. The "greenmail" craftsmen would then take their plunder and go on their way. The investors of the designated organization are the genuine washouts of "greenmail", because the administration of the company to back their insurance spends the investor's cash, assumes new obligations, and denies the investors of some benefit making capability of their portions. Michael Milken's gathering made bluffs to assume control over an enormous number of partnerships, including Walt Disney, Phillips Petroleum, and Avco. Saul Steinberg made what resembled the beginnings of a true threatening takeover of Walt Disney through Reliance. At a certain point, Reliance turned into Disney's biggest investor. Steinberg documented a changed 13D saying he expected to secure 25% of the partnership. The CEO of Walt Disney, was Walt Disney's child in-regulation Ron Miller. Saul Steinberg is a dear colleague with London's Jacob de Rothschild. Initially, Ron Miller (Stanford Univ. graduate.) and Ray Watson (a Bohemian Grove part from Stanford Unive.) of Walt Disney's administration acquired the Bass siblings to assist them with managing Saul Steinberg's takeover and to purchase and foster land (esp. in Florida). Beam Watson was Ron Miller's critical right-hand man to run things. The Bass siblings are mafia. Disney gained the Bass Brother's Arvida, and brought the Bass siblings into Disney's administration. The Basses sold their stake in Texaco back to the oil co. and then, at that point, utilized this cash to reinforce Disney. Sid Bass and Chuck Cobb (boss executive. Arvida) worked out an arrangement with Disney. Arvida (offered to Disney for $200 mil.) would benefit from creating Disney land in FL and Disney would benefit from the new monetary strength that getting Arvida would give. Arvida possessed oil fields, amusement stops, and had made arranged networks. For Ron Miller, on the one side was the Illuminati and the opposite side of things was themafia.

He didn't confide in either, however, Steinberg's takeover could take out Disney's administration, and both he (and RoyDisney) needed to save Disney from a takeover by Steinberg. From the get go, Roy E. composed a letter to Ron Miller and the other board individuals expressing his interests in the securing of Arvidafor Disney the executives, basically, the Bass siblings would allow Walt Disney to keep on making their family films. After the Bass siblings joined the Disney the board (and became one of Disney's significant investors), they before long got sides together with Roy

E. in an administration aftermath about whether Disney should purchase Gibson Greeting Card Company. With enough decisions on the board, they asked Ron Miller to leave for good. With Ron Miller, and those administration men lined up with Walt's side of the family gone, then, at that point, CEO Michael Eisner, Frank Wells, Rich Frank, and Jeffrey Katzenberg, and some others made the advanced Walt Disney Corporation. Disney's Touchtone studio which was referenced above in association with the film Alive was made in 1984 by Walt Disney's child in-regulation Ronald L. Mill operator. Ron Miller's administration style was dreary. The new administration has truly gone group busters. Even though Walt's side of the family is out of the administration end of Disney, they actually get monetary awards from different Disney endeavors. The Bass siblings procured more land for Disney in Florida. In any case, under their tutelage, Disney presently has a supervisory crew that is talented in land snatching methods. The Bass fortune started with Perry Bass, who made an organization called Bass Enterprises. In 1969, Perry resigned and surrendered things to his oldest child, Sid Richardson Bass. Sid has three more youthful siblings Ed, Robert, and Lee. The Basses claimed 27% in Prime Computer, as well as sizable land and oil property. The Bass siblings established a neighbourhood private academy in Ft. Worth, TX. Their HQs in Ft. Worth are brimming with present day craftsmanship. The Bass siblings were extremely astute in their arrangement with Disney. In return for their $14 interest in Arvida, they had moved past (a timeframe) 950 million dollars of Disney stock. In 1985, they sold Bass Brothers Enterprises and split the resources between the four siblings. Sid Bass had the option to move his inclinations from funds to culture and high society. One of the Bass siblings is associated with wineries in Napa Valley. The Bass Brother's monetary specialist was Alfred Checchi, presently of Beverly Hills, who has been an ally of Mishpucka part Sen. Dianne Feinstein (D-Calif.).

Roy is associated with crimes, and a few groups researching him have been obtusely cautioned that assuming they proceed, they will see their youngsters killed. Napa Valley's Illuminati action associates in with CIA exercises too. The Napa Valley Illuminati families all have CIA associations. For example, British tycoon Kenneth Armitage, who needed to escape from England to keep away from capture on various charges of robbery, double dealing, and bogus bookkeeping, had a portion of his old buddies in the Napa Valley, like Dr. John Duff, Johnny Beck, and others. Armitage has since bafflingly kicked the bucket in jail in England. Armitage had knowledge associations that connect to the nightfall universe of the crimes of the various insight abbreviation beasts. Additionally, his organization was approved to furnish individuals with Central American government archives. There is something else - significantly more to shameful undertakings which whirl around Roy Disney. Napa Valley, where numerous individuals from the Disney family live, has the Illuminati's Opus One sanctuary claimed by Rothschilds, as well as two streets fixed with fastidiously kept wineries possessed by Illuminati bosses and associated by means of mystery underground passages. To finish off this unimaginable assortment of Illuminati wineries (Rothschild's, Mondavi's, Rutherford's, Christian Brother's, Sattui's, and so on), on the north finish of a progression of wineries on roadway 29 lays the CIA's archaic looking Culinary Institute of America Greystone (at 2555 Main St., St. Helena, CA 94574), where various individuals have endured torment. The Greystone Culinary Institute of America as of late had the individual who runs their grounds store referenced in House and Garden, Sept. '96.

HOW TREAT KNOW ABOUT THE DISNEY FAMILY IN GENERAL?

A few individuals from the Disney family came to England with William the Conqueror. They were not known as Disney then, at that point, but since they came from the French Norman town of Isigny, they took the name 'Isigny, and anglicized it into Disney. Walt had two little girls, Diane Marie (bn. 12/18/33) and Sharon Mae.

Diane offered a few uncovering remarks when she said, he didn't pamper us. Like a great deal of young adult young ladies, I was wild about ponies, and I really improved at riding. I longed for my own pony, yet Dad wouldn't get one.

What's more, we had very little garments and different things." For being perhaps the most extravagant man in the country, Walt can't be blamed for having ruined his youngsters. He was additionally well known for his tenpenny tips at cafés, which turned into all the rage. Sharon Mae was taken on and shown up at the Disney home on 12/31/36. (She passed on in '93.) The reception was stayed discreet. The papers around the nation declared that Lillian had brought forth Sharon, and the Disney family kept up this lie for quite a long time. The explanation given for Sharon's reception was that Diane required a close friend. For quite a long time, Walt Disney didn't really like Sharon and only from time to time behaved like he even knew her name. Walt had needed a child, however, his better half needed to take on a young lady, so it was a wonderful young lady that Lillian chose to be an ally for her first little girl. At the point when Sharon was kindergarten age, Walt would take her to the merry go rounds in Griffith Park on Sunday evenings. Sharon was shipped off non-public schools. She went to Westlake School for Girls, and later was sent off to Switzerland to a young ladies' live-in school.

She had delicate fair locks and was appealing. In June of 1948, Walt took Sharon, who was then an appealing 12 yr. old to Alaska with him for around 2 months. For the majority of this trip, Walt and Sharon were separated from everyone else together. For, a disregarded dad Sharon throughout recent years, Walt was completely fixated on Sharon. He washed Sharon consistently, brushed her hair, washed her clothing, and painstakingly dressed her every night from head to toe prior to taking her to decent eateries. He even followed her when she dozes strolled. For what reason was Sharon a dissociative individual? That late spring in Alaska, Walt, and his own pilot went on an outing in August to Mt. McKinley, AK. Both were drinking scotch bourbon and they scarcely missed hitting a mountain, and nearly ran out of fuel prior to tracking down a runway. Sharon originally wedded a presbyterian Robert Borgfeldt Brown. Afterward, Sharon proceeded to wed William Lund. Years after the fact, Walt's significant other Lilly even kept a biographer from uncovering that Sharon was taken on. Sharon kicked the bucket somewhat youthful. It is vital to check out the Disney family rather than just Walt Disney in attempting to comprehend the Disney peculiarities. For example, in 1958, the Wall Street Journal referenced that Lillian B. Disney was a useful proprietor of more than 10% of normal Disney stock.

Lillian, Walt's widow, discreetly bought the property in Napa Valley and moved there in the last part of the 60's. She purchased the property through Walt's Retlaw Enterprises and the Lillian Disney Trust. Lillian and her 2 little girls ran Retlaw for a really long time. Diane Miller, her little girl, likewise purchased land and moved to the Napa region. The Lillian Disney Trust purchased the Silverado Vineyards, which Diane and her better half oversee as, gentlemen cultivators" as they call it. This side of the Disney family is evaded by the Illuminati insiders in the Napa Valley, as well as by the Roy O. side of the family.

Albeit exceptionally private, there are intermittent snapshots of exposure from Diane Disney Miller, when she gave wine for an asset raiser for the Planned Parenthood Shasta Diablo held at the estate Niobium-Coppola, claimed by chief/maker Francis Ford Coppola. Francis F. Coppola comes from an old mafia family. He possesses a major winery and coordinated Disney's Caption EO film. Local people in the Napa region don't confide in any of the Disney's, particularly the Roy O. side of the family. There is another Disney's that connect to the mysterious world. Wesley Ernest Disney, a 32° Mason and Shriner, who was a U.S. Senator, a state official, and a legal advisor in Kansas who had a sibling Richard Lester Disney- - who is a Rhodes Scholar and a Mason as well. Wesley Ernest Disney, by the way, started as a legal counsellor in Muskogee County (a Satanic controlled region), and was a Christian Scientist. He lived in Tulsa, a strong city of the Illuminati pecking order. Doris Miles Disney has been an author of mystery fiction, like The Magic Grandfather the Chandler Policy (1972) and Trick or Treat (1972) as well as numerous other occult novels.

A HISTORY OF DISNEY

"The tale of Disney's quiet movie profession isn't such a lot of a battle for imaginative articulation as it is a battle for business security." During the 1920's, Walt remained securely inside the bounds of comic activity as characterized by others, like the makers of Felix the Cat, Koko the Clown, and Krazy Kat. As such, when a significant number of the thoughts were coming from just himself, Disney's films were no greater than others. In the 1930's, Disney got probably the best ability accessible and he started to agree to simply the best outcomes from that ability. With the horde, and the Illuminati behind him, and driven by an obligation to them, Disney started to accomplish extraordinary outcomes inactivity. Somewhere in the range of 1924 and 1927, Walt Disney made a progression of 56 quiet Alice Comedies which utilized three distinct young ladies (6-year-old Virginia Davis, Margie Gay, and Lois Hardwick) to go about as Alice who frolics around in a make belief animation world. These kid's shows consolidated true to life and movement. When the series was done, Walt Disney needed to take a stab at working exclusively with activity. Margaret Winkler in NY (who wedded Charles Mintz) disseminated Walt Disney's Alice Comedies.

All along, kids were the focal point of all that Walt did. The mysterious world that supported Walt, as well as Walt himself, trusted that if they would draw out "the kid" (that piece of an individual called "the youngster" by different clinicians), then, at that point, they could engage the interest and sensations of the "kid" part of grown-ups. If it worked with grown-ups, they could do likewise with the youngster part in kids. They knew even in the 20's and '30 must be achieved in the mysterious Great Plan for a New World Order. The Illuminati Great Plan called for everyday life to be obliterated, for youngsters to oppose their folks, and for the world to turn out to be more savage. Youngsters expected to drench in pictures of viciousness so a fierce society could be made.

For example, the 1925 film Alice Stage Struck shows a young lady Alice lashed to a log prompting a buzz saw. They additionally needed to make mystery - black magic the normal conviction of the American public. The Illuminati felt they could acquire black magic in the event that they spoke to the interest of the kid in each grown-up. For example, the Donald Duck animation Corn Chips (1951) shows Donald bothering Chip and Dale who then, at that point, get back at him by taking a crate of popcorn and spreading everything over the front yard. Presently how treats animation like this educates kids? It helps that taking to reimburse resentment is O.K. also that doing tricks is entertaining. In Disney's 1920 movies, he shows kids cutting school, shoplifting, and taking an impromptu day off.

He shows Alice fleeing from liability to have experience. He shows detainees getting away and vagrants getting away from work. His movies are an articulation of trouble making being effective. How treats instruct youngsters? In the 1951 animation, Get Rich Quick Goofy successes cash at poker, and his at first irate spouse who tries to avoid betting pardons him when she perceives the amount he's won. Ridiculous demonstrates that they can have a spending binge by telling his better half, "What was easy to get is just as easy to lose!" The betting soul is an extremely strong soul that the Illuminati need to ingrain in this country. How could an animation that advances betting be healthy for kids? Lt. Col. Dave Grossman is a tactical master on the best way to condition individuals so they will kill. He writes in his great book On Killing (Boston, MS: Little Brown and Co., 1996) that the very cycle that the public authority has used to condition fighters to kill, is being utilized by media outlets. The only major distinction is that in the military, men are educated to kill just on order, while our youngsters are being instructed to kill at whatever point they need to by means of TV's "amusement." Grossman states on page 308, that the molding to kill starts with kid's shows. "It starts honestly with kid's shows and afterward continues to the endless actsof viciousness portrayed on TV as the childgrowsup. Then the guardians, through disregard or cognizant decision, begin to allow the kid to watch films mature rated because of distinctive portrayals of blades infiltrating and distending from bodies, remote chances of blood erupting from cut off appendages, and projectiles tearing into bodies and bursting out the back in showers of blood and minds." While kids see awful passing's on T.V., they figure out how to connect this enduring with diversion, joy, and their beloved soda, their most loved treat, and close private contact with their date. (See On Killing, p. 302) Disney resembles Wholesomeness; this appearance is very misleading. A nearby investigation of Disney kid's shows will uncover bunches of viciousness that couldn't be portrayed on the off chance that the savagery was really real and not a movement. It's the healthy front which is one of the duplicities that makes Disney kid's shows and movies so perilous.

Indeed, the picture of Disney has been that its kid's shows are healthy. No big surprise Illuminati mind-control software engineers have snickered at how guileless the American public is toward Disney. The Disney Gargoyles kid's shows are a TV series that is unadulterated demonology. The storyline is that a race of evil presences safeguards New York City. One of the Gargoyles is even named Demona.

The Illuminati software engineers are flabbergasted at how moronic the majority of individuals are, and how handily misdirected. How the Disney motion pictures are utilized as programming scripts is exceptionally involved so just one itemized model is given toward the finish of this part. The Illuminati and Mafia realized that Walthadwas able to take care of the business that the Great Plans called for. (Source: classified meeting.) They realized they had the "carrots and the sticks" to get him to participate.

There is no question that Walt was a diligent employee who thus expected elevated requirements from his employees.One associate of Walt expressed, "Walt offered a straightforward expression, that you can lick them with 'item' assuming you make your item sufficient, they cannotdeny it In Walt's assessment, all that was accomplished had to be executed with a lot of thought and artfulness." Neelands, Barbara, compiler. About Ben Sharps teenager, article by David R. Smith (second Impress.) Calistoga, CA: A Sharps teenager Museum Reprint, one major turn in Walt's standpoint toward quality came in April, 1927 when the head of Universal Studios composed a blistering report on the nature of Disney studio work. It constrained Walt to understand that up to then he had been slipshod and messy. He made plans to never take a simple way, however, to work with devotion toward making his drawings wake up with a character and fascinating circumstances. In 1922, Walt made the film Cinderella. This isn't to be mistaken for the later enlivened film additionally of a similar title delivered in 1950. The 1950 element was re-delivered various times. The Alice kid's shows were made with a 6-year-old young lady playing Alice. The initial six Alice comedies had broad true to life beginnings, and afterward went into animation. A couple of the 1920's Alice quiet animation titles include:

Alice's Wonderland (1923) Alice Hunting in Africa (1924)

Alice's Spooky Adventure (1924) Alice Plays Cupid (1925)

Alice Cans the Cannibals (1925) Alice Rattled by Rats (1925) Alice Chops the Suey (1925) Alice Charms the Fish (1926) Alice the Whaler (1927)

Alice the Beach Nut (1927)

After the Alice Series, Disney started a completely vivified series called Oswald the Lucky Rabbit. Here we see the mysterious idea of karma (who hasn't known about a fortunate Rabbit's foot?) being quietly advanced. Disney animation might engage, yet they additionally inculcate while they engage. In 1926, Walt Disney consented to an arrangement with Mintz and Film Booking Offices (EBO). Film Booking Offices were Illuminati top dog/horde manager Joseph Kennedy's organization. For at minimum the following years, Disney worked under the influence (protection) of Illuminati top dog Kennedy. All of the Disney pictures were enrolled by R-C Pictures Corp., one of the parent organizations of Kennedy's FBO. Joseph Kennedy likewise controlled the RKO studio which cooperated with the other huge studios to guarantee that no little studio would create as a contender. By 1937, every one of the enormous studios- - twentieth Cent., Paramount, MGM, Warner Bros., Cohn's Columbia Pictures, and Kennedy's RKO were permitting the crowd to skim cash from them. Kennedy's RKO gave Walt an assurance in 1937 that they'd appropriate Snow White without having looked at anything beforehand.

Walt Disney had their movies conveyed by Kennedy's RKO from 1936 to 1956. Another mostly secret detail is that in 1926, Leon Schlesinger (future maker at Warner Bros.) subcontracted activity occupations to Disney.

One of these was Universal's The Silent Flyer. In 1928, Steamboat Willie appeared. This was a vivified animation with a soundtrack featuring a mouse later named Mickey Mouse. It had taken loads of difficult work and assurance on Walt's part, yet it was the main animation with a sound track and it was effective. In 1929, the animation The Haunted House came out. The story is, Mickey Mouse is constrained by a tempest into a house brimming with apparitions who drive him to add to their creepy musicale. In 1930, Harry Cohn, quite possibly the most heartless and obnoxious person controlling a studio rescued Walt Disney of Walt's issue with rascal Pat Powers who was taking Disney's cash. Harry Cohn was a previous NY pool hawker and card shark who was acquired by Chicago financial backers to front their interests in Columbia Pictures, and run their studio. He wore a sapphire ring that the Chicago mafia man Johnny Roselli gave him. Roselli later turned into a rebel resource of the CIA, and affirmed before Congress (the Church Committee on Assassinations in '74) about a CIA contract which was given him.

Roselli worked for the Mafia Council of 9, which incl. Anthony Accardo and Sam Giancana. Harry Cohn was said by some to be the most despised man in Hollywood. His cash gave him "the force of a sovereign". His cash got him the best female tissue accessible which he utilized for his pleasure. He appeared to be all the time to show up from Las Vegas with rolls of new greenbacks, which had close partners pondering where all the cash came from that he generally got when he made excursions to Las Vegas. In 1931, Walt went into a long self-destructive sadness that endured into 1932. In the mid-year of 1932, he got away to attempt to recuperate from his mental meltdown. By 1932, Ingersoll had showcased its first release of Mickey Mouse watches. Disney items have filled in as a model of industrialism for the world. Disney watches have been made persistently starting around 1932 or '33. In 1932, eighty significant U.S. companies (like General Foods, RCA, and National Dairy) started to advertise Disney items. Ed Sullivan started routinely running stories that gloated with regards to Disney's work. Freemason Dr. Rufus B. von Kleinsmid, pres. of the Univ. of So. Cal., gave Disney an honor from Parents magazine for Walt's "work with youngsters". In 1932, a few craftsmen who had worked for William Randolph Hearst came to work for Disney. In 1932, Roy changed Disney from Columbia to United Artists. Joined Artists consented to front Disney $15,000 for each animation.

In the 1930's, the Illuminati' Bank of America financed Walt Disney. Years prior, the Bank of America had been unobtrusively made from Bank of Italy which was constrained by the very government that has run the Knights of Malta and renaissance Venice. The Bank of Italy was a strong bank in Hollywood's first years. It's delegates A.P. furthermore Atillo Giannini financed Walt during the 1920's with frivolous money to move him along, however insufficient to get him out of monetary servitude.

Joe Rosenberg of Bank of America was thoughtful to Walt. Joe Rosenberg, a Jewish investor, came to all of Disney's executive gatherings, sat next to Walt, and would exhort Walt on what bearing Disney Studios should take. Joe wasn't a board part, however, his recommendation got high need. Bank of America additionally bankrolled other Illuminati tasks and associations. Bank of America had one of their branch workplaces on Disneyland's Main St. from '55 until '93. They were open on vacations and Sundays for Disneyland. Bank of America is scheduled to be maybe the main bank to endure the monetary accident, when the Illuminati top dogs will permit their own banks to crash. Bank of America leader S. Clark Beise (who is a Scottish Rite Freemason) has been an individual from Disney's directorate from '65 to '75. Probably the greatest contributor to Bank of America is Roy E. Disney. Other Disney executives like Rich Frank have likewise involved Bank of America as their bank of decision.

The Bank of America bankrolled the Disney movement, Snow White. Walt figured out how to sell Joseph Rosenberg on the thought, when bygone era Hollywood individuals were prompting Rosenberg that Snow White must be a disappointment. Whenever Snow White was effective, Walt reported a beast party for all Disney laborers at Lake Neronian, close to Palm Springs, southeast of San Bernadino, CA where the expense of everything the Disney laborers needed to arrange - food or drink or whatever, eventual dealt with by the Disney's. Under the full moon, the Disney male and female specialists, at long last liberated from the tight principles at the studios, had what added up to a Roman blow out and an enormous bare thin plunge at the lake. Practically all of the Disney laborers partook in the bash and Disney had just two choices, 1. Fire them all or 2. Disregard that the party occurred. Walt picks the last choice, and after that nobody at any point is challenged to notice the party in his essence. In 1937, Walt and Roy went on an outing to Europe where Walt ate with the British Royal family, and met secretly with H.G. Wells, the masonic prophet! The organizer of what Wells and different bricklayers called "the New World Order". In Paris, the League of Nations (the precursor to the U.N.) gave him an honor. After the achievement of Snow White, Disney picked Pinocchio to follow it. Many have inquired as to why Pinocchio was picked by Walt. Assuming you take a gander at the content, the puppetmaker's better half is removed from the first content, and there is an accentuation on the little wooden manikin picturing turning into a tissue and blood child to the one who had made him. Here we have a kid with no spirit, who is told in the event that he really buckles down, he will be given one.

The content was most certainly different to have a storyline undeniably more helpful to mind-control programming. For the people who think Walt just reproduced fantasies on the screen, assuming one analyzes the progressions that are produced using the first storylines, they are changed to make them more helpful for mind-control. Both Snow White and Pinocchio have mysterious sort "passings and revivals". After W.W. II, Joseph Rosenberg convinced A.P. Giannini, his chief, to bankroll Disney again. Despite the fact that Walt was financed by the Mishpucka (Jewish Mafia), he would rather avoid the thought. Richard Rosenberg, a later Pres. of Bank of America, is additionally Mishpucka. Richard Rosenberg (his mom was a Cohen) was additionally accountable for Northrop Corp. what's more Marin Ecumenical Housing Assn. (Different instances of Mishpucka leaders are R. Goldstein, v.p. of Procter and Gamble, and Marvin Koslow, v.p. of Bristol Meyers Co.) In the 1930's, the world class advanced Disney's new kid's shows. In 1935, Walt Disney got the French Legion of Honor for his Mickey Mouse kid's shows. Additionally in 1935, the Queen of England (who perusers of my past articles will acknowledge is Illuminati, engaged with drug exchange, and is associated with the authority of Freemasonry) and the Duchess of York (likewise Illuminati) chose Mickey Mouse chinaware as presents for 600children.

This was after Walt invested energy with her in 1934. The League of Nations (the pre-W.W. II likeness the U.N.) invested in some opportunity to cast a ballot its endorsement of Mickey Mouse. (Finch, Christopher. The Art of Walt Disney from Mickey Mouse to the Magic Kingdom. NY: Harry N. Abrams, Inc., 1975, p. 53.) There is no question that Walt Disney had the ability. There is likewise no question from the record that influential individuals needed to advance him. Most likely his 320 Masonic participation and his DeMolay exercises helped help his help, and furthermore helped Walt's bowed toward the mysterious. How about we deviate just to let individuals in on Freemasonry's inclusion with acting and films. The well-known 233 Club was a masonic section for entertainers who were Freemasons.

Instances of entertainers who were Freemasons incorporate John Aasen, Gene Autry, Monte Blue and Humphrey Bogart, Douglas McClean, John Wayne. Then, at that point, there is T.V. DJ Dick Clark. Instances of Motion picture chiefs who were Freemasons incl. Ellis G. Arnall (Pres. of the Soc. of Ind. Movie Producers), Will H. Feeds (Czar of films 1922-45, and Pres. Movie Producers and Distributors of Amer. Inc.), Benj. B. Kahane (v.p.& dir. Assoc. of Motion Picture Producers, Inc.), Carl Laemmle, Frank E. Mullen David Sarnoff (Charm. of Bd. Radio Corp. of Amer. and, father" of American TV), Jack M. Warner (v.p. of Warner Bros.) and the President and dir. of Universal Pictures beginning around 1952. The Freemasons have made a big deal about Walt Disney's participation intheir enrollment attempts to sell something. Since the 2 Disney siblings' main commitments to the development of Disney films were the accounts and incidentally the thoughts utilized in a film, it is fairly misrepresentative of things that Walt Disney got all the credit for the achievement and nature of the Disney kid's shows. He was showered with 700 honours and praises from notable individuals, including 30 Oscars, and the Presidential Medal of Freedom (in '64). Walt Disney's extraordinary artists never got the credit they merited, however, nobody ought to fail to remember that Walt was the main impetus that enlivened and directed his laborers. In 1934, Walt Disney made an animation about a goddess of the Mystery Religions named Persephone. In the animation entitled The Goddess of Spring, the goddess Persephone is caught by Satan as his lady of the hour and shipped off the hidden world, with the arrangement she could get back to earth a half year of every year.

The Illuminati have ceremonies around Persephone. On December 21, 1937, Disney debuted the main full-length shading animation film "Snow White and the Seven Dwarfs." This animation had taken $1.4 in sorrow time cash and three years to make. North of 750 craftsmen dealt with the film. Walt Disney had gotten the thought from a quiet film of Snow White which he considered a kid in 1917. The film has a significant mysterious subject to it, and has been utilized for mysterious brain control programming. When the 1940 has begun, Disney was in monetary challenges. Now, Nelson Rockefeller employed his animation abilities to make kid's shows for South America, with the possibility that South Americans would stay faithful to the American industrialist authority, as opposed to moving to rise philosophies of one-party rule/Nazism, assuming they saw Walt Disney kid's shows. In Rio de Janeiro, Brazil on 8/24/42, Disney did its reality debut of Saludo Amigos, a 42-minute component about Latin America.

Ridiculous turns into a gaucho, a parrot helps Donald Duck to move the samba, as well as Disney craftsmanship showing different scenes of Brazil in the film. Be that as it may, the film The Three Caballeros, assuming it was intended to urge South American dependability to American free enterprise, totally fizzled.

The Three Caballeros showed a physically lustful Donald Duck who ofcolor attempts to make it with Latin ladies. The enchantment was likewise considered counterfeit. Albeit the Latin Americans despised the film, the foundation media's Look magazine lauded it. Another explanation that

Rockefeller sent Walt to South America was to move him so the public authority could settle the strike by Disney laborers.

Nelson Rockefeller was the public authority's Coordinator of Inter-American Affairs, a decent position thinking about the amount of South America the Rockefeller controlled. Rockefeller told Disney that Disney couldn't beat the strikers, however, that while Walt was in South America, FDR would make sure that the strike got settled. Whenever Disney returned, he submitted to the powers that were, and acknowledged the associations and the mafia's control. One more chance for Walt Disney was that in 1940, he and Roy transformed Disney into a "public partnership" and at first sold 755,000 portions of normal stock. The Illuminati Boston firm of Kidder, Peabody, and Co. were the financiers of the studio's public stock-contributions. By 1940, the Disney Studio at Burbank had turned into a smaller than usual city with 1,000 men and ladies' representatives and 20 structures on a 51acre plot of land. After the U.S. joined W.W. II, Disney Productions were made a piece of the American military foundation. The extremely following day after Pearl Harbour, the military moved onto the Disney Studio, which drives this writer to speculate that Disney was at that point part of the power foundation before the conflict breaking out. Disney made military films/kid's shows that showed the various parts of the military numerous things. They made purposeful publicity motion pictures for the partners. One series of movies was "The reason we battle." Disney made motion pictures for the IRS to get individuals to settle their expenses. A portion of the Disney films were top, secret, and concerned mystery military weapons or mystery mental strategies of the Americans. For example, one military film was "Armed force Psycho Therapy" which showed armed force men how to impart dread, and about the nuts and bolts of dread. Another military film was "Prostitution and the War". One more showed a transporter pigeon avoiding the Germans.

In 1940, Disney emerged with 2 full length enlivened kid's shows, Pinocchio and Fantasia, the two of which were before long utilized for Illuminati mind-control programming. Capriccio contains Schubert's hallowed Catholic music Ave Maria, which was utilized in a closing portion side to favor the profane Night on Bald Mountain melody, as well as six other old-style bits of ensemble music. As an element animation, it was a failure, however, as a programming instrument, it was fabulous. Capriccio gets a far-reaching clarification of how it is utilized for mind-control programming toward the finish of this section. Since a clarification of the utilization of a Disney film for mind-control is intricate, this clarification is put toward the finish of the section so it won't intrude on the progression of this present part's data. The Pinocchio film has been revamped and delivered multiple times throughout the long term. A portion of the following full length vivified movies to come out were: The Three Caballeros (1945) The Adventures of Ichabod and Mr. Toad ('49) Cinderella (1950) Treasure Island (1950) Alice in Wonderland (1951) The Story of Robin Hood and His Merrie Men (1952) Peter Pan (1953)20,000 Leagues Under the Sea (1954) Sleeping Beauty (1959) Very not long after the creation of these films, the Illuminati and their knowledge organizations involved them for Illuminati complete psyche control programming. To see their abuse as programming scripts one needs to see how the dreamlands of a modified different are made and the way that the film scripts are adjusted to program scripts. Vol. 2 gave many instances of how Alice In Wonderland and the Wizard of Oz scripts were utilized for programming scripts. At the point when Disney had his creature nature narratives, he altered and utilized portrayal to give the creatures human like attributes - something he'd effectively been doing with liveliness. Disney had a significant influence on the Illuminati's arrangement to hoist creatures and dehumanize people. One of the greatest Illuminati top dogs, and pioneer (Grand Master) of the Prieure de Sion was Frenchman Claude Debussy (bn.1862). Claude Debussy, a Merovingian, was Nautonnier (Navigator-helmsman) of the Prieure de Sion from 1885-1918. (See the report Dossiers insider facts, planche no. 4, Ordre de Sion, expounded on in Holy Blood, Holy Grail.)

In 1891, when a few mysteries coded materials (Merovingian records) were found by a French pastor Sauniere, he was guided by chapel authorities to visit with Emile Hoffet, a mysterious associate of Debussy. Debussy was dear companions with a large number of the top French soothsayers of his time. He is known to have been a dear companion to both the infamous satanists Jules Bois and MacGregor Mathers. Mathers began the Order of the Golden Dawn. Debussy was likewise a companion of the scandalous Papus (also known as Dr. Gerard Encausse) and W.B. Yeats. Papus was one of the ones who during his lifetime was important for the interlocking mysterious directorate of mysterious gatherings. Claude Debussy put a few works of the past P.d.S. Stupendous Master Victor Hugo to music. Debussy and his other strong mysterious companions were compelling with Monsieur Philippe, whose Russian mysterious circle affected the Russian Czars and Czarinas before Rasputin came around. Debussy headed out to Russia and Rome. A portion of Debussy's works became shows. Curiously, Walt Disney was incredibly restless to make an animation utilizing Debussy's Clair de Lane. The work was done; however, it was never displayed to the general population.

Disney never tracked down a spot to utilize it. It was initially finished with liveliness with flying cranes for theoccult event Fantasia, yet when the Fantasia wound up excessively long, Clair de Lane was cut and retired. It was again gotten ready for the film Make Mine Music, however, at that point, Blue Bayou was substituted in.

Walt utilized the Le Sacre du Printemps (the Rite of Spring) music for Fantasia. This piece of music was composed AS an agnostic ceremony were a virgin penances herself by moving to death. Disney's mobster Gunther Lessing had undermined Stravinsky on the off chance that authorization wasn't given for Disney to utilize the piece of music, it would be utilized at any rate. Dr. Julian Huxley engaged in the development of Fantasia. Aldous and Julian Huxley are notable by scheme scientists for their parts in the World Order. In the 1940's and 1950's, the Illuminati started involving Disney's Alice in Wonderland and the Wizard of Oz films as programming bases for their complete brain-controlled slaves. Alice in Wonderland had been done numerous years sooner by the Britisher William Cameron Menzies (who additionally did Freemason H.G. Wells' masonic estimate of the New World Order named "What might be on the horizon" in 1936, and the film Invaders from Mars.). In 1944, Illuminati Kingpin William Randolph Hearst (with some minor assistance from others) financed the Motion Picture Alliance, and Walt Disney turned into a fellow benefactor and its first Vice-President. In the mid 1950's, Walt turned his consideration from animated kid's shows to different ventures, for example, True-Life-Adventures, TV programs, and the creation of Disneyland.

Seal Island was his first evident life experience which was delivered to the overall population on May 4, 1949, and before long won Walt Disney an Oscar. Alfred and Elma Milotte had shot the film on a few Alaskan Islands named Pribilof Islands. James Algar had assembled the film. In 1952, Walter spelled his named in reverse to make the name of another enterprise, Retlaw". Roy and his family considered the transition to be an endeavor to remove them from the monetary picture. In 1954, Walt Disney and ABC settled on an understanding. ABC would straightforwardly contribute a large portion of 1,000,000 US dollars along with ensure $4.5

million in advances for the development of Disneyland. This made ABC 1/3 proprietor of Disneyland. Consequently, Walt Disney consented to deliver a customary TV series for ABC. Recollect too that ABC's leader Leonard Golden stein was an old buddy of Ronald Reagan.

On July 13, 1955, Walt and Lillian were endeavouring to commend their 30th wedding commemoration at a recreation area and eatery. Walt become too inebriated to even consider talking into the receiver, so he blew noisemakers into it, while Lillian hurried to haul him concealed. In 1961, Disney purchased out the ABC venture (likewise named Paramount) for $7.5 million with money and notes, and to bring this all state-of-the-art, later on, July 31, 1995, Disney converged with Capital Cities/ABC, with Disney in ostensible control. In reality, Capital Cities has for quite some time been a CIA front organization, so the consolidation put Disney unequivocally inside the CIA positions, despite the fact that it had been sleeping with them for the CIA's whole history. The Illuminati-controlled companies of Coca-Cola and the medication firm Johnson and Johnson became backers for Disney's initial TV shows. On 7/3/57, the Wall St. Diary declared that Atlas Corp. got 26% interest in Walt Disney Productions. Walt Disney worked unobtrusively with some consultants on the ideas driving Disneyland. His sibling and nephew attempted to forestall the task from happening.

Later they mentioned that Walt gives up Disneyland, Inc. to Walt Disney Productions, which Walt did. Walt kept 17.25 % of Disneyland possessions and Walt Disney Productions got the rest. Walt Disney Productions then, at that point, imparted their part to other people. The one who assisted Walt with financing Disneyland was the chief bad habit pres. of ABC Kintner. Walt Disney got the Illuminati's Stanford Research Institute to figure out what might be the best site for Disneyland.

A resigned Navy naval commander Joe Fowler was responsible for building both Disneyland and Walt Disney World. How do chiefs of naval operations squeeze into the power structure? Chiefs of naval operations are advised every day, and are given data concerning the mystery power structure. Most men who are at that tactical level are Illuminati or possibly all around constrained by the framework. Inside the most recent couple of years, there has been a serious work to remove any chiefs of naval operations who are not faithful to the Illuminati. Morgan-Evans, who lives in Malibu, and who might be of the renowned Morgan tribe, was the person who made the stupendous scenes for Disneyland, Walt Disney World, and

EPCOT in FL.

As per CIA sources went against to the NWO, CIA workers for hire were acquired to fabricate the underground passages under Disneyworld in 1977. These project workers were committed to mystery, however were just educated updated as the need arises why the CIA was engaged with a carnival. To deal with the mystery burrow project took an "Above Top Secret" leeway. A significant programming place was developed under Lake Holden. (A large number of the lakes in Florida are named Lake So-thus, rather than So-thus Lake.) The passage framework was worked for programming injury based all out mind-controlled slaves. It was worked of cement with steel support. Lake Holden lies just toward the northwest side of the Ornaldo International Airport and only south of Interstate 4. (It is near Range 29E on quad maps.) It is just (straight from one point to the other) around 12 miles from Disneyworld. Despite Draconian proportions of mystery, various claims (Fed. and State) were documented over the course of the years by casualties attempting to uncover the Disneyworld programming burrows, with the goal that at last the programming place was destroyed, tidied up and a, upkeep" burrow level and a, projecting" burrow level was opened to the general population. During its prime, the software engineers (military and insight men) had intriguing workplaces underground with strange programming gear. It doesn't take any creative mind to understand that assuming Disney conveyed mind-control programming above and subterranean, that they would require tight security powers to safeguard their privileged insights. Without a doubt, such is the situation. Disney event congregations have been conceded draconian abilities any place they have been fabricated!

The Disney parks have additionally utilized multitudes of spies dressed like vacationers to keep an eye on Disney's workers! On the off chance that event congregation laborers did anything somewhat awkward, they were (despite everything are) accounted for by the covert operatives in the camp, and they regularly have lost their positions. For example, one ex-specialist, who had 10 years with Disney, was found examining his separation with another laborer. Since separate doesn't fit the healthy picture that Disney needs, when the covert operative dressed as a vacationer detailed his discussion, he lost his employment. Numerous workers have attempted to recount their own harrowing tales of Disney's draconian principles and their draconian private police power, however, more often than not Disney has had the ability to stifle and threaten away an awful exposure. An exemption for that is the new Nov. 4, '96 Napa Valley Register article on page 2D named, "Pundits of Disneyland Say Security Abusive Inside Magic Kingdom." UCLA regulation educator David Sklansky remarked with regards to Disney's policy "One of the serious issues we have is no one truly knows what they are doing-how frequently they stop, question, or search individuals. They are not expose to similar kinds of administrative controls." It's practically unnecessary to let peruses know that Disney's carnival with its topic regions such as Fantasyland, Tomorrow land, and Adventure land was an extraordinary achievement. Everybody overall was interested to visit this diversion mecca to take part in something that had a perfect, healthy picture to it. The whole world framework arranged to guarantee that Disneyland got the picture and exposure that the main 13 Illuminati families and the different organizations needed it to have. For a very long time, they've done this. When something that everybody believes is perfect and healthy isn't assaulted by the world frame-work, that should cause a commotion among thinking individuals. Self-teaching, figuring out how to peruse phonetically and other healthy exercises for youngsters have been violently assaulted and disparaged by the laid-out media. Why has Disney gone immaculate? Disney Studios for a really long time endeavored to have an exceptionally spotless picture.

Laborers had clothing standards, and any movement with respect to workers that wasn't ethically moderate was justification for moment excusal. Obviously, the exemptions were all around concealed, for example, a representative who utilized entrancing to get many of the female's workers to strip down until bare. John L. Hulteng, creator of The Messenger's Motives (Englewood Cliff, NJ: Prentice-Hall, 1976, p. 213) illuminates us, "As correspondence specialists have underlined, the best effect the media have on the arrangement or change of general assessment is as far as impressions developed over a significant stretch." [bold added] The healthiness of Disney is a picture that has been worked throughout an extensive stretch of time. Disney's mysterious subjects of world citizenship, black magic, humanism, and excessive admiration have additionally been long running impressions that have been creatively executed upon this country, so long that they started before this present writer's - - and most likely the peruser's - birth.

Individuals don't connect film resembles Consenting Adults with Disney, or The Corpse Had a Familiar Face with Disney. Indeed, as recently referenced, when Disney needed to put out more "grown-up" films, they did a skilful deception and made the name Touchstone films so that individuals wouldn't relate motion pictures like Splash (which showed what resembled exposed bosoms) with Disney Productions. Another name, Hollywood Pictures, was made by Disney to assist with dispersing Touchstone films. At first, the work force of these organizations was basically Disney's staff, however as time continued, they got their own creation faculty.

On Oct. 27, 1954, Walt Disney's Wonderful World of Color appeared on TV. The TV show observed Disney's film wins. The words Wonderful World of Color are not poorly picked. As indicated by an Illuminati mind-control developer, when Disney dealt with his kid's shows, and carnivals, colors- - extraordinary tones and shading blends - were explicitly picked for mind-control programming purposes. Great World of Color under different names, for example, Disneyland circulated for a very long time over the broadcasting companies. In 1955, Walt Disney made his animation character Mickey Mouse genuine by making a fan club- - the Mickey Mouse Club, which circulated five days per week generally similarly as youngsters returned home from school. 24 kids called musketeers would help Mickey, and they would move and sing and do dramas.

The Mickey Mouse Club loved the special, adorable little beanie Mickey Mouse covers with their huge ears mounted to each side of the beanie. In the 1950's, most child watchers of the show needed their own "Mouse Ears" and to turn into a Musketeer, particularly youngsters who were getting Mickey Mouse scripts in their absolute psyche control programming. Disney utilized his Mouseketeers to assume every one of the parts in an Oz film Rainbow Road to Oz, which was never displayed to people in general. Grown-ups today (the two men and ladies) who got Mickey Mouse programming during the 50's through 70's can in any case be seen with Mickey Mouse stickers, watches, lampshades, trinkets, tee shirts, and so on Years after the fact the children who watched can in any case recall "Twist and Marty" and the Mickey Mouse signature melody. The picture that everything was amazing including Mickey was depicted by the Club's T.V. program. Still in some way the American public started to utilize "Mickey Mouse" as an equivalent for a senseless, imagine the approach to getting things done. It became normal for individuals to say, "He mickey-moused it together." to mean he made a less than impressive display assembling it. On Jan. 30, 1957, Walt Disney had a TV program broadcasted named "About Magic" where a Magic Mirror clarifies about wizardry. The Magic Mirror likewise contains a "Bibbidi-bibbidi-Boo" succession. In 1959,

Disney purchased 8 little submarines from Todd Shipyards for $2, 150.000.

Whenever ABC wouldn't allow Walt to make a TV series out of a storyline where an enchanted ring changes a kid into a canine (a brain control programming subject) - - on the grounds that ABC didn't figure the general population could swallow the story line- - Walt quit ABC for NBC. Walt then, at that point, made a downsized variant of this mysterious storyline entitled The Shaggy Dog. Ahead of schedule in the 1960's, Walt and his sibling Roy went subtly searching for a region on the east coast to fabricate another Disney Park. Walt the more youthful of the two, passed on in 1966, and Roy completed the task. Starting in 1964, 30,000 sections of land were subtly bought at $200 a section of land in the Orlando, FL region only west of NASA's Cape Kennedy. Utilizing fake names and paying money, Disney purchasers purchased the land and swore the vendors to the mystery.

The Magic Kingdom has been duplicating. In 1971, Walt Disney World was opened to people in general. Sway Hope and others partook in a Disney unique on Oct. 29, 1971 "Thousand opening of Walt Disney World". From the hour of its opening until Oct. 12, 1995, Disney World determined 1/ 2 billion individuals visited DisneyWorld. This event congregation is in Orlando, FL on the north of 27,400 sections of land and incorporates the EPCOT Center (presently likewise called just Epcot). The EPCOT focus was one more long for Walt Disney's (but more than marginally altered from Walt's unique EPCOT thoughts.) EPCOT initially represented Experimental Prototype Community of Tomorrow. It was to be an augmentation of the gigantic psyche control being completed at Disney World. The first EPCOT city planned by Walt was to continue its business (traffic) by means of underground streets and passages like the Disney Theme parks. After Walt Disney passed on, his replacements changed the proposed trial city into another amusement park essentially called Epcot. It is actually normal to see hordes of the north of 48,000 individuals plunge on Walt Disney World and the EPCOT focus in a solitary day. A few guests show up through a monorail. Guests can purchase 5-Day World Hopper passes which permit them to skip around with admission to every one of the locales for seven days. As such, a few families stay for seven days at Disneyworld.

Bad-to-the-bone guests can get Annual Passports which give limitless utilization of Walt Disneyworld for a whole year.

As a general rule, numerous guests to Disneyworld start the day energetic, and following a day of blistering sun and holding up in long queues with enormous groups for impersonations of the real world, the travelers are zombie-like and anticipating returning to their lodgings. Many individuals have felt the rides were not almost what they anticipated. A portion of the rides are superior to other people, and some commonly get remarks like, "It was inept." Some of the creepy occasions like Snow White's Adventures, or the larger than usual tops of the Disney characters strolling around can leave the little preschool youngsters unnerved and bewildered for the remainder of the day. Conversely, more seasoned kids, who ordinarily seldom show tolerance at home might show the amount they need to go on a specific Disney ride, by holding up 90 minutes in the warm sun for a ride. Outsider Encounter is a Walt Disneyland include that welcomes travelers in for a "showing of interplanetary instant transportation." When the "exhibition" as arranged "separates" an, outsider" with asocial attributes shows up among the crowd and threatens the crowd. An adorable animal is revoltingly singed, distorted, and afterward spewed into space shouting. Here are a few remarks from guests to this Walt Disneyland fascination:

"Outsider Encounter is one of those rides I can say I've seen and that I have no aim of ever doing again. Truth be told, guardians who take youngsters younger than six oughts to be raised on kid misuse." Woman, from MI "Alien Encounter was the WORST insight for my kid (and pretty much every kid in there). It begins charming enough during the preshow, yet the real show is a fiasco for youngsters. My little girl shouted and cried in dread all through it. I thought the Disney alerts were ambiguous and incorrect. At the point when we left, there wasn't one kid with dry eyes (even durable looking 12-year-old young men were crying.). I think an age necessity of 13 or 14 is more suitable. I conversed with a couple of grown-ups and we even concurred that the embellishments were very undesirable in any event, for us. This show isn't a Disney family experience-- its ATROCIOUS!!" A mother from Phillipsburg, NJ.

"We went to Alien Encounter...The preshow is misleading. It sort of breaks you into thinking "this isn't genuinely terrible." When the principle part came up, I concede the experience gave me the outright heebie-jeebies. ..I'm at absolutely no point doing that show in the future - it was excessively extraordinary for me, and I'm presently 27 years old! from a family in Laurel, MD Michael Eisner, the President of Walt Disney Co., at first dismissed Alien Encounter for not being unnerving enough when it was being considered as an expansion to Disneyworld. One considers what he would have preferred! Snow White's Adventures, which was a fascination at Disneyland, was one of whatthe Disney individuals called "dull rides". Inevitably a sign showed up with a witch advance notice individuals that the fascination was terrifying. Later in 1983, they renamed it Snow White's Scary Adventures. It very well may be fascinating to bring up that when the first Snow White and Seven Dwarf's film came out, that England prohibit the film to be seen by any youngster under 16 except if joined by a grown-up in light of the alarming substance of the film.

How far we have come from that point forward. Schools in the Florida and California regions additionally make field outings to the Magic Kingdom that are organized with Disney. EPCOT gets a huge number of youngsters this way during March, September, and October. Secondary schools utilize the Magic Kingdom for proms or senior evenings, and a few couples utilize the offices of the Magic Kingdom for weddings. Modem Bride positioned Orlando as the main special night objective on the planet. Bunch conversations of individuals who took special nights to Disney World have had an agreement that the promotion isn't generally so extraordinary as the truth. A few weddings are finished with animation characters. Disney offers "fantasy" wedding bundles. An incredible arrangement for two psyche-controlled slaves. They can build up their programming while at the same time getting hitched. The Disney fantasy wedding regularly has its service on a structure on an island in the Seven Seas Lagoon with the Cinderella Castle as a background. The fantasy wedding can then be followed by a Fantasy gathering with a selection of topics like Beauty and the Beast or Aladdin. The dream programming can go on as the lady of the hour is conveyed to a "Cinderella's Ball" by a real glass carriage drawn by six white Disney horses. A costumed divine helper and stepsisters are likewise at the ball. Desert is served in a white chocolate shoe.

One of the after-dull shows is Illuminations which comprises of music, firecrackers, ejecting wellsprings, unique lighting, and laser innovation done at the World Showcase Lagoon. EPCOT has a show Cranium Command at the Wonders of Life in the Future World segment where visitors sit in a performance center that capacities as an order control space for a kid's cerebrum. In 1980, Disney emerged with the movies flop The Devil and Max Devlin. In 1984, Roy E. Disney acquired Michael Milken, of garbage bond notoriety to help Disney out monetarily. In 1985, Disney purchased MGM's privileges to Leo the Lion logo and started utilizing the MGM Wizard of Oz material. Later a revamp of Alice in Wonderland turned out in the advanced theme of Honey I Shrunk the Kids. In the 1990's, Illuminati controlled organizations proceeded with their advancement of Disney. For example, the Nestle family's Nestle organization advances Disney films on their chocolate bars. The Nestle family is uncovered in this current writer's booklet Illuminati Control Over Foods and Grains, p. 4 as one of the world class Black Nobility families. In 1996, Walt Disney World made a real private town named Celebration on its property. This independent local area has 20,000 and a school, a theatre, a fiber optic data network connecting business, as well as different elements.

SOME DISNEY People of Interest

Throughout the long term, the nearby partners of the Disneys' are extremely uncovering. General society can figure out Disney's mentality toward Illuminati bloodlines in the Disney film The Happiest Millionaire which is about Anthony J. Drexel Biddle and Angie Duke. Perusers of this current writer's past compositions will perceive the Biddle and Duke names. Indeed, the film depended freely on a book composed by Cordelia Drexel Biddle about the Biddles X.Atencio. His first name was Xavier, however was nicknamed and called X. He chipped away at the haunted mansion of Disneyland with WED undertakings. He joined Disney in 1938, and was an associate illustrator of Fantasia.

Warren Beatty. (b. 1937 in VA) This entertainer is from the Illuminati Beatty family and featured in Disney'sDick Tracy. The Dick Tracy film significantly involves shading, and this connects to the shading programming of the brain control. Some absolute brain-controlled slaves have programming in view of Disney's Dick Tracy moviefor them to find and kill "targets" (individuals). Warren's sister is the popular (or scandalous) Shirley Maclaine. Shirley "MacClaine" isn't what she shows up for. Her dad was an educator who was a CIA resource. She was utilized by the CIA as a sex slave. She became famous with the studios since she headed to sleep with the right individuals. Her abilities were utilized to get her as a knowledge slave into places that a conspicuous insight specialist couldn't go. She was hitched to a man in the NSA for almost 20 years. Her embraced name Maclaine (allegedly her mom's original last name) is a play on words on McLain, VA where the CIA modified her. Shewas utilized by the CIA in an activity in Australia, where the CIA involved her as a sex slave to think twice about Peacock, an Australian MP, so they could lay out the Nugen-Hand bank for their grimy tax evasion and so on She is companions with satanist Stephen Nance who has furnished her with a portion of her lessons. Lowell McGovern thinks of her material. The CIA has customized a large number of their New Age captives to worship Shirley MacLaine. An illustration of this is Christa Tilton, one of their psyche-controlled slaves, who uncovered in a meeting how she viewed herself as a brought back to life Christian who had gone through a large portion of her time on earth in Oklahoma, yet had strangely been attracted to Shirley MacLaine. During her life she has gotten rehashed "clairvoyant urgings"- - that is compelling impulses to get things done and end up in a good place, which she's not sure where these urgings came from. After spellbinding, Christa drew photos of the specialist who customized her. Christa has had a government specialist screen her continually. Her significant other has seen this specialist, who has made an appearance on her entryway step and settled on decisions for her. She names the specialist John Wallis (no doubt a cover name). This specialist has a total information on her life, and government specialists have taken photographs of her during her as far as anyone knows "outsider kidnapping" encounters. Christa is only one of many casualties who have been customized to revere Shirley MacLaine. (Christa is referenced here on the grounds that she is one case that this creator knows about.) Warren Beatty, who peppers his discourse with four-letter words was an understudy at the Stella Adler Theatre Studio in NYC.

Dark, Shirley Temple. Shirley Temple Black sat on the Disney directorate. Her movies were utilized for a portion of the mid 40's and 50's customizing and showing slaves body developments/dance. She wedded somebody in a world-class Network family from San Francisco named Charles A. Dark. Charles A. Dark was a Lt. Col. in the Pentagon who inhabited Bethesda, MD. Was Shirley an early illustration of cerebrum stem scarring to get virtuosos? Shirley's sibling seems to have created "Various Sclerosis" from cerebrum stem-scarring. It was Shirley Temple who helped to establish the International Federation of Multiple Sclerosis Societies, and was an individual from its executive. board of trustees. Shirley addressed the U.S. at the UN General Assembly in 1969, has a place with the Sierra Club, and has been embellished with the Cross of Malta. Shirley has shown hints that she might be an Illuminati mind-controlled youngster protege.

Stephen Bollenbach. Bollenbach was important for Walt Disney the board, and was a key figure who aided designer Disney's $19 billion buyouts of the CIA's Capital Cities/ABC, as well as offered the plan to Eisner. He is the CEO of the Network's Hilton Hotels Corp. He as of late has been engaged with attempting to purchase ITT, to assemble the world's biggest in gambling club blend. Bollenbach has a broad foundation in the gaming-betting industry. At the point when the Justice Dept. started investigating the consolidation of Disney with Cap. Urban areas/ABC, Bollenbach surrendered his Disney position. Certain individuals feel his renunciation was required for Disney to get the Justice Dept. to support the consolidation, since his past was defenceless against being uncovered.

Warren Buffett. A significant investor in Walt Disney. He likewise possesses 40% of Berkshire Hathaway Inc. which likewise possesses bunches of portions of Disney stock. As indicated by S.F. Analyst, Buffett himself possesses 24 million shares of Disney. Warren Buffett is important for the Ak-Sar-Ben organization and Monarch slave victimizers who were uncovered in the Nebraska Saving and Loan outrage. He is maybe the second most extravagant man in the country, and excessively strong for anybody to contact. In the head honcho versus top dog fights, certain individuals near within consider Buffett to be a hero. Perusers need to concentrate on the Lincoln Savings and Loan outrage and the embarrassments associated with modified youngster slaves at Boy's Town to get more data on this Disney investor. Robert G. Hagstrom, Jr., who is the portfolio director of the common asset Focus Trust, which has shares in Walt Disney, composed the book The Warren Buffett Way. Hagstrom has a part on Disney in his The Warren Buffett Way. He cites Buffett as incredibly energetic with regards to Disney's consolidation with Capital Cities/ABC. Due to his energy Buffett says, the chances are incredibly high that we will have an extremely enormous measure of Disney stock."

Salvador Dali- - This odd surrealist Spanish craftsman was a companion of Walt Disney. After Salvador was kicked out of Spain for Franco's conviction that he was a socialist, he came to America, and worked with Disney Studios in 1946. Salvador, an unconventional who had no specific work propensities, portrayed himself, "The main distinction among me and a crazy person is that I'm not a psycho."

The Tommy Dorsey Band, This band has had various men in it who are Mind-control slave victimizers related to the Network. Honest Sinatra, a sexual slave client, stumbled upon the opportunity of a lifetime with this band. This band performed at Disneyland in 1984 at the Plaza Gardens. Tommy Dorsey was important for the Network's fashionable elite. Whenever he was on a USO Tour with Bob Hope, he wounded entertainer Joe Hall and tossed him out of a window. Joe needed to have 32 fastens. However, Joe didn't get equity, the adjudicator excused his argument against

Tommy.

Michael Dammann Eisner, Chairman at Disney is a CIA resource and associated with the horde. A few insiders accept he is associated with components of the CIA and horde that are hostile to NWO. All things considered, these enemy of NWO groups additionally utilize mind-control. Eisner disregarded a danger by Red China to blacklist Disney items assuming he made a film about the country Tibet that China controls with draconian power. The U.N., the Commerce Dept. what's more the State Dept. all attempted fruitlessly to get him to withdraw on the film. Documentation interfacing Michael Eisner and Walt Disney Co. to mind control is their help of the Boys and Girls Club of Napa Valley, which is utilized for a stock of kids for pedophilia and brain control. The Boys& Girls Club is utilized to supply caddies for the Silverado Country Club, where these youngsters are likewise utilized as brain-controlled slaves for the sexual depravities of the world-class. Notice that Napa's Silverado Country Club welcomes in superstars, (for example, CIA resource Pat Boone, Joe DiMaggio ex of sex slave Marilyn Monroe, Engelbart Humperdinck a slave controller, Digger Phelps Notre Dame's mentor who uses slaves, and Jack Valenti CEO of Motion Picture Assoc. and Bohemian Grover) for a golf competition which is charged as a, benefit for the Boys and Girls Club". The advantage for kid slaves is they get to assist and physically administer world-class debases. Michael came from old American cash of a family that has been rich shippers and attorneys. Michael experienced childhood in sumptuous Park Ave. as well as his family's "nation place" in Bedford Hills close to Mt. Kisco, NY. He went to a world-class non-public school Allen-Stevenson, which is popular for its youngsters' ensemble.

At 14 years old, he then, at that point, went to Lawrenceville School, which is a private academy for Princeton, whose educational cost in '56 was $3,000. Eisner's class incl. NY's lead representative's child, and different children of influential men, for example, the child of Saudi Prince Turki al-Faisal. The school is a private academy for the foundation's media outlet.

Understudies are simply permitted to see their folks on significant occasions. Eisner was in the Periweg Club, the school's theatrics society. His helpless educational exhibition implied that he needed to go to a little aesthetic sciences school, rather than Princeton or Harvard, for example, was family custom. For example, his granddad had gone to Phillips Exeter Academy and Harvard. His granddad has served in numerous government commissions and had a place with the Harvard Club, the American Club in London as well as a few yacht clubs. Between his lesser and senior year in secondary school, Eisner was a page at NBC's HQ in the Rockefeller Center. In 1966, he found some work in the programming division of ABC. He had a place of authority. Eisner had one great break for concluding TV programming. He was 21 when the ideal interest group was 21 years of age, and when he was 35, the objective age of the entertainment world was then 35. He has been portrayed as having "powerful excitement" coupled with a lifetime mission for untested thoughts.

Rich H. Candid, was Executive Vice-President with Walt Disney until his abrupt abdication about a year prior to this was composed. He worked one next to the other with Katzenberg and left after Katzenberg surrendered in a question with Disney's director Eisner. Rich Frank was President of Walt Disney's TV-Media Division. He procured the bequest of VanHoffenwiggen, when VanHoffenwiggen escaped the nation and disappeared when Lendvest started to be uncovered. VanHoffenwiggen was a significant figure associated with Lendvest Mortgage Inc., a medication washing activity and medication pirating activity working out of Napa Valley. It was likewise the quickest developing land contract organization in northern California until its medication carrying started to be uncovered. Lendvest did a few stunts ala Nugen Hand Bank. A great many dollars of financial backers and leasers have vanished leaving loads of harming individuals, and the home loan organization petitioned for insurance from banks inU.S. Liquidation court, and is as yet inactivity. Global agent Edmond Safra's private bank, the Republic National Bank of NY, launders cash from the Medellin drug cartel. Safra's bank sent Lendvest bunches of fresh new $100 notes. The Safras are connected to the Rothschilds. (The Safras are apparently ongoing land owners in St. Helena close to Napa (through Good Wine Co. which is the Spring Mountain Wineries), close to where Lendvest was HQ. Edmond's nephew, Jacob Safra, has an association in Napa Valley's Good Wine Co.

The Rothschild's Citicorp empowered Republic National Bank to give worldwide (world) carrier bonds ("monetary orders") The Luxembourg/ Belgium part of Bank Nacional de Paris gave a conveyor bond that was associated with the Lend vest drug running activity. In Britain, a U.S. resident Mike Spire ran the British activity of Lendvest and In Vest. Land Vest's parent was In Vest which has worked in the U.K., Switz., Saudi Arabia, and Paraguay. The boring tale made short, LendInvest has been a worldwide CIA-Mafia drug running activity, with Illuminati hints and associations with it. In light of this, it is peculiar, that Walt Disney's President of its TV-

Media Division, Rich Frank, purchased the palatial house of John 0. Many vanhoffenwiggen vanished from the nation when prosecutions and captures started to be made of individuals associated with Lendvest. As indicated by insiders, Rich Frank is likewise one of various Napa Valley individuals engaged with the illicit naming of wines. Rich Frank was a critical figure in Disney's customizing adventure with three local Bell Telephone organizations meeting up. Chime Telephone needed to get into satellite TV. Michael Ovitz framed a rivalgroup of 3 other Bell Telephone co.. Calvin Robinson, who connected to Land Vest, worked with Boyce, who thus worked for TRW Co., in Redondo Beach, CA. Boyce was condemned to 40 years for offering US reconnaissance privileged insights to thesoviets.

Daniel Hillis, the prime supporter of a supercomputer maker Thinking Machines from MIT, is responsible for the Walt Disney Imagineering unit. Hillis assisted Disney with fostering an augmented experience ride at Disneyland in light of the Aladdin animation.

Jeffrey Katzenberg, has been the executive of Disney's film studio, is a forceful laborer, a model Type An individual., Ask 50 individuals to depict Jeffrey Katzenberg, and most will say determined. 'In the event that Jeffrey was any more forceful, he'd be in prison." says the maker, Dan Melnick." Katzenberg is the dad of twins, which individuals' joke was normal of his productivity. Katzenberg managed the development of Star Trek. The greater part of his films has been filming industry victories. In the '70's, Katzenberg worked for NY Mayor John Lindsay.

Sanford Martin Litvack. Sanford is the Executive Vice Pres. of Disney and is accountable for "HR" for the enterprise. He is a Jewish legal counselor who was taught at the Jesuits' Georgetown University. He is onthe bd of dir, of Bet Tzedek.

Vincent Price. The cost has been one of the major persuasive mediums thathave furnished the world with many occults' shock books and scripts. He worked for Disney some, and was the voice for Ratigan in The Great Mouse Detective. Vincent Price's old buddy John Hay Whitney is an Illuminati head boss and bad habit pres. of the Pilgrim Society and was raised into the Illuminati through the Yale Scroll and Key brotherhood. His companion Whitney likes blood and gore flicks.

The Osmond Brothers, Merrill Osmond's young men were "found" at Disneyland when they were visiting the site in 1962. The Disney individuals on Main St. simply "occurred" to perceive the ability of the five young men and marked them up soon for their first expert singing agreement.

The Osmond Boys did some TV appearances for Disneyland like Meet Me at Disneyland, and Disneyland into the evening. (Considering the psyche control programming done to these Osmund kids, these TV shows were an awful joke.) Of the singing Osmond kids, Donny is the close to the most youthful, and his sister Marie is the most youthful. Both Donny and his sister Marie are modified products who are slaves, who have been exposed to a great deal of misuse. They have great front modifies. Their dad has made millions from medications, pornography, and white servitude and is essential for the Mormon Illuminati front. The Mormon front of the Illuminati has gotten a great deal of good exposure off of the Osmond's. They sang for Andy Williams whose French spouse was once summoned on murder allegations. Later they sang for the evil Network's Lawrence Welk show. Swedish complemented Lawrence Welk has been essential for the Network. Marie Osmond has grown up, and she has embraced 3 of her 5 youngsters disregarding her bustling singing timetable which incorporates approx. 200 singing shows a year at places like Mafia controlled Atlantic City. As far as mysterious families, took on youngsters are frequently modified kids, so this is a sign that her kids have been customized as well.

Michael Ovitz. Ovitz was the no. 2 man at Walt Disney for some time until close to the furthest limit of '96. Michael Ovitz was a secondary school cohort in VanNuys, CA with Michael Milken (later the garbage bond wizard), and there are a large number of similar individuals associated with the two men. Whenever Michael Ovitz's National Mercantile Bancorp (a saving and credit) started getting into the sand trap of a few claims and embarrassments, lawyer Robert Strauss addressed him. Illuminati part Robert Strauss has been a legal counselor associated with drug running and the mafia. He was additionally an FBI specialist from '41 to '45 with Hoover. He is conceded to the Wash. D.C. bar. Pres.

Shrubbery delegated him U.S. Diplomat to Russia. He has been on the leading body of dir, of the Illuminati's PepsiCo, Archer-Daniels-Midland (ADM), and General Instruments (which have been uncovered in different compositions by this creator.) He was additionally a board individual from the Illuminati-mafia run MCA. Strauss is found in Wash. D.C. as an in the background power specialist. Strauss addressed Michael Milken partner Ronald 0. Perelman, Charm. of Revlon, who made a $600 mil. killing off of the first Gibraltar S&L. Strauss addressed MCA, which the Bronfmans took over in 1995. The book Knoedelsder, William. Stiffed-The True Story of MCA, The Music Business, and the Mafia. NY: HarperCollins Pub., 1993, works really hard of associating MCA to the crowd, the Network, and IranContra.

Time magazine 2/24/97 conveyed a page tedious account about Michael Ovitz being out of a task. In the article, they revealed that he was investing energy in his new yacht The Illusion, visiting Joe Silver's bequest in So. Carolina, visiting his property in Aspen, CO, and having lunch with speculation counsel Richard Salomon of Spears, Benzak, Salomon, and Farrell. Gordon Crawford of the Capital Group is cited in the article applauding Ovitz, and saying he would put resources into an Ovitz adventure. Ovitz is accepted to be mafia by individuals in a spot to know. He has additionally been known to compromise individuals utilizing mafia terms, for example, Vanity Fair reports Ovitz undermining Bernie Brillstein, a maker, with his "foot fastens". The San Francisco Chronicle statements the most recent issue of Columbia Journalism Review about an occurrence where a correspondent Anita Busch who was exploring Ovitz became viciously ill from the MSG in her food as she talked with him. To finish off everything off, Ovitz followed up her story which scrutinized his activities, by sending her a gift-wrapped bundle of MSG with a single word note: "Appreciate.". Michael Ovitz has had the clout to manage Illuminati boss Edgar Bronfman no holds barred. He mentioned and got Bronfman to keephis father utilized, which was obediently finished. Edgar Bronfman Jr. had truly considered having Ovitz head Seagram's MCA/Universal combination.

Candid G. Wells. Candid was the President and the Chief Operating Officer of The Walt Disney Co. Wells was additionally on Disney's top managerial staff. He was a Rhodes Scholar, and an attorney in 1955. The individuals who have perused past books by this writer know how the Rhodes Scholars fit into things and are important for the Illuminati. He worked intimately with Eisner and Katzenberg. Forthcoming kicked the bucket in a helicopter crash in the spring of 1994 while heli-skiing in Nevada. His enduring sister is Molly Wells Chappellet who goes around in Illuminati circles. Molly Wells Chappellet has been highlighted a few times in Betty Knight Scripp's magazine Appellation. Betty Knight Scripp was hitched to a Bohemian Grove part. Betty has been old buddies with: the late Pamela Harriman (who was a new U.S. representative to France and associated with the Rothschilds), as well as old buddies with Her Imperial Highness the Grand Duchess of Vladmir of Russia, who claims the Chateau Margaux in Bordeaux. Betty Scripps by and by screens with tend to think about what is placed into her mind-blowing magazine Appellation. She has a section's "Who in the Wine Country" where the Chappellets have shown up on paper various times.

Virtually every one of Disney's 1920 films had a dark feline in them. Many had mysterious inclinations to the contents. The mysterious inclination never left from Disney subjects.

DISNEY and Its MOB Connection

At the point when this creator addressed the co-creator's more profound Illuminati adjusts about Disney, they responded that Disney had been depicted to them when they were in the Illuminati as "an organization inside an organization." They said that while in the Illuminati, they knew that Disneyland had their own administration, their own guidelines, and their own police power. They were a criminal organization inside an organization. What this Illuminati changes nonchalantly referenced, was checked by this creator the most difficult way possible through research. One Disneyland Security Supervisor said, "There is no Constitution at Disneyland. We have our own regulations." Once, when Walt Disney got annoyed at a Hollywood police officer, Walt said, "I'll have your identification." If Disney monitors choose to, theywill get extremely harsh truly with individuals, and attack them in any style they see fit. Individuals they keep are regularly tossed into minuscule cells at Disneyland where they are kept without the advantage of a call, without the advantage of a latrine or water. The legal framework chooses to disregard anything that Disney police do. Many individuals pay Disney to get their kids out of a Disney cell, and never get fair treatment by any law.

This kind of treatment has continued for a really long time, and is right around a day-by-day event at Disneyland. The Anaheim Police power is extremely amiable with the Disney private police power. Additionally, at a certain point, the Burbank Chief of Police was the brother by marriage to Disney's Chief of Security. As of late, when a couple documented an unfair passing suit against the Magic Kingdom of Disney in Florida, the territory of Florida shockingly has seemed to have eased off from their customary conduct of safeguarding Disney's power. An article on the suit said, "there is proof of some apprehension with Disney's relative independence." (San Francisco Chronicle, article "Mickey's Dark Side" Oct. 1, '96, p. C6) A lawyer for the situation said, "Disney World's security individuals aren't simply cops, they are awful ones. I don't think there is any company that has at any point had the apparent influence that Disney has." Richard Fogle song, an educator of legislative issues at Rollins College in Winter Park expressed, "On the grounds that Disney World controls such a great deal it's corporate and city universe, it can't resist the urge to act in an awkward way to brutally safeguard its personal responsibility. They have immunity from state and neighbourhood land use regulation. They can fabricate an atomic plant, disseminate liquor. They have abilities neighbourhood networks don't have. Do they mishandle it? As I would see it, yes." In accordance with Disney's past oppressive approaches on their properties, Disney's new city called Celebration won't have any chosen government.

Since the city is unincorporated (a perfect Disney stunt) the chairman is selected by Disney. A few Disney "semi government'" bodies control residents of the city. For example, the Celebration Residential Owners Association, which takes part in restricting all occupants to a Declaration of Covenants, a lawful fastener of decides that inhabitants should live by. Obviously, the Declaration of Covenants was composed by Disney. These standards incorporate such finicky things as, something like two individuals can rest in a similar room, no pickup trucks can be left before homes, and in the event that Disney authorities try to avoid your feline or canine they can persuasively eliminate the creature from your home. Disney Corp. has executed various double dealings on the inhabitants, incl. disgraceful work on their homes, and working for their "public" school with Disney comrades. All things considered, the inhabitants that have moved into Celebration are sparkling with acclaim for the town notwithstanding the way that the city is completely run by Big Brother Disney Corp. Obviously, the individuals who don't adore it, before long leave. So much for the American custom of self-government.

Since the city is unincorporated (a slick Disney stunt) the chairman is named by Disney. A few Disney's semi-government'' bodies control residents of the city. For example, the Celebration Residential Owners Association, which takes an interest in restricting all occupants to a Declaration of Covenants, a lawful folio of decides that inhabitants should live by. Obviously, the Declaration of Covenants was composed by Disney. These standards incorporate such finicky things as, something like two individuals can rest in a similar room, no pickup trucks can be left before homes, and in the event that Disney authorities would rather avoid your feline or canine they can coercively eliminate the creature from your home. Disney Corp. has executed various trickeries on the occupants, incl. terrible work on their homes, and working for their "public" school with Disney sidekicks. In any case, the inhabitants that have moved into Celebration are gleaming with acclaim for the town despite the way that the city is completely run by Big Brother Disney Corp. Obviously, the people who don't cherish it, before long leave. So much for the American practice of self-government.

Some MOB HISTORY

Customarily, the horde kingpins have had a yearly culmination. In 1928, they had their yearly meeting at Cleveland. In 1929, they had their mysterious yearly meeting at Atlantic City. In 1931, they held their mysterious yearly conference at Wappingers Falls, NY. At the Wappingers Falls meeting, went to by around 300 masters and troopers, the tops of the family factions examined their wrongdoing family plans. They concluded where the primary public Mafia show was to be held. When the Mafia had the option to hold their yearly private-public gatherings, they had the option to organize their exercises, as well as choose such things asthe course of public and inside activities, and long-range plansthe advancement of new bosses'choices on turf and rank, wares &cash working through unions or questions with the Mishpucka, Triads, FBI, Illuminati, and so on and consciously working with others. The mafia families would then leave the yearly culmination gatherings and finish in their space of tasks, until they would meet the following year, audit their victories and disappointments, get new tasks, and choose new short-and long-haul objectives. In 1927, the Mishpucka worked with Mafia to highjack a contraband shipment of bourbon making a trip from Ireland to Boston for the Kennedy Illuminati family. The majority of Kennedy's gatekeepers were killed in the shootout, and J.P. Kennedy had the widows of the watchmen attacking him for monetary help. Billy Graham's old buddy Mafia Chief Joseph Bonanno was one of the bosses who went to the yearly conferences. He likewise met with J.F. Kennedy in the Winter of 1959. John Kennedy was known to have said that mobster Sam Giancana worked for his Kennedy family. The horde/ Illuminati unions and infighting are too mind boggling to even consider managing in this book, however, the two gatherings needed to set strategies in motion to manage the nullification of Prohibition, which would end their worthwhile smuggling. The transient arrangement for the Mafia was to control the entertainment world in Hollywood, and to infiltrate the associations better. The drawn-out plans called for sending their next couple of ages of kids off to the top schools and getting them into authentic decent corporate positions. By learning the intricate details of legitimate, lawful activities, they could then blend in the illicit tasks in with their lawful ones and look lawful. They intended to broaden their power base into governmental issues, the Harvard-Stanford business colleges, as well as the best corporate board rooms. They expected (and have succeeded) in getting a portion of their posterity to deliver/direct T.V./films. They would include an expanding presence inside the Bohemian Grove participation, as well as a portion of the other incredible social and business clubs. Their arrangement to assume control over the entertainment world relied on their association command over associations and theaters. The Chicago horde controlled the International Alliance of Theatrical Stage Employees Union. The horde controlled the projectionist's association, and in the event that the producers had the theaters where their films were shown closed down, what great could it be to make motion pictures? The producers and the mafia both had influence and cash. As opposed to battling an extended conflict, they made an arrangement. The significant studios would give about $50,000 per year to the mafia, and the little ones $25,000, to be permitted to work. Different arrangements were likewise reached. Horde thugs Willie Bioff and George E. Browne were horde lieutenants who coordinated the crowd's "Hollywood takeover".

Countless dollars were emptied by the Mafia & Mishpucka into land in southern California, by utilizing authentic neighbourhood finance managers to launder the cash. Hollywood was pronounced a "free zone" where all the Mafia/Mishpucka families could work without a feeling of dread toward a turf war. Allow us to backtrack marginally to 1930. Columbia circulated Disney kid's shows from 1930 until 1932, when Disney changed to United Artists, since Columbia wasn't trying to pay Disney the cash they owed. In 1930, Cohn, Pres. of Columbia Pictures, got Disney off the monetary snare with Powers by scaring Powers with some road endures conveying a lawful suit. In the event that Disney wasn't obligated to the mafia previously, he was by then. Biographers have been perplexed why Disney went into such an awful misery after Henry Cohn "made a difference" him. Troublemaker Henry Cohn ensured Walt realized who was chief. His demeanour was that Walt ought to be content to be paid by any stretch of the imagination by him for the kid's shows Walt provided Columbia. After this, Walt would secure himself in his room and sob wildly for quite a long time. He was outside the realm of possibilities for anybody to coexist with. He couldn't zero in on anything, and would gaze for significant stretches out the window. Biographers pin Walt's conduct on the way that his significant other was pregnant. They likewise put it on his companion Iwerks surrender to another organization. In all honesty, Walt had dealt with Iwerk like a canine, and where it counts probably known why Iwerk left such a harmful relationship.

To guarantee that he sobbed for quite a long time consistently in light of the fact that he understood he could turn into a dad is a lot to swallow. Whenever Walt was asked years after the fact about for what valid reason, he was so discouraged he said it was the pressure of the monetary circumstance. Walt said, "I had a mental meltdown. Costs were going up; each new picture we completed expense more to make than we had figured it would acquire when we initially started to design it.I laughed hysterically." This writer submits to the peruser that a piece of his breakdown might have without a doubt been the monetary pressure from having gone under the impact point of the mafia. They had every one of the resources to represent the deciding moment him, and he had no real option except to give up to their staggering ability to extort and obliterate him OR to escape the business.

How this treated spot Walt in a position where his two most grounded characteristics needed to conflict - his mind-boggling fixation to work for himself, and his imaginative fixation to make a movement that was wrapped up with his inner self and his profound fears and mental necessities. His psyche couldn't surrender its autonomy nor its innovativeness without extraordinary mental torment, and accordingly, Walt was extremely disheartened, realizing that he would need to concede rout, and clasp under the impact points of the enormous young men. Exactly when he wanted consistent encouragement his significant other planned to have a youngster, and his best artist left. Walt had deserted Iwerks years prior, and Walt's significant other had needed a youngster for quite a while. Iwerkstakeoff and his showing up youngster don't in themselves represent the long exceptional mental meltdown that Walt experienced.

Biographers bring up that Walt was exceptionally hesitant to have kids, and that he was weak with ladies including his better half a significant part of the time. His impotency to do ordinary sex might assist with clarifying his mysterious sexual propensities. Walt's masonic sibling Carl Laemmle offered Walt a decent arrangement to assist him with recuperating from Henry Cohn's oppressive control of Walt, yet Carl needed the copyright to Mickey Mouse as a trade-off for the assistance, and Walt wouldn't leave behind Mickey Mouse. All things considered, Walt marked an agreement presented by Joseph Schenck of UA (United Artists), who was one of the Mafia's unlawful medication head bosses. In 1935, the horde's unlawful drug dealer Joseph Schenck continued to establish twentieth Century, Inc. which later converged with Fox in '38 to shape Twentieth Century-Fox, whose top managerial staff would incorporate two Illuminati bosses, William Randolph Hearst, and Malcolm MacIntyre. Joseph Schenck's siblings Nicholas Schenck and Marcus Loew combined Metro Pictures and Goldwyn Pictures and named Louis B. Mayer as its head. In the interim throughout the long term, MCA, headed up by Illuminati Kingpin Lew Wasserman acquired an imposing business model over the American entertainment world with the mysterious reserved alcove bargains that they made with Ronald Reagan's Screen Actors Guild and Petrillo's American Fed, of Musicians.

(Incidentally, Lew Wasserman would attempt to restore Reagan's acting vocation in the mid '60's. Honest Sinatra and Walt Disney were the two companions of Ronald Reagan, and each of the three put the stock at the top of the priority list control.) Ronald Reagan and Petrillo thusly worked with the Mafia's NCS Council of 9 (which incl. Anthony Accardo and Sam Giancana), which at one point partitioned the U.S. into 24 horde domains. After J. Schenck went to prison (momentarily), he was supplanted as Pres. of the twentieth Cent. Fox by Spyros Skouras. Prior to his capture, while Schenck was as yet responsible for the twentieth Cent. Fox, he made various proposals to Disney for Disney to fuse his studio as a development of the twentieth Cent. Fox. Disney labored for a couple of years with them circulating his films, yet he would not relinquish attempting to be autonomous. The FBI and American Intelligence went to the crowd to help them as the U.S. entered WW II. Maybe Walt's horde association added a catalyst for his recruitment.

Walt went to various American Nazi gatherings before Pearl Harbour. This creator accepts from knowing Walt's character that Walt might have been on task, rather than a Nazi supporter. All things considered, for what reason does one of Disney's Pre-Pearl harbour kid's shows show an insignia? Disney's Epcot Resorts is near the horde's Atlantic City Board Walk with its dance club. The hotel was planned by Robert A.M. Harsh. (This creator doesn't be aware of Robert Stern, however, there are customized products and Illuminati individuals inside the Stern family.)

At Walt Disney World, the club there was named "Enclosure", and afterward '8 TRAX". Parody Warehouse, which is a dance club at Pleasure

Island in Walt Disney World opened on May 1, 1989, and has involved slave entertainers too having individuals who are mind-control victimizers. On Feb. 11, 1987, Walt Disney Co. was reincorporated in Delaware. Delaware is the main express that permits all out the corporate mystery. Nobody can discover who truly is running a Delaware enterprise, and numerous different privileged insights can be concealed under Delaware's partnership regulations. Capital Group has significant offers in Disney, as well as 29% of the portions of the Robert Mondavi winery at 7801 St. Helena Hwy, Oakville, CA. Wellington Group and Mellon bank likewise have shared. Behind Capital Group are crowd-controlled gatherings like DeBartolo Realty Corp. what's more La Quinta Inns (a Bass brother. activity.) Sam Bronfman works with Sterling and Monterey Vineyards. There are incalculable individuals strolling around that have felt the heartless, unoriginal, controlling, cash snatching side of the Disney Corp. Additionally, there are various writers who have encountered directly the mystery and distrustfulness that the Disney company has. Most writers are not used to the mystery that invades Disney. Since Disney has formed the legends of America for a long time, the public takes more worry over who is running Disney, than they would different foundations. Since the greater part of America trust in the picture that the Illuminati have worked for Disney, they are pulling for it to succeed.

How the Disney Executives have sorted out some way to take land across the U.S

Throughout the long-term Walt Disney has fostered a few exceptionally tricky solid strategies to gain land. They secure land through their leaders and enormous investors and relatives of the executives and investors. After every one of the arrangements is made in a space, and when everything is set up throughout some stretch of time, these individuals then, at that point, surrender their property to Disney. Disney works with government authorities and nearby brokers to arrange extraordinary arrangements so they can prevail in their arrangements. After everything is arranged, the organization declares its arrangements and goes ahead. This system has been utilized over and again, for example, the American History Theme Park in the Manassas Civil War combat zone area of Virginia for which Disney has procured 1,800 sections of land and approaches something like 1,200 more. In Nov. '94, after another Virginia lead representative was chosen, the Virginia "Disney's America" project was declared, and Virginia casted a ballot in a split second for the cash for transportation and foundation enhancements to the region so that Disney's amusement park would be feasible. Disney set up 3 banks in Napa, CA. Their banks made advances to old families in the valley. The trusts and the wills for these families were made up by Stanford Univ. graduates. These individuals set on the sheets of these banks or associate with the sheets of these banks. They charge enormous expenses, and know each stunt in the book to deny individuals of their homes and their residing trusts. The Stanford graduates, who associate in with insight organizations and the crowd utilize specific code words when they set up their organizations, like RESOURCE, EVERGREEN and PACIFIC. There are various frightened landholders who are being threatened to sell their territory in the Napa Valley district.

DISNEY And the GOVERNMENT

Only before W.W. II, the FBI enrolled Walt Disney. His occupation was to keep an eye on Hollywood or whatever else that looked dubious. Archives acquired from the Freedom of Information Act, notwithstanding weighty editing, obviously show that Walt Disney turned into a paid Special Correspondent resource of the FBI. He answered to FBI specialist E.E. Conroy. In 1954, Walt was elevated to Special Agent in Charge (SAC) and that implies others answered to him. Subsequent to "leaving" the CIA, ex-DCI (ex-top) of the CIA William Hedgcock Webster turned into a legal advisor for the Wash. D.C. based firm of Milbank, Tweed, Hadley, and McCloy. In 1993, when news broke with regards to Walt Disney's FBI participation, ex-CIA head Webster worked with the Disney family to conceal to the public that Walt Disney was an FBI specialist. Webster went on TV and had meetings to spread the manufacture that Walt was not associated with the FBI. Why? One of the innumerable things that Disney was engaged with was the examination concerning the vanishing/assault of a six-year-old kid Rose Marie Riddle on 1/12/61. As per archives gotten from the Freedom of Information Act, W.G. Simon was the FBI specialist who met with SAC Walt Disney in L.A. regarding the case. W.G. Simon has been one of those individuals who has been openly lying by asserting that Walt Disney never was an FBI specialist. The documentation demonstrates in any case. For what reason is it so essential to the FBI and CIA to conceal that Walt was an FBI specialist? Walt additionally worked for the CIA, despite the fact that documentation of that isn't accessible. This creator guesses that the explanation the FBI and CIA are so delicate with regards to telling individuals that Walt worked for the public authority is that the Network knows how the FBI and CIA cooperated to acquire kids for mind-control programming purposes. Since Disney and Disneyland played, for example, a colossal jobs in Mind-control, Disney's association with them, albeit on the surface an apparently minor truth, is as a general rule a minor reality setting on top of a huge loathsome mystery. Whenever W.W. II began, the public authority consolidated the Disney studios into the conflict machine.

The military paid Disney $80,000 for 20 preparation kid's shows, which cost Disney $72,000 to make. Disney studios likewise made a few mystery films for the military. Mickey Mouse and Goofy kid's shows were skewed to have war subjects, for example, the Goofy drawing of 1941 "The Art of Self Defense" and "How to be a Sailor" in 1944. Maybe out of appreciation for the commitment Disney had put forth to the conflict attempt, "Mickey Mouse" was the secret word of the Allies for a large number of men on the huge D-Day intrusion on June 6, 1944. Walt Disney created an animation showing Donald Duck paying his expenses reliably. The film was entitled The New Spirit. It was exceptionally effective in getting Americans to consent to the IRS. In 1946, Disney made a film for the government funded schools for sex instruction entitled The Story of Menstruation.

For the United Nations, Walt Disney made "You never know who might turn up in the course of your day" fascination for UNICEF for the '64-65 World's Fair. This fascination was moved to the amusement parks and has been a significant component of mind-control. In the wake of learning of the tremendous measure of brain control programming continuing during night-time stealthily burrows at Disney as well as in the public offices, it seems OK why the Russian Premier Nikita Khrushchev would be denied a visit to Disneyland by the U.S. government "because of safety contemplations" when he was visiting the U.S. in Sept. 1959. Khrushchev clearly had his own security working pair with American security and the insight individuals for whatever reason(s) didn't need the complexity of these Russians going to a significant programming site. A few strong military men have been associated with Disney films. Two previous chiefs of the USS Alabama atomic sub were specialized counselors for the Disney film Crimson Tide. Walt Disney was attached to the U.S. government, and ongoing revelations show that he was attached to the FBI. Walt utilized his FBI association to obliterate the existence of Art Babbitt, who had driven the negative mark against Disney in 1940. Babbitt observed that all that he endeavored in life after the strike was destroyed by some secret power. Was Walt a piece of maritime insight connected to the FBI? Might it be said that he was important for the FBI that is engaged with kid acquisition and brain control? In the 1950's the Illuminati started sorting out covens on the West coast and started setting their power. (This comes from a few autonomous sources.) Likewise, obviously, Disney didn't have the clout in 1953 with nearby states, that it does today.

Walt Disney was ineffective when he attempted to get authorization from the city of Los Angeles and the Burbank City Council for the development of Disneyland (called Disneyland around then), in the Burbank region. One Burbank councilman told Walt, "We don't need the carny climate in Burbank." Inconsistently, inside a couple of years, they allowed to Universal to fabricate an event congregation in Burbank, which opened in 1964. Disney then, at that point, ask the Stanford Research Institute to find a spot for Disneyland (Disneyland), which they found in Anaheim. Lately, Disney concluded they needed to construct another entertainment mecca (called California Adventure) opposite Disneyland. To do as such, the Interstate thruway should have changed, and the Anaheim city chamber is expected to support the enormous 55-section of land development. Rather than the Burbank City Council in 1953, Anaheim's City Council was excited with regards to the extension notwithstanding bunches of neighborhood resistance. Local people whined at chamber gatherings to the City Council that the city should not be going countless dollars into an obligation to help a corporate goliath. (Anaheim will issue $400 million in bonds.) Locals additionally raised worries that the government funded educational system in Anaheim is anxious to the limit where they are thinking about going to half days, and that Disney Corporation should give as much thought for the younger students of Anaheim as they do to their Amusement Park. Disneyland's Pres. Paul Pressler boasted with regards to Disney's new California Adventure event congregation, "Disney's California Adventure is truly a celebration of the tomfoolery, the excellence, individuals and the achievements of this enchanted state. We truly have embarked to attempt to catch a touch of what the California dream is about." (Sounds like the fantasy is to be affluent and control individuals. The world class would prefer to give us BREAD and CIRCUS than schooling.)

The Dragnet films were done to some degree at the Disney studios. In an Office Memo from the 66-new LA SAC FBI specialist to Hoover (12/16/54), which was gotten by means of the Freedom of Information Act, the composed reminderstates, Mr. Disney has chipped in delegates of this office complete admittance to the offices of Disneyland for use regarding official matters..." Historically, we presently realize that Disney's utilization for "truly matters" included psyche control.

J. DISNEY and MIND CONTROL

When the peruser knows about the programming scripts, the peruser just requirements to watch the Disney "Undertakings in Wonderland" that come on TV in the first part of the day to see Disney mind-control at work. Inside a couple of moments one morning, this writer had seen a white bunny make "a world to you" (the statement is what the show said!) with a ring, watched Alice go through the mirrors, watched a White Rabbit [the programmer] read a book to a young lady, and the TV audience be told by the show "The White Rabbit is our main expectation!" The more deeply changes of Illuminati slaves who are modified for surveillance, for spying and coercion, and enchantment and death, are given programming to live in a dreamland. They never connect with the real world. Quite a bit of this kind of programming has continued at Disneyland.

Disneyland guests are taken in a boat where dolls sing an around-the-world signature tune "You never know who might turn up in the course of your day". These doll world pieces of the event congregations are utilized for programming death and undercover work adjusts. The tune and dolls assume significant parts in these change's brain control programming. A few slaves at around age 19, have this kind of programming tried to ensure it is decidedly set up. The tune, you never know who might turn up in the course of your day" was formed by the Sherman siblings for Disney initially as a signature melody for a ride at the '63-'65 NY World's Fair. The Sherman siblings were abilities that Disney found. They were brought into the world in NYC, and both moved on from Beverly Hills High School. They composed Disney tunes for somewhere around 29 movies.

Mind-controlled slaves, who over and over catch one another, however, don't have the foggiest idea why, will be tracked down saying, "It's a little, little world." Both ceremonies and programming continue at Disney carnivals during both the day and night. Steven Rockefeller and Walt Disney voyaged and hung out with Dr. Hadley Cantril, a foundation master on human conduct.

Whenever Walt Disney started Walt Disney World, he sent Card Walker to the Florida cash-flow to demand renumeration, and the lead representative gave it to Disney. What that implied is that Disney's property in Florida was completely controlled under Disney's ward, they had their own regulations, their own police power, their own medical clinics, and their own assessment rate. No external authority would obstruct Disney's purview. Disney World's funds would be distant and far away by the territory of Florida. Never had such a lot of force been parted with. Disney World turned into its own criminal organization inside the organization. Disney event congregations are likea city inside a city. They have their own security powers, and the nearby police permit the Disney security powers to deal with their turf. Disney has their own arrangements (regulations). A portion of the security powers can be recognized in regular clothes with clean-trim haircuts and have communication devices.

The security powers have a central command room where TV screens show to experience the leave focuses at Disney as well as different areas. America's Most Wanted has a genuinely huge document on kids who have been captured at Disney Amusement Parks. One mother, who got isolated from her youngster while getting off a train, wildly told a gatekeeper her kid was absent. The watchman took her to the screen room, where they saw the hijacker did the offspring of the recreation area with the kid stooped behind him. For that shy of a period, the criminal had sedated the youngster, trim his hair unique, and set an alternate shirt on him. As composed previously, white bondage is important for what's truly going on with Disney. This mother was one of the lucky rare sorts of people who figured out how to track down their hijacked kids. An insider expresses that the Disney police are most certainly part of those moving and mishandling honest youngsters got for mysterious ceremonies. Moreover, the Disney security powers spy on their own workers.

Representatives don't enter the amusement parks like the guests, nor do they move around like the guests. They have underground passages and underground doors and offices for that. One casualty of all out mind-control referenced that a passage entrance was at the Matterhorn Mountain at Disneyland. (The Matterhorn was opened by Walt and his old buddy Richard Nixon, who rode in the primary vehicle down the mountain.) The Disney creations have given the Illuminati the cover to unite Illusionists, entertainers, and enhancements specialists without anybody being dubious. A portion of these men had the option to apply their gifts toward programming kids. To act as an illustration of their gifts, Disney embellishments specialists had the option to make 16 sensible looking bodies for the 1989 film Gross Anatomy. Walt Disney, Inc. has collaborated with Los Alamos and Sandia Labs, two different gatherings which are vigorously engaged with mind-control and individuals' control to foster body sweeps, marking, and access codes for the guests to Disney's amusement parks. Every one of the Disney Theme parks, for example, Disneyland, DisneyWorld, EuroDisney, and so forth have tremendous underground offices. These underground offices permit a considerable lot of the specialists to get to the ride regions through underground entries. Each topic office likewise has an immense foundation underground to keep up with it. The underground regions contain closet plan and fix units, fitting rooms, bathrooms, cafeterias, security units, PCs, cargo slopes, utility encasements, and enormous associating burrows. The underground regions additionally have programming rooms. They have their own power plants and water frameworks and their own police power.

Disney organization utilizes 71,000 individuals in a few areas, tone ongoing TV show utilized the figure 40,000 Disney employees.] People are going back and forth 24 hours at the Disney amusement parks.

Three movements keep up the 24-hour business. The night groups keep up with and fix the parks for a great many individuals that will before long show up toward the beginning of the day. Disneyland makes a characteristic prop for doing mind-control. The things they sell are likewise normal props-- like the Goofy watch ($19.95) which has hands that go in reverse to befuddle a slave with respect to what time it is. Was Walt Disney mindful of how Disneyland was utilized for programming? There is no question. Disney lived a lot of evenings at Disneyland, and had a condo at the firehouse close to the train station on Main St. Around evening time, on the off chance that he was not doing anything more, he'd wander the grounds of Disneyland writing notes on his own unmistakable blue paper, which he'd pass on for laborers to follow the following day. The notes would agree that such things as "Supplant these blossoms," or "Move that seat". Walt Disney knew all that continued in his Magic Kingdom. The Epcot Center and the Disney entertainment meccas market a wide range of mysterious triggers, including precious stones, rainbows, wizards, and so forth that support the programming. The Epcot Center has two glass pyramids alongside its "Excursion into Imagination". Disneyworld has the Island of Atlantis on its sub visit. Fantasyland is one of the most involved voyages through Disneyland for mind-control purposes. It has merry go rounds, joyful music, a fantastic palace, boat rides, story book characters, and so on Resting Beauty Castle with its blue turrets and gold towers is the focal visual object of Disneyland. You cross a drawbridge to get into it. Inside Fantasyland are Illuminati programming locales, for example, the Mad Hatter teacups, the King Arthur merry go round ponies, and Snow White's Forest.

In the furthest corner of Disneyland's New Orlean's Square is the Haunted Mansion. This chateau is intended to alarm and frighten, it has a brilliant plan and numerous enhancements and deceptions. Practical apparitions, a shrieking raven, yelling voices, and other terrifying things invite the guest. Life size visualizations are made at the Haunted Mansion, and move in a state of harmony with the music and afterward grow dim at specific places. There is a multi-dimensional image of a lady's head in a precious stone ball that gabs constant. A genuine decent snicker for the software engineers of a young kid. At the point when you are at the end, you will get an opportunity to investigate a mirror where a visualization apparition will settle up adjacent to you.

Star Speeder is one more extraordinary programming area at Disneyland. It was the formation of George Lucas and the Disney Imagineers. The innovation is acquired from Star Wars, and is like pilot training programs utilized by the military to prepare pilots. Disneyland Hotel offers Character Breakfasts, where youngsters have breakfast with Disney characters, to individuals who make exceptional game plans. U.S. Exceptional Forces, which does mind-control, possesses two lodgings close to Disney World, and the Mormons have one moreover. Knott's Berry Farm with its Ghost Town, Amusement Park, and its Charlie Brown topics and characters is close to Disneyland. One of the Disney leaders started one of the most over the top terrible injury-based personalities control programming focuses in Los Angeles called Magic Castle a satire stockroom. This ER had awful dungeons.

Youngsters were acquired from South and Central America to be customized at the Magic Castle. A valiant

L.A. police officer uncovered the spot - for which he lost his employment, and at last, had the option to get the site shut. One of Disney's new pursuits in them

Disney Institute, which Newsweek named "the Disneyland of the Mind". An exclusive hangout called Club 33 at Disneyland found higher up in the New Orleans Square is accepted to be associated with mind-control. Offspring's Den regulates youngsters' exercises at the Wilderness Lodge Resort at Walt Disney World.

At Disney-MGM Studios, the significant fascination is the Twilight Zone Tower of Terror. Visitors go on a weird unnerving outing through the inn, where visitors are at last sent into a lift that exits control 13 stories. The ride has been promoted on TV. Disneyland presently has a Temple to the Forbidden Eye- - which is basically a Temple to the All-Seeing Eye, the Illuminati image. Guests, who have the persistence to stand by inline, can lash themselves in for a ride that resembles a drill that jostles the rider through a sanctuary loaded up with snakes, rodents, and mummies. One high impact exercise instructor couldn't stroll for three days after the jostling ride, which appears to be, corny". The experience is more damaging than fun, however at that point perhaps that is the thing that was planned.

DISNEY VACATIONS FOR THE ELITE

Year's prior, this current creator's bulletins uncovered Hilton Head Island, SC as a watering opening of the strong first-class incl. resigned commanders and chief naval officers, and the site for the first class's Renaissance Weekend "meat market".

Keep in mind, that at one time Hilton Head Island was private, with imported crocodiles in the water around it. An individual was just permitted on the island by passing through security doors with a leeway. In a later bulletin, Disney's Hilton Head Island Resort was referenced. This hotel, worked by Disney Vacation Development, Inc., is situated on a 15-section of the land private island connected to Hilton Head Island by a thin extension. Individuals to the Disney Vacation Club can trade time for get-aways at Disney and different retreats around theworld.

MELODYLAND

Right smack opposite the entry to Disneyland is the Assembly of God's Melodyland Christian Center, the origin of TEN (Trinity Broadcasting Network). The Assembly of God category has been vigorously invaded by the Illuminati, and has been intensely utilized as a front for customized slaves. Paul Crouch, leader of Trinity Broadcasting Systems, Inc., was associated with Melody land in 1973 when TBS was getting everything rolling. Around then, Melodyland was a rich intensely invaded alluring church, with its portion of customized products. In 1973, wardrobe gay priest Jim Bakker, and his significant other Tammy Faye, a customized numerous was with Paul Crouch in Anaheim at Melodyland. Paul Crouch had been the associate minister of Bakker's home church in Muskegon, MI. Hunker's right-hand man was Alexander Valderrama, an appealing Roman Catholic. TBS involved a neglected army installation as their TV complex, involving holders as studios. For the mid 70's, ABC set Bakker and Crouch's initial shows on their associate stations on Sunday morning. Bakker had effectively gotten his profession started off with Illuminatus Pat Robertson and his 700 Club.

Jim Bakker split and went toward the east coast. To assist Bakker with his cash, Bill Perkins, who had been a monetary examiner for the World Order's psyche control research at Sandia National Labs in Livermore came to assist Bakker with running his service's accounts. Afterward, TV preacher Bakker started fabricating Heritage USA, which was to be a major cash resort. Bakker recruited individuals who had worked for Disney to develop Heritage USA. Bakker concentrated on Disneyland, Disneyworld, and other Disney places as a model for Heritage USA. After Disneyworld opened in Florida, Jim Bakker was a REGULAR guest to it. Legacy USA's Ft. Legacy was designed according to Disney's Ft. Wild, Main St. was designed according to the Magic Kingdom's Main St., and Disney's created iron fencing was additionally duplicated. A great many people know about Jim Bakker's $265,000 result to Jessica Hahn to stay quiet about her sexual administrations to him, his long-lasting gay relationship with his right-hand man David Taggart, and his jail sentence. James Orson (named after Orson Welles) Bakker was from Muskegon, the very spot that Cathy O'Brien, a liberated Mind-controlled slave came from. He was conceived pre-mature, and made theirinterestedin family circumstances that make his family suspect.

While Cathy O'Brien got customized by means of the Catholics, Jim was important for one more group which additionally was into programming, the charming Assemblies of God. His granddad, who resided nearby to Jim, and where Jim invested a lot of youth energy with was prominently referred to around as a "peddler", and nicknamed Kingfish after the manipulative person on Amos and Andy. Tammy his better half experienced childhood in International Falls, MN in neediness in the home of her stepfather and mom. Other than having a "shopping evil presence," she has had her portion of fears and mental issues, as can be anticipated from somebody who has needed to endure programming. It would merit calling attention to who has acted the hero when he was enduring an onslaught. For example, on Thursday, Oct. 4, 1984, when Jim was enduring an onslaught, Jim Bakker's show had six individuals give supports and commendation of Jim Bakker. Those were Ronald Reagan, Dale Evans, Robert Schuller, Oral Roberts, Billy Graham, and Rex Hubbard. Of those, this creator knows without a doubt that all are bricklayers, aside from Rex, who could conceivably be. Robert Schuller, Billy Graham, and Oral Roberts are "Christian pastors" who take part in utilizing and taking care of psyche control slaves. These three pastors all take part in covertly Satanic ceremonies. The last couple of passages has given just a problematic image of the personal connection between Disney Mind-control and the magnetic development and its utilization of injury based complete brain control.

DISNEYANA FOR THE PROGRAMMED AND OBSESSED

For individuals who have been customized with Disney programming and who are fixated on Mickey Mouse and all the other things about Disney, and for others who simply have the gathering soul for Disney memorabilia, there is a gathering called Disneyana. Disneyana, was coordinated in the 1980's, and comprises of individuals who are clique like in their commitment to anything genuine Disney. Some of them to communicate their commitment obviously tatoo their bodies with Disney characters. This gathering holds its yearly show at the Contemporary Resort in FL. One Disneyana at the yearly show said, "We gather to keep the positive sentiment inside." Another when talked with said, "To this end, everything unquestionably revolves around adoration." The creator knows as a reality a portion of the ones who are fixated on Mickey Mouse and Disney things are modified products. One of Kenneth Anger's mysterious companions has had the world's biggest Mickey Mouse assortment. Who is Kenneth Anger? Kenneth Anger, an individual from LaVey's Magick Circle and later his Church of Satan, is a medium and an underground producer.

Kenneth Anger (he pick the last name Anger) was raised in the Wizard of Oz books. His biographer Bill Landis composes that the Oz books "laid the basis for Ken's appreciation for Crowley, the medium who might modify Rosicrucian idea into his own otherworldly framework." Ken was fixated on Crowley's life and sorcery. As a kid, Ken had hit the dance floor with Shirley Temple in a contest after she turned into a youngster star. Ken Anger cherished the OTO's sun powered phallic religion, and was additionally fixated on Mickey Mouse. He invested a piece of his energy concentrating on his companion's Mickey Mouse assortment. Ken Anger did his projecting for his film, Lucifer Rising" by telling mysterious companions and colleagues that they could experience their goddess or god power-trip dreams by representing him. The British government's National Film Finance Corp. fronted 15,000£ for Lucifer Rising's creation. Renowned mysterious performer Jimmy Page did the sound track complimentary. Ken

Anger went about as the film's Magus and caused his Magus job to look like Mickey Mouse in the film Fantasia. (The job Fantasia plays at the top of the priority list control programming will follow as the last piece of this section.) "Lucifer Rising"also begins with Fantasia-type volcanoes. One more of his notable movies was "Conjuring of My Demon Brother."

MIND CONTROL FEATURES IN DISNEY MOVIES

The components inside Disney films that are deliberately placed in for mind-control would take volumes to depict. An itemized portrayal of how only one Disney film is utilized as a programming script before long follows. Capriccio was chosen as the model. Arbitrary inspecting of elements in Disney motion pictures for mind-control programming could include:

Cogis worth the charming mantle clock in Beauty and the Beast.

The person's Door Knob, which is a door handle depicted as an individual in the Disney animation Alice in Wonderland, is helpful for programming entryway knob alters.

The Blue Yonder is a Disney film on the time travel of a young man. Time travel films are used for programming to wreck the casualty's sense of time.

Disney film "Vivified Alphabet" has letters that wake up, which is helpful for programming. Also, shouldn't something be said about the '82 Disney film "PCs are People, as well!"?

All the Illuminati individuals this creator knows about who has gotten injury-based complete brain control were educated to astrally project and study on the astral plane what they expected to realize. A Disney film that depicts this is Goofy over Dental Health. This is an instructive film delivered by Disney in '91 and again in '93, where Goofy places an enchanted toothbrush under a kid's cushion, with the goal that the kid astral ventures to a dental specialist office and keeping in mind that on the astral plane examinations how to have sound teeth.

Illuminati changes accept that trees and blossoms are alive. The 1932 Disney film Flowers and Trees is a tale of two trees who experience passionate feelings for. The film depicts the mysterious conviction that trees can talk and sing. Inside, change frameworks will be developed with singing trees and blossoms that address individuals and which are adjusted. The singing trees give out inner codes to move changes inside where they need to go. Get back to Oz. (1985) This Disney film starts its story line about a young lady who is remembered to have mental issues due to her stories of Oz. She is cautioned not to discuss Oz with her family members. She is taken to a major ruby analyst ring, who lets Dorothy know that electroshocks won't hurt her, and that we are at the "beginning of a New Age." Dorothy is informed that her recollections are, simply dreams" that originate from an abundance of electrical flow in the mind. She is shipped off a psychological establishment to get shock medicines for talking aboutOz.

A lightning storm permits her to get away from the shock medicines and when she rests, she rises and shines in Oz. In Oz, she goes through many psyche control situations, ruby shoes, mirrors, and so forth, and at the end visits with abhorrent Mombi, Princess of Oz who keeps Ozma (Dorothy's twin) as a slave. Mombi in the end projects a spell and charms Ozma into a mirror. Science fiction creator J.D. Vinge in her Return to Oz in light of the screenplay composes on pg. 211-212, "Dorothy looked at herself in the mirror, seeing her own appearance, and recalling the second when she had checked out herself and seen another person there, somebody so like her that it might have been her sister." Parts of this film were shot close to Stonehenge, Eng. Disney has placed out a few movies on the Wizard of Oz subject, which were all utilized for programming. The first series of Oz books were by Baum. In '39, MGM did the renowned Wizard of Oz film. In the Disney film Tron (1982), a youthful PC virtuoso goes into a modified state where he winds up turning into a PC program. Subsequent to overcoming the MCP, he gets back to this present reality. This is just a programming script. An embellishments group made a three-dimensional world, showing how gifted Disney enhancements individuals can be in causing something to appear to be genuine. This film should show individuals their psyche control abilities. Numerical Applications Group, Inc. (MAGI) was one of the gatherings that made the designs. Disney emerged with 3 recordings of new undertakings in Wonderland which are mind-control programming.

In the mornings here from 9-9:30, on station 21, Disney has a Wonderland Show each day which is mind-control programming for youngsters. Inside a couple of moments, this creator had seen a young lady stroll through a mirror, the 3 existences of Thomasina referenced, and a little tune "I'm a little tea kettle" where an individual turns into a tea kettle. They likewise had an "under the umbrella" scene. This was generally unadulterated programming, right on TV. Obviously, they show the White Rabbit as a focal figure. ABC Under the sponsorship of Disney created an extensive 140 min. film Wild Palms which portrays Illuminati mind-control and life. One peruser of Vol. 2 expressed that the Wild Palms film would have pretty much no clue aside from that having perused the Vol. 2 books, the film appeared to be legit in the radiance of Vol. 2's disclosures. The film portrays how kids are abducted, exchanged upon entering the world, modified through TV kid's shows, customized to kill and utilize immobilizers, and so on.

The film portrays Illuminati bloodlines and organized relationships. Albeit the name, Illuminati" isn't utilized, in the event that watchers substitute in the name "the dads" for Illuminati fathers, they will get an insider's perspective on life at the top. The principle regulators are tended to by their slaves as "Father" or "Daddy" or "Mother". This is consistent with life. An individual went against to the dad's states, "One day we will awaken and find we don't possess this nation and nobody will mind." The film expresses those occasions are not happening arbitrarily. The film shows an underground passage framework that has an entry concealed by a pool. Many real programming codes were said during the film, for example, "down, down, down through the pool of tears..." and "we will go down the yellow block street now." The film was made by Bruce Wagner, who clearly is an insider concerning injury based complete psyche control. The reality the film was made shows the presumption of the software engineers' convictions that their crook acts in programming huge number of young kids won't be uncovered, and that individuals will be too inept to even think about understanding that what is put out as fiction is really reflecting what's going on. It's like they trust their own content that IF individuals discovered "nobody will mind."

For Mickey Mouse programming they emerged with Thru the Mirror, where Mickey Mouse ventures through his room mirror and winds up in a different universe (adjusted state). Not all of the Disney motion pictures that have mind-control programming subjects got delivered to the general population. One unreleased animation had Penelope escaping from an evil looking Grandfather Clock which is conveying her to a different universe, and has one more scene where Penelope attempts to clutch somebody who represents the Wind. George Lucas, who coordinated the celebrity Wars, which was a film arranged by the Illuminati and utilized for Illuminati programming, additionally coordinated Disney's film "Commander EO". Skipper EO (who appears as though a satanic substance) goes to protect the Queen (who appears as though the prostitute portrays as Mystery Babylon in the Bible). The Queen is in imprisonment just on the grounds that she and her kin have confidence clearly (which address great and fiendishness).

Whenever they repudiate such a conviction, they are saved by Michael Jackson (in genuine life a brain-controlled slave) playing Captain EO. It's a New Age black magic film through and through. Incidentally, Michael Jackson has gone to Disney event congregations commonly, once in a while in camouflage. It is public information that his Jehovah's Witness family has been exceptionally oppressive intellectually and truly to their youngsters. Disney has placed out a few motion pictures on how the psyche functions, like the instructive film The Brain and Nervous System in 1990. Their film Runaway Brain is an animation where Dr. Franke Nollie transfers Mickey's mind into a beast's body as well as the other way around. A 1994 film, Puppet Masters shows the govt's. secret Office of Scientific Intelligence attempting to save the U.S. from outsiders who live in human bodies. Lately, Bette Midler has been Disney's fundamental entertainer.

In the Vol. 2, it was uncovered that she is potentially a Monarch Mind-controlled slave. She is renowned for her "temperament swings" (switches in character), and she had a "psychological episode" in 1985. Her eyes and body signals are those of a customized various. She has gone out on a visit to Disney without making - cash, and she is best of companions with Jeffrey Katzenberg (second in order at Disney). Jeffrey Katzenberg by the way is incredibly hated by his partner Sid Sheinberg. Bette Midler plays Stella in the film Stella.

Stella is a mysterious name. In the film, the content appears to be custom-made for Bette Midler and for somebody who is a customized slave, rather than the entertainer fitting the job. At the film's end, Stella (Bette Midler) goes to her own little girl's marriage by looking in a window and watching from an external perspective. This is the content they give so many of the pieces of a slave, so they feel disgraceful and feel like they are outwardly examining 100% of the time at life. Many parts (characters) of slaves find it difficult to interface with reality, since they believe they are outwardly examining. And afterward, in evident Disney design, Disney had Bette Midler assume the part of the lead witch in Hocus Pocus. The film Hocus Pocus does some hocus pocus of its own. While professing to ridicule black magic, they really instruct black magic. They in all actuality do make the 3 witches look diverting. Coincidentally, the 3 witches represent the lady, mother, hag combo that the Illuminati adoration. Disney quietly works in profound mysterious things, for example, the all-powerful eye on the front of the book, the young lady promising the feline (who is a recognizable soul) that her relatives would constantly focus on it (valid, on the grounds that the feline was a generational soul).

The feline is killed in the film yet can't bite the dust. What's more Bette Midler as a lead witch in her ensemble, which has some mother-of-Darkness symbology on it, states as she prepares to end the existence compel from an honest young lady, "We need to live always, so we end youngsters' lives." This is healthy amusement for kids? The Disney limit with respect to misdirection stretches out to its own specialists. PR men select youngsters for its Disney College program. They let the youngsters know what an extraordinary venturing stone it will be for their professions. They have been known to make it sound like the best thing in your life. Kids come from everywhere in the country because of the smooth enrolling strategies to work for Disney. They are then housed in Disney lodging, given modest positions, and paid low wages. The vast majority in the College Program leave frustrated. Assuming the laborer ends up coming up with something incredible, Disney authorities have been known to take the thought, and in light of the fact that the specialist was working for Disney, the specialist will observe that they can't get any credit or cash for the possibility that Disney takes and makes millions off of. One unaccredited maker of a Disney deal thing said, in a real sense, they're involving everyone for everything."

K. POINT BY POINT SCRIPT ON HOW THE DISNEY FILM FANTASIA IS USED FOR PROGRAMMING TRAUMA-BASED MIND-CONTROLLED SLAVES

During the 1950's, '60's, and '70's somewhere around 90% of the Illuminati's injury-based brain-controlled slaves were exposed to watching Disney's Fantasia film for them to fabricate the fundamental symbolism of the psyche control. Kid mind-control casualties had their eyes taped open, and afterward sat one-on-one with their essential software engineers so the developers could give the contents as the kid watched Disney's Fantasia again and again. What made Fantasia one of a kind as a programming device is that it had nearly all that the software engineers expected to make the basic symbolism for their injury-based psyche control. To fabricate a trustworthy change framework implies that the universes need a strong establishment. Capriccio has given the resources to get a strong establishment for the inside universes that the Illuminati slaves work to them. It is additionally a work of art in planning tone and music.

The Disney film Fantasia which debuted on Nov. 13, 1940 (at Broadway Theater in NYC) was a monetary catastrophe as a film, however was an Illuminati programming show-stopper. The film was delivered to theaters in '40, '46, '56, '63, '69, '77, '82, '85, '90 to get each age of youngsters. The video was delivered in 1991. During programming, a large part of the youngster slave's brain will watch the film. One specific part (adjust) will be compelled to remember everything in the film. This little part (little change) is all around concealed to each victim. This little change, who has a distinctive and comprehensive recollection of the film Fantasia, is locked cautiously away so ONLY an entrance code will pull him/her up. Watching the tape Fantasia won't pull this change-up. The software engineers pull this modify up when they have a fresh start adjust. At the point when they are taking a fresh start of the psyche, they will pull the tidy part up and have the modify who has retained Fantasia toss its memory onto an inside big screen. The inward Outer space (otherwise known as Rubicon) is formed like an amphitheatre, and capacities as a major immense screen for replay. There is an interior ball or sun made by means of the lighting impact of the film Fantasia, so the film seems projected in the psyche as on a globe.

Furthermore, the Fantasia film pictures hit this interior globe and go round in the brain and twist through the framework. The software engineer will then, at that point, tell the new part "THIS IS WHAT I WANT YOU TO CREATE. THIS IS WHAT WE NEED." In this style, Fantasia has given the developers their essential instrument for taking a separated fresh start part of the brain, and controlling it to turn into another useful part inside the framework. The youthful part that holds the whole Fantasia memory is decisively positioned in the framework so it very well may be called up from wherever in the framework. Regardless of where the software engineer is working in the framework, he can get to this little modify whose capacity is to recall the film. The majority of the framework will go into a daze rest whenever shown in the film. The front (as well as the greater part of the framework's changes) will be absolutely amnesic to having at any point seen the film. Since the programming put in with Fantasia is so central it should not shock anyone that the developers have worked really hard in safeguarding this programming from everybody, including the slave. Abreacting the film for some, modifies could tear the framework separated, in light of the fact that after the film is retained, extreme injury starts to be overlaid and joined to the film. There might be a few little changes that actually convey smidgens and bits of memory of the film, however just one will truly recall it.

The accompanying content will be a running record of how Fantasia has been utilized as a significant preliminary film for Illuminati injury-based psyche control to prepare the brain control casualty's brain to have the option to envision the programming that will be layered in. The time clock will start when the element film's activity starts, and afterward will run its whole 116 minutes. This will give the specialist of the brain control a pass up blow depiction of how a Disney film is utilized for programming. The film was regularly displayed to kid casualties around 3 to 4 years old with a wide screen while the youngster was under a directed LSD trip. (Before the utilization of LSD a few different medications were utilized.) A Grande Dame or Mother-of-Darkness regularly worked with the Illuminati software engineer as an Assistant Programmer.

The contents and the programming have as of now been talked about preceding the appearance of the kid in the movie, so the software engineers know the course they need to take the kid, and will fit some of what is shared with the kid casualty to individualize the programming. At the point when a three-or four-year-old is shown Fantasia on a mesmerizingly ready and controlled LSD trip, the colors & impacts of Fantasia are expanded multiple times. The film is more real than genuine to the kid. The film won't be shown only a single time, however again and again with the goal that the contents are imbued into the psyche. The symbolism for the kid's interior world will be grounded, in light of the fact that the big screen film improved by both the medications and the brilliant shades of the craftsmanship will appear to be more genuine than life itself. Right now, the kid is a different, yet the dividers between the different pieces of the brain are not strong, but rather like the dividers between inner self states in a grown-up non-numerous. An enormous piece of the 3-or 4-year-old kid's framework will be permitted to see the framework, including the Christian parts. Then, at that point, the whole framework (with the single exemption of the modify conveying the whole memory of the film) will be mesmerizingly told to neglect having seen the film. Years after the fact, the front changes won't recall having seen the film, yet they might have an unusual abhorrence for the film. They might observe that they can't distinguish where their sensations of aversion to the film originate from. The kid casualty will watch the film with its developer and collaborator software engineer one-on-one, with no different kids in the room. The kid will watch the film more than once and be barbecued with regard to what is in the movie.

The youngster will see the film so often in such a striking structure and will be tied to the point that the film will be remembered. However, it will be mesmerizingly secured up in the subliminal by the software engineers, with the goal that it shapes a base for the brain to start building programming, yet will stay stowed away from the cognizant. At the time the Fantasia film was made, the Illuminati had been making prepared products for quite a long time, yet they realized they needed to program the various characters as per the best psyche control methods of the day. Therefore, the Fantasia film was prepared of time, with the goal that it might actually fill in as a programming help. The film is quiet (practically no words) aside from music so it tends to be utilized for mesmerizing perception, so the mother of Darkness and the software engineer can fill in the programming script with the youngster casualty as they watch the film. As it ended up, their arrangements were fruitful. The New Age writer David Tame states in his book The Secret Power of Music, that Fantasia is."A wonderful marriage between the visual and melodic expressions. A large portion of the successions. new Age film was expected to be!" The force of the film to impact the psyche sticks out. To make the film, Disney utilized a few in number arm strategies on a couple of individuals. The film was a film industry flop when previously delivered in the 1940's, however, at that point, it was made for the mysterious world in any case. By the 1960's, the Illuminati had made a medication culture and had loads of imperceptible psyche-controlled slaves going around that had been modified with Fantasia. In the 1960's, Fantasia turned into a hit with the medication culture which had its portion of Illuminati slaves profoundly engaged with it. Another update, the sentences that are "ALL CAPS" in the content are things that the developers are sharing with the youngster casualty as the kid watches the film. (Remember, that the youngster watches the film over and over, so not all things indicated in this content by covers that the developer says will essentially be said in one appearance.)

SYNOPSIS

Since the peruser takes care of so a lot, the accompanying statements (with strong accentuation's additional) take on significantly more profound meaning: Joe Flower in Prince of the Magic Kingdom, Walt Disney was fixated on creation, headed to construct supernatural universes not, as numerous craftsmen are, out of paint and material, or words, or even film, yet truly, out of cement, wires, smoke, power, and exceptionally customized workers."

Julian Halevy in Nation criticizes Disney for bringing this country into a "float to dream." He adds, "one feels our entire culture heading up the dim stream to the source that heart of murkiness where Mr. Disney deals with pastel tinkered evil for gold and ivory." For the people who comprehend programming Aubrey Menen remarks about Disney's prosperity are significantly proper, "the most grounded want a craftsman knows...to make his very own universe where everything is similarly as he envisions it." John Ciardi was not really decent, he named Walt Disney as "the shyster in the reserved alcove of deception." Eliot said, "While his recorded pixie tales may have showed up from the get go to be light and fanciful, upon closer assessment they appeared to be more bad dreams of deconstructed reality allied with the time's driving neo-Freudian Modernists."

You have now wrapped up perusing a never-before-heard, extraordinary Warning with regards to the Dark Reality of the Disney's Magic Kingdom, and how it finds a place with Mind-Control. Most Americans when reviewed say they trust in God, generally, go to chapel, and many accept they are brought back to life. Due to the Illuminati' s misdirection crusade north of a few ages, the American public, and the world overall has been persuaded to think that Disney was great, and that Walt Disney was a decent man. Due to his picture, individuals suspended judgment about Disney and Disney films. They shared their kids with him. Individuals had been maneuvered toward a mood, an inclination that anything that emerges from Disney is great. They shared their youngsters with taking in what Disney took care of their kids' little personalities consistently. The public's inclination of trust was utilized to present Illuminati convictions and their political plan, and to complete a tremendous program of injury put together psyche control with respect to countless little youngsters, whose minds and spirits were taken from them. Since a considerable lot of the youngster slaves, who are customized with Disney-subjects, are modified with jobs in acquiring the Anti-Christ, Walt Disney and his family have played a major job for the Anti-Christ. Furthermore, now you can perceive how exact the Word of God is the point at which it says, what is exceptionally regarded among men, is a cursed thing to God. To start with, there will be an Overview of the kinds of sources utilized, and afterward will follow an incomplete Bibliography on this Disney Section.

CHAPTER FOUR

THE MCDONALD BLOODLINE

At the point when one thinks about the name, McDonald one promptly thinks about the inexpensive food cheeseburger chain which has establishments everywhere. The McDonald's Corp. has been reputed for quite a long time to be associated with Satanism. Truth be told, a book that attempts to expose faith in a Satanic intrigue entitled Satan Wants You revealed the gossip that Mc Donald's proprietor Ray Kroc gave to the Church of Satan.

Beam Kroc invests energy with NWO elites and is an individual from the Bohemian Grove. There is no question that the McDonald's Corp. has an inside track with the Illuminati, in light of the fact that the U.S. government has given by one source 40 million dollars openly charge cash to McDonalds to assist them with setting up McDonald Restaurants in far off nations under the camouflage that this was cash spent on international strategy. In 1991, the complete of McDonald outlets (cafés) in the 3 essential European countries of Britain, France, and West Germany added up to 959restaurants.

Notwithstanding the large numbers of dollars of expense dollars, the U.S. has given to McDonalds Corp., the cash doesn't appear to be straightforwardly associated with the McDonalds family, in light of the fact that the McDonalds family (Richard and Maurice McDonald known as 'Dick" and "Macintosh") what began the cafés in 1937 were purchased out by Ray Kroc around 1954. When Ray Kroc had purchased out the McDonald siblings, they had an extremely fruitful business going. The McDonald's siblings lived in the rich segment of San Bernardino, and had around 11 McDonald's restaurants.

The siblings made about $100,000 benefit a year and were very substance. The McDonalds had planned the brilliant curves and had assembled the inexpensive food idea and had been selling establishments. Nonetheless, the Mcdonald's were excessively content. The McDonalds would have rather not extended and when Ray Kroc shaped McDonald's System. Inc. on Mar. 2, 1955, subsequent to purchasing out the siblings with acquired cash, he energetically went to attempt to form McDonald's into the International Franchise that it is. Beam Kroc lived efficiently for a long time placing for what seems like forever into developing the McDonald's establishment. It was his drive that took a smart thought and transformed it from an achievement in Hollywood and San Bernardino into a global achievement. Beam Kroc knew a smart thought when he saw it, and created others' smart thoughts into an incredible achievement.

James A. Collins, administrator of Collins Foods International, presently the biggest Kentucky Fried Chicken franchisee and the administrator of Sizzler Restaurants discussed his experience with the McDonalds in 1952, 'There was a clique of us, and all of us saw the McDonald's in San Bernadino and essentially replicated it after the young men [the McDonald siblings gave us a visit." "We as a whole took our examples from the McDonald siblings," Collins recollects. The idea of the establishment pay for the McDonald siblings was given out free, and Collins pivoted and started getting $100 a day preparing individuals from Carnation, with the ideas that the McDonalds had shared. Henry's Drive-ins and Ken's were McDonald clones that began from individuals prepared by Collins. Glen Bell who began Taco Bell, who disparaged the McDonald's fundamental eatery in San Bernadino began Taco Bell from thoughts from McDonald's. The main year Collins imitated McDonald's with his own drive-through joint, Collins made $80,000 a year salary. The McDonald siblings turned into a piece of the nearby tip top of San Bernadino, CA close by such rich neighbourhood families as Guthrie, Stater, and Harris. Perusers are helped to remember every one of the articles in my bulletins regarding how San Bernadino is a significant base camp for the Illuminati and Satanic Hubs since there are such countless professionals of dark enchantment in thearea.

I in all actuality do know from working with overcomes of the Illuminati that the McDonald family has part of their kin in the Illuminati. How far back does the McDonald family go in the mysterious? The McDonald family was a Scottish group that was important for Druidism. A large number of the McDonald have proceeded to serve Christ. However, there is as yet a huge strong unforeseen of the McDonald family which is associated with the Mystery Religions, and which has relatives who are essential for the Illuminati. Every one of the significant Scottish factions had a region that they controlled of Scotland. The McDonalds controlled the islands and waterfront regions on the west bank of Scotland. Whenever the Knights Templars tied to abuse, to get away from the different British armadas, they cruised a course that took them to western Scotland. During the hour of King Philippe IV of France. the McDonalds were associated with the development of the Knights Templars. The Knights Templars had taken on Gnostic/evil works on during the hundreds of years they protected the pioneers in the Middle East. The Order had additionally turned into the International Bankers of Europe and huge landowners in Europe. The King of France curved the Pope's arm (in a manner of speaking) to get him to oblige a mission to wipe out the Knights Templars. Since the McDonald family was in private still agnostic. they were able to assist the Knights Templar with getting away from the Pope's announcement against the Templars.

The Knights Templars were not by any means the only International Bankers to move north. Afterward, during the sixteenth and seventeenth century, the world class sinister financial families moved their activities from southern Europe to Antwerp Flanders and afterward on to

Amsterdam. A large number of the Knights Templars misled Scotland, where they helped Bruce, the King of Scotland. At the point when the English attacked Scotland, they were crushed by Bruce in a significant fight named Bannockburn. Bannockburn kept Scotland liberated from England for the following 289 years. The Knights Templars battled with Bruce in the fight under the order of Angus Og McDonald, who was a huge Scottish landowner and a companion of Bruce. Angus Og McDonald had already in the 1308-time span given insurance to the Knights Templars. The Knights Templars brought their fortunes and their military could to Scotland and to the McDonalds. Large numbers of the Knights Templars continued to the Orkeney Is., yet some remained in Scotland and became significant in the mysterious world. The descendents of these Knights are as yet protecting a few significant mysterious relics, which might be uncovered in the following not many years. The Sinclair family has been important for the Prieure de Sion, Freemasonry, and the Illuminati. Bad habit pres. of the Sinclair Oil and Gas Co. in Tulsa in '59-'61 was Marshall McDonald, who was a functioning Freemason who wedded into the Collins family. Note that the urban communities/towns Tulsa, Wagoner, Muskogee, Broken Arrow in Okla. are completely constrained by the Illuminati. The climate in these little towns SW of Tulsa has been portrayed as abusive and inclined to viciousness by individuals who have lived in them. One of the cabin frameworks set up by the Illuminati was the Jacobin Club (initially known as Club Breton).

Its Jacobite individuals got financing from the Illuminati and were a major piece of the reason for the French Revolution. The Jacobites likewise assumed a part in the early history of the United States and the American Revolution. The Jacobites had various blue-bloods who were likewise secret Satanists as their chiefs. They had a hotel in Rome. One of the Scottish Jacobites was Flora Macdonald. She saved Prince Charles Edward's life. Etienne Jacques Joseph Alexandre Macdonald (Scottish blood) was a 33-degree Freemason and additionally an official who battled on the French Revolution. He proceeded to turn into a Marshall in the French armed force. In 1805. he turned into the Grand Administrator of the Grand Lodge Symbolique in France.

The McDonalds and MacDonalds (and a portion of the Donalds) are descendents from King Somerled. Lord Somerled ousted the Vikings (Norsemen) from Scotland. Ruler Somerled's child was Ranald and Ranald's child was named Donald. The grandson then, at that point, became Argus

Mor McDonald (macintosh signifies "child of") Argus' grandson wedded MacRorie and became Lordship of the Isles. The McDonalds were the heads of that area. Families that looked for their security once in a while took their name as well. Thus, it isn't unfathomable that a portion of the Knights Templar bloodlines wound up for sure as McDonald. The strong McDonald of Glencoe lived in Glencoe until the 1692 slaughter by the English government against Francis Stewart supporters. **Francis Stewart** was the Grand Master of the black magic covens around there of Scotland and the McDonalds were allies of him. Additionally, in the seventeenth century, the Mcdonald's had to take an interest with others in theft.

There are a few strong Stewarts (likewise spelled Stuart) in the Illuminati today, some of who are companions with the Rockefellers. No less than one Stewart intermarried with a Rockefeller. Another Stewart has relatives who own a progression of theaters in California that have secret passages to day care focuses so kids can be ceremonially mishandled and modified. (This Stewart had a dad in Satanism who was related to the Hungarian castle.) James C. Stewart, an individual from the Illuminati, fabricated the Mormon's capital structure in Salt Lake City, 60 Wall Tower in NY, and the Savoy Hotel in London that the Illuminati used for their Pilgrim Society central command. James had a place with the Pilgrim Soc. as well. Since the peruser knows this, the person will comprehend the reason why this creator did a twofold take when I stumbled into Stewart McDonald, who was the overseer of Savoy Plaza Hotel, in New York. a spot regularly visited by the tip top. Stewart McDonald was the leader of Army War Shows in '42-'43. See the article on the Van Duyns in this pamphlet to comprehend the associations between the Army War Shows and the mystery mind-control operations done in W.W.II under the sponsorship of the Illuminati.

Stewart McDonald was likewise the police chief in degenerate St. Louis, MO, and the Fed. Lodging Administrator for Wash. D.C., as well similar to an automobile producer. There is a Stuart who really has a more grounded guarantee to the privileged position of England than Queen Elizabeth. He is eleventh in line as a petitioner, while she is just thirteenth. His case is a painstakingly saved mystery by the media. Sovereign Elizabeth is of the Hannover Dynasty which is essential for the thirteenth Illuminati bloodline. This Stuart inquirer was as of late inquired as to whether he might want to have the lofty position of the recently shaped country of Estonia, yet he dismissed it. The Stuart bloodline and their associates have been a significant piece of the initiative of Freemasonry as the centuries progressed.

The Scottish Stewart family, as well as the Cameron, Campbell, Douglas, Hamilton, and Montgomery Scottish families were initially strong families that came from the Flanders region (presently Belgium and north. France) which is today a solid point for the Illuminati. These families emigrated to Scotland in the twelfth century and were essential for the solid mysterious connections among Scotland and the Flanders region. (Today, Flanders is split between northern France and Belgium.) Later, Flanders turned into a financial community for the International Bankers. The Hungarian mysterious world additionally associates with Scotland with such antiquated verifiable figures as Saint Margaret (a Hungarian honorable), whose spouse Malcolm Ceanmor killed, all things considered, Macbeth. Her child David brought feudalism into Scotland, and she, when all is said and done, acquired Catholic Priests. There are many mysterious ties between Scotland. Flanders, Hungary, and Rome. Portions of the McDonalds keep on rehearsing Druidism, which was the first religion before the Christians. The McDonald legacy returns to the Picts and Gaelic individuals. A portion of the McDonalds has become a piece of the Catholic order. I accept I am aware of five MacDonalds that have become Air Marshalls (high level) in the British RAY.

The names of these RAF Marshalls are: Someried Douglas McDonald, Thomas Conchar McDonald, Sir William McDonald, Air Commander John C. McDonald, and Major General John Frederick Matheson McDonald. The NWO has been known as the Air Dictatorship in light of the fact that the NWO's air power will be so significant, so it is critical that the RAF has had such countless high officials who were MacDonalds. Only one illustration of the connections, the British Minister of Aviation Roy Jenkins (64-65) has been important for the Trilateral Commission. Thomas Conchar MacDonald did secret exploration for the Air Ministry after WW II. He went to the Univ. of Glasgow. Another Marshall Sir William Laurence Diary) MacDonald was engaged with British Air Force Intelligence. Various other McDonalds has worked for insight offices too, incl. David George McDonald, James Nlichael McDonald, Jr., and so forth William McDonald was a specialist who worked with FDR in 1925.

Henry Ford additionally invested energy with a specialist named William McDonald. Various McDonalds are Bankers (or significant in the Stock Markets) and trying to keep this article brief I'll simply show some of them: Andrew Jewett McDonald (Yale, USAF), Archibald MacDonald,

Allen Colfax McDonald, Angus Daniel McDonald, John Garwin McDonald, William Henry McDonald (Can.), and Witten McDonald. Archibald McDonald is head of Joseph Freeman, Sons and Co., Ltd. as well as being significant in different things.

The Freeman family is one of the best 13 bloodlines and interfaces with the Prieure de Sion. Sir Peter George MacDonald has been the overseer of Guardian Assurance Co. Ltd. which likewise has associations with the Freeman family and the Prieure de Sion. There is an extensive rundown of McDonald's who have served different legislatures all around the world in administrative roles. Danny Lee McDonald of Tulsa, OK served on the bad Federal Election Commission ('82-'83) as its bad habit director, and from '83 ahead he filled in as its executive. William C. McDonald was the primary state legislative head of New Mexico from 1911-17. The Freemasons ran the state around then.

This writer would wear the peruser's tolerance ragged by portraying all the McDonald's who have been in significant government occupations. The cop who observed **Lee Harvey Oswald** after JFK was shot was a McDonald. This police officer was then relegated to safeguard Marinna Oswald (the widow of Lee Harvey Oswald). These heavy police officer McDonald (who goes to the Oakridge Christian Church) has showed up on TV as of late, for example, on Channel 32, on Top Cops at 7:25 p.m. where he revolts against paranoid ideas in the JFK death. The whole capture of Oswald by M.N. McDonald is loaded up with questions.

Jack Ruby was in a similar theater. Oswald attempted to fire McDonald with a dumped firearm. Some obscure individual had warned McDonald that Oswald was in the theater, and the police had for reasons unknown previously concluded Oswald was liable because while capturing him the cop was heard saying by witnesses, "Kill the President, will you." And yet the Warren Commission said that Oswald was not a suspect until some other time. This is only one spot of numerous where the McDonald family interfaces in with the bigger Satanic connivance. Jack Ruby was engaged with the Carousel Club which was attached to the Monarch Project. The death of JFK was done through the Perm index, which was set up by Louis Mortimer Bloomfield, who worked for the Illuminati in SOE (British Special Operations Executive) inside the US Army Intelligence. He worked for OSS and ran the FBI's Counter Intelligence Div. 5, while working for British SOE and the Illuminati.

George DE Mohrenschildt, Oswald's dearest companion or nearest contact was himself an ex-Nazi government agent who worked for the CIA. The Mob's associations with the Top 13 Illuminati families are clarified in the Van Duyn family article in this pamphlet. Remember, the crowd had betrayed JFK as well. In synopsis. A portion of the McDonalds have stood firm on significant footholds for the Illuminati, and part of the McDonald descendants are in the Illuminati. You will likewise track down McDonalds extremely dynamic in Protestantism and Catholicism. The McDonald family's association with the mysterious goes clear back to Druidism, and afterward the insurance and initiative they provided for the Knights Templars. Today, a portion of the McDonalds are Barons, some are Bankers and some are driving insight and military men.

A news story that shows Linda McDonald was granted quiet cash by the Canadian govt. and the CIA for MK-Ultra Mind Control programming.

Indoctrinate casualties to get $100,000. Ottawa rejects obligation for tests. By Bob Cox

The Canadian Press

OTTAWA - The national government will pay $100,000 each to casualties of conditioning tests financed by Canada and the CIA somewhere in the range of 1950 and 1965, Justice Minister Kim Campbell reported Tuesday. Ottawa is paying the cash to keep away from lawful cases by casualties or the examinations done by Dr. Ewen Cameron at Montreal's Allan Memorial Institute.

Upwards of 80 individuals were Involved, however, It's not satisfactory the number of areas yet alive and qualified for the installments. Campbell said the public authority actually doesn't concede any lawful obligation or obligation, however, is paying the cash on caring and philanthropic grounds. However, Linda Macdonald, a Vancouver lady who sent off the legal dispute that constrained the settlement, said she thinks about the instalments as an affirmation of obligation and an emblematic expression of remorse. My greatest concern has forever been that the central government recognize its liability in subsidizing the trials, so we can trust that such maltreatment of patients' privileges won't ever occur in the future in this country," she said. Macdonald, presently 55, went through "de-designing" at Allan Memorial in 1903.As a mother of five kids under four years of age, she was shipped off the Institute experiencing weariness and discouragement. She was treated as a schizophrenic, however, never analyzed all things considered. She was vigorously medicated, kept sleeping for 86 days, given more than 100 electroshock medicines. She arose five days after the fact, scarcely ready to work. She was unable to peruse or compose, utilize a latrine, drive a vehicle, cook a feast or make a bed. She didn't recollect her better half, kids or the initial 26 years of her life." I acknowledge the states representative expression of remorse through remuneration, yet no measure of cash can repay me for the deficiency of memory. Also, the colossal troubles my family and I have endured".

McDonald said in a proclamation. She was in Los Angeles on Tuesday conversing with film makers about her story. Previous patients at the Allan Memorial have looked for remuneration from both the Canadian and U.S. government for quite a long time. The US. Focal Intelligence Agency, needing to dive deeper into indoctrinating and psycho-consistent de-programming, secretively gave $85,000 to Cameron somewhere in the range of 1957 and 1962. Canada, as a feature of a public program of medical care awards, gave about $70,000 somewhere in the range of 1950 and 1954 and again somewhere in the range of 1961 and 1964. The analyses finished in 1965. Canadian authorities later said they didn't know about the CIA financing. In 1988, the U.S. Equity Department came to an out-of-court settlement that gave about $100,000 to every one of nine Canadians treated under Cameron's CIA-supported trials. The Canadian government helped take care of lawful bills for those Canadians who sued the United States, yet shied away from paying Its own pay.

A 1986 report by George Cooper, a Halifax legal counselor and previous Conservative MP, acquitted Canadian specialists of any fault and depicted Cameron's work as "in mindful yet not flighty." But Thomas Berger, Mc-Donald's attorney, introduced a report to the public authority in 1990 testing Cooper's decisions One U. S. specialist compared Cameron's examination to conditioning strategies utilized In Chinese jails. A Justice Department official said he didn't have the foggiest idea of the number of individuals is qualified for the $100,000 installments. Various previous patients have as of now kicked the bucket. Just individuals still alive can apply for remuneration.

CHAPTER FIVE

WORLD WAR'S

WORLD WAR 1

The First World War, a war that set world history apart, A war that has ruthlessly massacred more lives in the world, the war that ended the British rule that turned the world into its own colony, the war that caused the United States to spill the ashes of war on the bloody European nations and cause the American superpower to rise dramatically, is to say the least, why did the First World War, which was bloodied in the pages of history, occur? Why did more than two crore people die in the war? Were millions of people murdered for the death of a Crown Prince?

A car was speeding down the road in Austria on July 28, 1914. In the blink of an eye, two bodies fell on the road. The story of the First Crusader, while on a quest to find out who was responsible for the death of the Crown Prince of Austria, revealed that his investigation revealed that the Serbian conspiracy was to wage war on Serbia to get the title of the Crown Prince, and it was at this point that the two teams split into world nations as supporters of Serbia and Austria. Ready for war? It was in this context that Germany sought to colonize the countries under British control, and Germany immediately jumped into battle to use the event as its instrument. Like Germany, Britain, France, Russia, the United States, and Italy began to extend their tongues of war, so that Germany, Britain, France, Russia, the United States, and Italy fought in support of Austria, and almost any of the nations were determined to support thousands. On August 4, 1914, World War I began, and it was triggered not only by the death of Ferdinand, the Austrian nut-bourgeoisie. Capitalist society emerged in Europe in the late nineteenth and early eighteenth centuries. The three major European countries are responsible for this socio-historical change. It was the seeds of the Industrial Revolution in Britain, the Philosophical Revolution in Germany, and the People's Revolution in France that changed the course of history.

In this context, on the twenty-eighth of July, 1914, the market began to search for countries and enslave them, so that the colonial powers appeared on the world stage, on the one hand, and on the other hand, countries such as Germany, France, and the United Kingdom began to try to divide the colonies within themselves or to create new colonial nations. Crown Prince Ferdinand is being overthrown, and only then do the dominant nations hide their faces from the colonial powers and prepare for war by dusting off the weapons of war. In fact, the First World War The historical reality of the day was that the war was not waged to seek justice for the death of Crown Prince Ferdinand of Austria, but for the sake of patriotism. There is a need to explore the history of that period if we are to know and kill. The quest for dominance in the navy between Britain and Germany erupted in the same context in which the European countries sought to occupy Alsace-Lorraine, a French-occupied territory, at the end of the French-Persian War, which led to a major feud between France and Germany and a hostile war between France and Germany. The merger was not accepted by Germany, which considered Britain, France, and Russia to be united against it. It was seen as a key colony at the outbreak of World War I, as well as the issue of Serbian nationalism as a major issue in World War I. Serbia's ambition was to unite the scattered Serbian population in the countries around it.

This was possible by annexing the areas inhabited by the Serbian people, mainly under the Austrian Empire. Serbia feared that the Austrian Empire, which feared that if the Serbian people under its domination seceded from their own country, the Hungarians, Germans, Italians, Romans, etc., who could live in their own country, would claim a separate country. The British agreed to confirm the rule of France, against whom Germany backed the Sultan of Morocco. Germany thought that the treaty between France and Britain, which were once rivals, could not last, and that Britain, Russia, Italy, and Spain, contrary to German intentions, had rallied around France to secure French domination in Morocco. The system developed, and the conflict between Serbia and Austria escalated as France prepared to roll the German shirt against Britain, urging Austria to launch an immediate offensive against Serbia in the wake of the assassination of Prince Ferdinand of Austria and Germany to offer unconditional assistance.

Following Austria's invasion of Serbia in 1914, Russia ordered the full mobilization of its forces. The turning point was that Germany, which had planned to enter France via Belgium, had to face the most serious counterattack in areas where it thought it could most easily invade Britain, which could have been Belgium's bodyguard, and thus the potential for European countries to prepare themselves for the great catastrophe that the European nations were preparing for that would lead to the Great Depression. Hungary, and Bulgaria joined Germany, splitting in favour of Serbia. Britain, France, Russia, the United States, and Italy were also involved in the war. World War I broke out on August 4, 1914, when the United States initially intervened but aided France and Britain. The heavy use of submarines and warplanes caused extensive damage to the Allies, and the most important turning point in history must be seen in this place where the Allies used heavy talkie forces. The name is America, and then the dream of a superpower became a nightmare for the whole of Europe. This is where world history was split in two, that is. One way is the division of the capitalist country based on the rich into two socialist countries based on the people of the other way. If necessary, the United States as a country for capitalism and the Soviet Union as a socialist country that respects the labour of the people were formed during the First World War, during which the Soviet Russia Revolution erupted. They point to the Tsar's misguided military policies as the main reason for the revolution's success.

During World War I, German troops attempted to wage war on Tsar King Russia. The King said that for any Tsar who enslaves himself, our first act would be to overthrow the Tsar, who would win the war against Germany again in World War I and regain the status of the Tsar in Russia while the war was raging in Russia. Lenin signed a peace treaty with Germany and withdrew from the war in the late 1917s.Then the Russian army was on the offensive against the Tsar Banner. Lenin used it as a tool to revolt against the Germans. It was celebrated that, in direct opposition to these historical events, a single nation arose during the First World War itself, which means that one of the main reasons for the outbreak of World War I was the inability of European nations to tolerate the development of the war in Germany, the display of new weapons of war by Germany, and the increase of German war equipment as naval forces, posed a threat to countries such as Britain, and thus frightened European countries into invading Germany. went to war to control the United States, which had been quiet at the beginning of World War I, and decided to take advantage of the situation.

That is, the evolution of the European pulses, realizing in the absence of Europe the new weapons of war that Germany had during World War I, the United States produced and sold munitions, and the United States soon became a superpower. At the same time, the United States stood on the world stage as the first country for wealthy capitalists, an important event that made history from the remnants of World War II. Each country began to use separate war tactics, mainly German forces, to use poison gas. All countries agreed that poison should not be used in war, but in defiance of this, Germany initially used poison, and eventually, the forces of the three nations, Britain, France, and the United States, rushed toward Germany. Germany panicked and joined the League against King Kaiser, who sent troops to subdue the people. The German forces engaged in the war were shooting at their own people.

The war, which lasted one hundred and sixty-one days, claimed the lives of two million people. Two million people died worldwide after the end of the war due to poisoning, and forty trillion dollars' worth of property was destroyed. It remains to be seen why Germany, which had worked to establish its dominance in World War I, embraced defeat and was defeated by Germany's illusion that it could easily be sold off in the war by the force of its weapons and force. Germany's war plan was to capture France on Germany's western border in six weeks and recapture Russia on its eastern border, but the biggest challenge was to wage war on both sides of the country, as France was unable to capture France in six weeks as planned. The heat of the devastating World War I infected Austria, which not only failed when it sought to invade German-occupied territory defended by Britain, the United States, and Japan, but also aroused the wrath of the United States, which had until then neutralized Germany's defeat in World War I. Food, clothing, and weapons were brought into Allied Germany without their permission. The biggest setback for Germany was the invalidation of essential commodities, including sugar. Germany had a military structure, but all the countries that were allied with Germany were major German aid states, and tens of thousands of powerful nations supporting them on the battlefield led to Germany's defeat in the First World War.

Most of the Asian countries, including India, were under British control, and India had to support Britain without hesitation. About fifteen lakh Indian soldiers participated in the First World War from the states of

Punjab, Uttar Pradesh, Maharashtra, Tamil Nadu, and Bihar, especially those who fought in the West Frontier countries of East Africa, Mesopotamia, and Egypt. One of the reasons volunteers participated in the war was the good pay they received, as well as the social status of those who went to war due to the custom of treating them as Chhatris. He volunteered at a hospital for injured soldiers, and won about a thousand heroic medals in Britain. The highest award, the Victoria Award, was given to twelve Indian soldiers. Sixty-five thousand Indian soldiers died in the war; sixty-five thousand were wounded; ninety-eight Indian nurses went on duty; and there is no information about ten thousand soldiers.

After the completion, India was left disappointed, and at the end of the war, Germany decided to pay compensation to the Allies, and France seized some of Germany's prosperous areas. The war caused great divisions in politics and relations with other nations throughout the rest of the twentieth century. As a result, the world community felt that such a world war should never happen again, for which an international union was formed in which many nations joined, but the United States, which had made great efforts to form the union, did not join in panic. The German Empire was overthrown. It lost much of its territory and, as a result, reached the borders of Europe and the Middle East. Many commonwealth states and republics were formed, especially in place of the old monarchies.

Despite the fact that Europe, the United States, and other countries were responsible for the First World War, Germany bore the entire burden of blame due to its failure, and it was Germany's humiliation on the world stage that led to the rise of dictator Hitler and the conduct of World War II.

Hitler in World War 1

CHAPTER SIX

WORLD WAR II

World War II taught the people of the world the lesson that an atomic bomb could have an impact on people's lives. The problem that began among the nations of the world as to whose moon power rose ended only after it had amassed crores and crores of lives. The power map of the world was turned upside down. The world's ruling powers are the nations that emerged as powers at the end of World War II. World War I brought about great political change on the European continent. In World War I, Austria-Hungary, Germany, Bulgaria, and the Ottoman Empire was overthrown. Large-scale casualties had been exacerbated, and nations formed at the World Conference in Paris in the 1910s to prevent a future war, with the aim of preventing armed wars between nations and resolving international conflicts through negotiations. Unrest persisted after the war. This war brought about great political change in many countries, and in some countries, this war changed the maps. The German Empire lost thirteen percent of its territory due to the peace treaty signed after the war, and the massive loss of life and economic loss caused the People's Revolution there, leading to the fall of the German Empire and the formation of the Democratic Empire. Tensions in the nursery then rose due to clashes between nationalists and communists.

In 1913, he was imprisoned for one year after the failure of Hitler's efforts to establish rule in Germany. Shortly afterward, in 1913, Hitler declared his dictatorship by concealing democracy. The various actions of Hitler were against the peace treaty. A similar situation prevailed in Italy during World War I when Italy accepted the leadership of Benito Mussolini, who seized power from the Allies with the aim of creating a new Romanian empire. Mussolini made a number of policy changes to hide democracy and make Italy the centre of the world. In the meantime, strengthening France-

Italy friendship supported Italian colonial rule over Ethiopia, and in the same color, the annexation of the Tsar's Basil to Hitler's Germany led to the preparation of weapons against the peace treaty and the enlistment of large numbers of troops in Hitler's, resulting in a tense situation on the European continent. France, Italy, and England formed the Stress Brand in April 1935 to control German domination, which imposed some military sanctions on Germany but lifted those restrictions in June of the same year. The UK alone imposed a naval agreement with Germany without third-party restrictions. Germany's rapid military growth Germany's actions aimed at annexing most of Eastern Europe became a headache for the Soviet Union, so the Soviet government entered into a Franco-Soviet treaty with France. The League of Nations, which was formed to promote peace between nations, acted nominally, and the United States, which oversees itself, decided to neutralize the problems caused by the devastation of World War I, while tensions between China and Japan erupted on the Asian continent. China's Kuomintang Party through various campaigns to unite the territories in the occupied territories and the civil war between the Communist Parties in the Kuomintang and the occupied territories in favor of Japan, thereby capturing the Manchuria region of China. The League of Nations condemned Japan's tendency to appeal to the Occupied Territories, and Japan withdrew from fear.

After that, the two countries fought on many fronts until the signing of the 1933 Third Year Peace Agreement, although Chinese rebels occasionally fought in the occupied territories of Japan, in which case the Axis Pact was signed between Germany and Italy in October 1939. One month later, Germany and Japan signed the Anti-Comintern Pact Agreement against the Communist Party, which Italy joined in a few months. The agreement was passed against communist policy. Although the beginning of World War II is said to be in 1913, various political events in Europe and Asia preceded it. Hitler and Mussolini aided the nationalists in the Spanish Civil War. In the same vein, the Soviet Union extended its support to the Spanish refugees who ruled Spain. Both Germany and the Soviet Union used the war as a time to test their readiness and tactics. The war was won by pro-German and pro-Italian nationalists. The leader of the nationalists, Francisco Franco, was installed as president. Although Spain was said to be neutral, it sent troops in support of the Axis powers in the Eastern European region. The border issue between Japan and the Soviet Union continued, and in 1919, the war between the two countries began as Japanese troops entered the

Soviet Union. Although Japan advanced at the beginning of the war, it fell to the Soviet Union. A faction of the Japanese government preceded the peace agreement to prevent Soviet Union intervention in the Japan-China war, which resulted in the signing of the Japan-Soviet agreement, which the Japanese government wanted to focus on in the United States and Europe in the Pacific Ocean instead. At the same time, Germany and Italy were openly dominating Europe. Germany annexed Australia in March 1938. But large-scale regimes did not emerge from other European countries, which favoured Hitler. So, he began to take steps to annex the southern-eastern part of Czechoslovakia, inhabited by the Germans, to the Germans.

The United Kingdom and France did not oppose the German occupation when the Czechoslovakia government opposed it, as Germany promised that no further land would be claimed. The United Kingdom and France vehemently opposed the occupation of Poland, Romania, and Greece by the British and French occupiers, who had pledged their independence. Tensions continued to rise in the European region. The dominance of Germany and Italy continued to grow. This called into question the existence of England and France. In early September 1919, Germany and the Slovak Republic invaded Poland. Within two days of the attack, Britain, France, and its allies declared war on Germany. The Germans were paralyzed by the sea to destabilise the German economy and control the war. The Soviet Union, which had declared a ceasefire with Japan, attacked Poland on September 17th. Poland, attacked from many angles, refused to surrender and continued to fight, forming a shadow government with the help of the Allies.

The German infiltration of Denmark and Norway in April, the year following the infiltration of the Millennium, prevented the export of iron ore from Sweden. Germany easily captured Denmark. Despite the help of the Allies, Norway was unable to overcome German forces and surrendered. Germany, which had also started a war against the neutralized European powers, sought to capture Belgium, the Netherlands, and Luxembourg, thereby plotting to overthrow France. The following year, in June of the same year, France declared war on Italy, France, and England. The French force fell, unable to cope with the German and Italian forces. Both countries invaded France. The Luftwaffe's air force began its offensive against Britain in early July, occupying large parts of Europe, but German warplanes crashed into British warplanes, forcing Germany to suspend war. Although the United States decided to remain neutral, it did provide economic assistance to allies, including China. The United States began aiding the British military after the French occupation. The majority of Americans protested. Franklin Roosevelt, the then President of the United States, said that he was opposed to military aid, but that US aid was needed to defend democracy. The United States has taken a number of actions against Germany. Italy occupied British-occupied Egypt during the war in Europe. Italy, seeking to expand its borders, sought to invade North Africa off the Mediterranean coast. It was thwarted by Italy, which wanted to extend its dominance as far as Greece. The governments of Italy and Romania began to invade Russia together. Hitler did not like the existence of a communist state in Russia, even though there was German support and a neutral ceasefire agreement with the neutral Soviet Union due to the agreement signed between the two countries, so he indirectly plotted against Russia. Most of the forces were moved toward the Soviet Union by the Axis powers to seize the Soviet Union. Taking advantage of this, Britain began to devise its own strategies.

This caused problems for Stalin, the Soviet president who helped Germany during the Polish occupation. Following this, in July 1940, England and the Soviet Union signed a military treaty against Germany. After that, the Middle Eastern countries captured the fields of Iran and strengthened themselves on the Iranian front to strengthen their team. The United States, which had provided its support and military without participating in the war, promised to put economic pressure on Japan to ban the trade in fuel, which was a major headache for Japan. The talks sought to improve Japan-US relations but forced the US to withdraw its troops from neighbouring countries, including China, without heeding Japan's efforts. The United States, the Netherlands, and the United Kingdom also signed an agreement to protect their territories. Because of this, Japan is preparing for war against the United States. In December 1919, Japan attacked Pearl Harbour, a U.S. port near the island of Hawaii, as it waged war on the United States and the British colonies in Southeast Asia. This attack led the United States into World War II. The United States is ready to launch an attack against Japan. In the Pacific Ocean, US and British forces launched an attack on Japanese forces.Between 1920 and 1923, Japanese forces continued to occupy British and US-held colonies on the Asian continent. In this situation, the British-dominated Indian forces opposed the Japanese forces on the Indo-China border. Australian forces fought in the Ugine areas. Within two years of the start of the war, Germany had taken control of its neighbors. Countries such as Poland, Denmark, Norway, the Netherlands, Belgium, Luxembourg, and France also came under German control. Germany was victorious as long as the United States remained neutral in the war. Germany, a key member of the Axis Powers alliance, did not even report war on Japan and Italy, with whom it had signed treaties.Interested in invading neighbouring countries, Hitler failed to predict his troops. The continuous wars without fulfilling the requirements of beating them left the soldiers exhausted. The players could not bear the heavy pitfall of Europe. As a result, war-torn Russian forces erupted.

By July 1913, one by one, the cities of the Soviet Union, which had been under German control, came under Stalin's control. The bourgeois United States participated in World War II because of Japan's invasion of itself. Opposing the Axis powers by making a pact with the Soviet Union, which had communist policies against their own. Winston Churchill, Prime Minister of the United Kingdom, and Roosevelt were scheduled to meet with Chiang Kai-shek in China. The result was the annexation of Japanese-controlled islands in the Pacific Ocean. In the same vein, the Allies met with Soviet President Joseph Stalin in Iran and plotted to control the domination of Japan and Germany. This caused a slight setback for the Japanese forces that dominated Asia. The British Indian forces fought against the Japanese forces while Japan advanced its forces until there was no Assam in India, which was under British rule. At the same time, Japan withdrew its troops from Burma in the face of Chinese opposition. As the United States and the Soviet Union joined, England, which had initially fought with the Axis powers, became stronger. Germany's success was hampered by a series of setbacks. Allied forces surrounded and defeated the German allies without much effort. The advance of the Allies saw a stagnation in the course of the Italian National Forces. In the year 1945, Soviet troops occupied major German cities and parliaments. The changes in US politics during this period added further strength to the allies. Harry Truman was sworn in as the new president. Mussolini was assassinated on April 28, 1945, by the movement's nostalgia for revolution against Mussolini's fascism. Due to this, Italy withdrew from the war. Germany, besieged by the Allies at both besieged ends, agreed to surrender on the twenty-ninth of April. The next day, the dictator, Hitler, committed suicide in Germany. Following that, German forces withdrew as the Ceasefire Agreement was signed unconditionally on May 7 and executed on May 8. Despite the surrender of Germany and Italy, Japan continued to fight.

At the beginning of 1945, a joint effort by US and Philippine forces in the Philippines was called to expel other troops. Troops were mobilized to capture Manila, the capital of the Philippines, in March 1919. The fighting continued until Manila was captured. Clement Attlee was elected Prime Minister of the United Kingdom after the defeat of Winston Churchill, the Allied leader of World War II. The United States and the United Kingdom prepared to launch a war against Japan in early August, in violation of the Treaty of Japan, which had been signed on July 27, 1945. The city of Hiroshima in Japan was hit by a bomb called the "Little Boy" on August 6. More than one and a half million people were killed in the attack, and more people were exposed to radiation. The Batman Atomic Bomb was dropped on Nagasaki on August 9, three days before Japan recovered from the attack. Fifty thousand people were killed in this blast. This attack was a major blow to Japan in World War II. Unable to deal with US forces, Japan surrendered to the war. On the fifteenth day of August in the year one thousand nine hundred and ninety-five, Japan declared war and agreed to surrender. But finally, on September 2, 1945, the United States came aboard and surrendered. Japan surrenders and World War II ends.

The war caused heavy casualties. The embracing nations also lost their great wealth. The war for supremacy in Europe marked a major turning point on its map. In many countries, this war brought about great political change. Germany split in two after the war. Countries such as Poland, Hungary, Romania, and Albania became supporters of the Soviet Union. Many countries in Asia were liberated from European and American colonial rule. The Allies formed the United Nations to bring peace to the nations of the world. This organisation was created not as a nominal organisation like the World Nations Association but as an authoritative organization. Member states have common policies to uphold human rights among the nations of the world. Its permanent members were the United States, the United Kingdom, the Soviet Union, China, and France, the major powers in World War II. The UN Security Council was formed to include these members. Memorandums of Understanding were also signed between the countries for the use of nuclear weapons. Although many wars have taken place since the impact of this war, which led to the independence of countries including India, diplomatic talks have been the solution to its solution.

CHAPTER SEVEN

COLD WAR

Think about America's tricks. Let me remind you once again that in World War II the United States joined hands with the Soviet Union, which was directly opposed to its policy, to strengthen its side. At the end of World War II, the nations that were the power of the world were Great Britain, the United States and the Soviet Union. But Britain's dominance waned as the colonies gained independence. The strongest nations now are the United States and the Soviet Union. After the end of World War II both countries predicted a competitive entry for the two of them as they were countries with opposite policies. But did not fight directly but rather indirectly fought to keep his ally country. To put it bluntly, arguing with my wife and me is like spending our friend's money on alcohol and ruining things in a friend's house without a direct confrontation.

The Cold War was a time of international strain between the United States and the Soviet Union and their individual partners, the Western Bloc and the Eastern Bloc, which started after World War II. History specialists don't completely settle on its beginning and finishing focuses, yet the period is, for the most part, considered to traverse from the 1947 Truman Doctrine on March 12th, 1947, to the 1991 Dissolution of the Soviet Union on December 26th, 1991. The term "cold conflict" is utilised in light of the fact that there was no enormous scope for battling straightforwardly between the two superpowers, yet they each upheld major local contentions known as "intermediary wars." The contention was based on the philosophical and international battle for worldwide impact by these two superpowers, following their impermanent partnership and triumph against Nazi Germany in 1945. Aside from nuclear weapons stockpile development and conventional military organization, the battle for supremacy was communicated through covert means, for example, mental fighting, propagation crusades, secret activities, extensive bans, contention at games, and mechanical rivalries, for example, the Space Race.

The Western Bloc was led by the United States and other First World countries that were, for the most part, liberal majority countries but were tied to an organization of dictator states, the majority of which were their former provinces. The Eastern Bloc was led by the Soviet Union and its Communist Party, which had an impact throughout the Second World and was also affiliated with a dictatorial organization. The US government upheld conservative states and uprisings across the world, while the Soviet government subsidised left-wing gatherings and uprisings all over the planet. As essentially every one of the pioneer states accomplished autonomy in the period 1945–1960, they turned out to be Third World front lines in the Cold War.

The principal period of the Cold War started soon after the end of the Second World War in 1945. The United States and its partners created the NATO military union in 1949 in the dread of a Soviet assault and named their worldwide strategy against Soviet impact regulation. The Soviet Union shaped the Warsaw Pact in 1955 because of NATO. Significant emergencies of this stage incorporated the 1948-49 Berlin Blockade, the 1927–1949 Chinese Civil War, the 1950–1953 Korean War, the 1956 Hungarian Revolution, the 1956 Suez Crisis, the 1961 Berlin Crisis, and the 1962 Cuban Missile Crisis. The US and the USSR sought to make an impact in Latin America, the Middle East, and the decolonizing territories of Africa and Asia.

Following the Cuban Missile Crisis, another stage started that saw the Sino-Soviet split between China and the Soviet Union confound relations inside the Communist circle, while France, a Western Bloc state, started to request more prominent independence of activity. The USSR attacked Czechoslovakia to stifle the 1968 Prague Spring, while the US encountered inner strife from the social equality movement and resistance to the Vietnam War. During the 1960s and 70s, a worldwide development of harmony flourished among residents all over the planet. There were developments against atomic weapons testing and for atomic demobilization, with a large enemy of war fights. By the 1970s, the two sides began considering harmony and security, introducing a time of détente that saw the Strategic Arms Limitation Talks and the US opening relations with the People's Republic of China as an essential stabiliser to the USSR. Various self-broadcasted Marxist systems were framed in the final part of the 1970s in the Third World, including Angola, Mozambique, Ethiopia, Cambodia, Afghanistan, and Nicaragua.

Détente imploded toward the decade's end with the start of the Soviet-Afghan War in 1979. The mid 1980s were one more time of increased strain. The United States expanded political, military, and monetary tensions with the Soviet Union when it was experiencing financial stagnation. During the 1980s, the new Soviet pioneer Mikhail Gorbachev presented the changing changes of glasnost ("receptiveness") in 1985 and perestroika ("rearrangement") in 1987 and ended Soviet association in Afghanistan in 1989. Pressures for public sway developed further in Eastern Europe, and Gorbachev declined to militarily uphold their legislatures any longer.

In 1989, the fall of the Iron Curtain after the Pan-European Picnic and a tranquil flood of upheavals (except for Romania and Afghanistan) toppled practically all socialist state-run administrations of the Eastern Bloc. The Communist Party of the Soviet Union itself was completely let go in the Soviet Union and was prohibited after an unsuccessful uprising in August 1991. This thus prompted the proper disintegration of the USSR in December 1991, the affirmation of freedom in its constituent republics, and the breakdown of socialist legislatures across quite a bit of Africa and Asia. The United States was left as the world's only superpower.

The Cold War and its occasions have left a critical heritage. It is regularly alluded to in mainstream society, particularly on subjects like reconnaissance and the dangers of atomic fighting. For the ensuing history, see international relations beginning around 1989.

COMPANIONS - 1776–1945

The Russian Revolution of 1917, followed by the Russian Civil War, caused a crack between the Soviet Union and the United States. In any case, when President Franklin Roosevelt got to work in 1933, discretionary and exchange relations between the two nations continued. The relationship was stressed once more after the USSR attached the Baltic States and signed a peace agreement with Nazi Germany.

In spite of their disparities, the Soviet Union and the United States ended up as partners after the German intrusion into Russia in June 1941. As the conflict in Europe started to slow down and triumph was in sight, the two nations had totally different perspectives with regards to what the post-war world would resemble. At the Potsdam Conference, not long before the nuclear bomb was dropped on Japan, Stalin needed to put Eastern Europe under the Soviet range of prominence, setting the circumstances for the Cold War to begin.

IRON CURTAIN – 1945-1947

As wartime gave way to peacetime, a resurgent United States enjoyed financial prosperity, while Europe was left to recover from the effects of war. Stalin's dreaded cleanses have continued in the Soviet Union, and the country is on the verge of starvation. Germany is compelled to surrender a portion of its eastern region to Poland, and the Germans residing in that space are ousted from their homes. Stalin starts to expand his grip on Eastern Europe, introducing socialist systems yet choosing to avoid the Greek Civil War.

The United Kingdom, depleted from the conflict, sees its once-strong realm go into decay. As food deficiencies compromise the solidity of Europe, a more confident United States starts to challenge the USSR's impact in both Turkey and Iran.

MARCHALL PLAN 1947-1952

The Marshall Plan was an American drive authorized in 1948 to give an unfamiliar guide to Western Europe. The United States moved more than $13 billion in financial recuperation projects to Western European economies after the end of World War II. Swapping a previous proposition for a Morgenthau Plan, it worked for a long time, starting on April 3, 1948. The objectives of the United States were to remake war-torn areas, eliminate exchange obstructions, modernise industry, further develop European success, and forestall the spread of socialism. The Marshall Plan required a decrease in highway obstructions and the disintegration of numerous guidelines while empowering an expansion in usefulness as well as the reception of present-day business techniques.

The Marshall Plan's help was split between the member states, generally on a per capita basis. A bigger sum was given to the major modern powers, as the predominant assessment was that their revival was fundamental to the overall European restoration. More guides per capita were also directed toward Allied countries, with fewer directed toward those that had been important for the Axis or remained nonpartisan.The biggest beneficiary of Marshall Plan cash was the United Kingdom (getting around half of the aggregate). The tremendous expense that Britain brought about through the "Loan Lease" plot was not completely re-paid to the US until 2006. The following most elevated commitments went to France (8%) and West Germany (12%). Somewhere in the range of eighteen European nations, some got Plan benefits. Despite the fact that it offered investment, the Soviet Union declined plan benefits and, furthermore, obstructed advantages to Eastern Bloc nations, like Romania and Poland. The United States gave comparable guide programmes in Asia, but they were not part of the Marshall Plan.

Its part in the quick recuperation has been discussed. The Marshall Plan's bookkeeping mirrors that help represented around 3% of the combined public pay of the beneficiary nations somewhere in the range of 1948 and 1951, and that implies an expansion in GDP development of not exactly a large portion of a percent.

After World War II, in 1947, industrialist Lewis H. Brown composed "A Report on Germany," which filled in as a nitty-gritty suggestion for the remaking of post-war Germany and served as a reason for the Marshall Plan. The drive was named after United States Secretary of State George C. Marshall. The arrangement had bipartisan help in Washington, where the Republicans controlled Congress and the Democrats controlled the White House with Harry S. Truman as president. The Plan was to a great extent the work of State Department authorities, particularly William L. Clayton and George F. Kennan, with assistance from the Brookings Institution, as mentioned by Senator Arthur Vandenberg, administrator of the United States Senate Committee on Foreign Relations. In a speech at Harvard University in June 1947, Marshall expressed a strong desire to aid Europe's recovery.The Marshall Plan was created to aid in the economic recovery of countries following World War II and to secure the United States' international clout over Western Europe.To battle the effects of the Marshall Plan, the USSR fostered its own monetary arrangement, known as the Molotov Plan, disregarding the way that a lot of assets from the Eastern Bloc nations were paid to the USSR as restitution for taking an interest in the Axis Powers during the conflict.

The expression "likeness of the Marshall Plan" is frequently used to describe a proposed enormous-scope financial salvage program.

In 1951, the Marshall Plan was, to a great extent, supplanted by the Mutual Security Act.

BERLIN BLOCKADE – 1948-1949

The Berlin barricade was a worldwide emergency that emerged from an endeavour by the Soviet Union, in 1948–49, to drive the Western Allied powers (the United States, the United Kingdom, and France) to forsake their post-World War II purviews in West Berlin.

In March 1948, the Allied powers chose to join their different occupation zones in Germany into a solitary financial unit. In the fight, the Soviet agent pulled out of the Allied Control Council. Incidental to the presentation of a new Deutsche mark in West Berlin (as all through West Germany), which the Soviets viewed as an infringement of concurrences with the Allies, the Soviet occupation powers in eastern Germany started a barricade of all rail, street, and water correspondences between Berlin and the West. On June 24, the Soviets reported that the four-power organisation of Berlin had stopped and that the Allies no longer had any freedoms there. On June 26, the United States and Britain started to supply the city with food and other imperative supplies via air. They likewise coordinated a comparative "carrier" the other way, of West Berlin's enormously decreased modern commodities. By mid-July, the Soviet multitude of occupations in East Germany had expanded to 40 divisions, compared to 8 in the Allied areas. Before the end of July, three gatherings of U.S. vital planes had been sent as fortifications to Britain. Pressure stayed high, but the war didn't break out.

Notwithstanding desperate deficiencies in fuel and power, the airdrop pushed life along in West Berlin for a considerable length of time, until on May 12, 1949, the Soviet Union lifted the barricade. The carrier went on until September 30, at an all-out cost of $224 million and after conveyance of 2,323,738 tonnes of food, fuel, apparatus, and different supplies. The finish to the bar was achieved due to countermeasures forced by the Allies on East German interchanges and, most importantly, given the Western ban put on all essential products from the Eastern coalition. Because of the bar and carrier, Berlin turned into an image of the Allies' eagerness to go against additional Soviet development in Europe.

KOREAN WAR – 1950-1953

The Korean War was a conflict fought between North Korea and South Korea from June 25, 1950, to July 27, 1953. The conflict started on June 25, 1950, when North Korea attacked South Korea following conflicts along the line and uprisings in South Korea. North Korea was supported by China and the Soviet Union, while South Korea was supported by the United Nations, primarily the United States. On July 27, 1953, the fighting came to an end with a truce.

In 1910, majestic Japan added Korea, where it governed for a very long time until its acquiescence toward the finish of World War II on August 15, 1945. The United States and the Soviet Union isolated Korea along the 38th parallel, dividing it into two zones of occupation. The Soviets regulated the northern zone, and the Americans managed the southern zone. In 1948, because of Cold War pressures, the occupation zones became two sovereign states. A communist express, the Democratic People's Republic of Korea, was laid out in the north under the extremist socialist administration of Kim Il-sung, while an entrepreneur expresses, the Republic of Korea, was laid out in the south under the tyrant dictatorial initiative of Syngman Rhee. The two legislatures of the two new Korean states professed to be the sole genuine administration of all of Korea, and neither acknowledged the boundary as long-lasting.

On June 25, 1950, North Korean military powers crossed the boundary and crashed into South Korea. The United Nations Security Council reprimanded the North Korean move as an attack and approved the arrangement of the United Nations Command and the dispatch of powers to Korea to repulse it. The Soviet Union was boycotting the UN for perceiving Taiwan (Republic of China) as China, and China (People's Republic of China) in the central area was not perceived by the UN, so neither could they uphold their partner North Korea at the Security Council meeting. The 21 nations of the United Nations in the end added to the UN's power, with the United States providing around 90% of the tactical stuff.

After the initial two months of the war, the South Korean Army (ROKA) and American powers quickly dispatched to Korea were on purpose in shame, withdrawing to a small region behind a protective line known as the Pusan Perimeter. In September 1950, an unsafe land and/or water-capable UN counteroffensive was sent off at Incheon, removing KPA troops and supply lines in South Korea. The individuals who got away from envelopment and catch were constrained back north. UN powers attacked North Korea in October 1950 and moved quickly towards the Yalu River, the boundary with China—yet on October 19, 1950, Chinese forces of the People's Volunteer Army (PVA) crossed the Yalu and entered the conflict. The UN withdrew from North Korea after the First Phase Offensive and the Second Phase Offensive. Chinese powers were in South Korea by late December.

In these and ensuing fights, Seoul was caught multiple times, and socialist powers were pushed back to positions around the 38th equal, near where the conflict had begun. After this, the front settled, and the most recent two years were a conflict of whittling down. In any case, the conflict in the air, in any case, was never an impasse. North Korea was dependent upon a gigantic US bombardment effort. Stream warriors engaged in an aerial battle without precedent in history, and Soviet pilots secretly flew in support of their socialist partners.

The fighting came to an end on July 27, 1953, when the Korean Armistice Agreement was signed.The understanding made the Korean Demilitarized Zone (DMZ) the isolation zone between North and South Korea and permitted the arrival of detainees. Despite this, no truce was ever declared, and the two Koreas were still at war, locked in a frozen conflict.In April 2018, the heads of North and South Korea met at the DMZ and consented to pursue a settlement to officially end the Korean War.

The Korean War was one of the most damaging conflicts of modern times, with roughly 3 million conflict fatalities and a higher corresponding civilian loss of life than World War II or the Vietnam War.It brought about the obliteration of essentially every one of Korea's significant urban areas, a large number of slaughters by the two sides, including the mass killing of a huge number of suspected socialists by the South Korean government, and the torment and starvation of detainees in battle by the North Koreans. North Korea has become one of the most intensely besieged nations ever. Moreover, a few million North Koreans are estimated to have escaped from North Korea throughout the conflict.

DIVISION OF KOREA-1954

A global commission reviewed the Korean Armistice Agreement.Beginning around 1953, the Neutral Nations Supervisory Commission (NNSC), made up of individuals from the Swiss and Swedish Armed Forces, has been positioned close to the DMZ.

In April 1975, South Vietnam's capital was captured by the People's Army of Vietnam. Supported by the accomplishments of the Communist upheaval in Indochina, Kim Il-sung considered it to be an amazing chance to attack the South. Kim visited China in April of that year and met with Mao Zedong and Zhou Enlai to request a military guide. Regardless of Pyongyang's assumptions, in any case, Beijing wouldn't help North Korea with one more conflict in Korea.

Since the cease-fire, there have been various invasions and demonstrations of animosity by North Korea. From 1966 to 1969, an enormous number of cross-line invasions occurred in what has been alluded to as the Korean DMZ Conflict or the Second Korean War. In 1968, a North Korean commando group fruitlessly endeavored to kill South Korean President Park Chung-hee in the Blue House Raid. In 1976, the hatchet murder occurrence was generally well received. Starting around 1974, four invasion burrows prompting Seoul have been uncovered. In 2010, a North Korean submarine obliterated and sank the South Korean corvette ROKS Cheonan, bringing about the passing of 46 mariners. Again in 2010, North Korea discharged ordnance shells on Yeonpyeong Island, killing two military staff and two regular folks.

After another rush of UN sanctions on March 11, 2013, North Korea guaranteed that the truce had become invalid. On March 13, 2013, North Korea affirmed it finished the 1953 Armistice and proclaimed that North Korea "isn't limited by the North-South presentation on peace". On March 30, 2013, North Korea expressed that it had entered a "condition of battle" with South Korea and announced that "The long-standing circumstance of the Korean promontory being neither settled nor at war is at last finished". On April 4, 2013, the US Secretary of Defense, Chuck Hagel, informed the press that Pyongyang had "officially educated" the Pentagon that it "confirmed" the expected utilisation of an atomic weapon against South Korea, Japan, and the United States of America, including Guam and Hawaii. Hagel also expressed that the US would convey the Terminal High Altitude Area Defense ballistic missile destroying rocket framework to Guam due to a sound and sensible atomic danger from North Korea.

In 2016, it was uncovered that North Korea was moving toward the United States about leading proper harmony conversations with officially ending the conflict. While the White House consented to secret harmony talks, the arrangement was dismissed because of North Korea's refusal to examine atomic demilitarisation as a feature of the deal.

On April 27, 2018, it was reported that North Korea and South Korea had consented to converse and end their continuous 65-year struggle. They invested in the total denuclearization of the Korean Peninsula.

In his discourse at the United Nations General Assembly on September 22, 2021, South Korean President Moon Jae-inemphasized his call to officially end the Korean War in his speech.

RED – 1948-1953

Apprehension about each other pervades the eastern and western authorities, streamlining down to the populace. The House Committee on Un-American Activities in the United States started research affirming socialist penetration in media outlets and discretionary corps. In the USSR, an expanding clique of characters is being developed around Stalin, and a more severe police state is grabbing hold. In light of Yugoslavia's free international strategy, the Soviet Union pushed a progression of cleanses in Prague as an advance notice to other satellite nations that might wander from the Soviet approach. Dread and constraint in the USSR hit their pinnacle just before Stalin's abrupt passing in 1953.

AFTER STALIN– 1953-1956

After Stalin's abrupt demise, Nikita Khrushchev assumes control over the Soviet Union, changing a portion of Stalin's harsh strategies. Khrushchev likewise restores relations with Yugoslavia, and in a mysterious discourse given to the Soviet authorities, he impugns Stalin's unforgiving strategies. In the meantime, West Germany starts to rearm, driving the USSR to lay out the Warsaw Pact accordingly. Attempting to keep up with the Soviet impact in Eastern Europe, Khrushchev sent troops into East Germany, Poland, and Hungary to put down revolts.

SPUTNIK – 1949–1961

Unbeknownst to the United States, the Soviets had kept an eye on the U.S. improvement of the nuclear bomb, and they immediately made their own after the Second World War. This ignited an atomic weapons contest between the two superpowers. With the successful Soviet launch of Sputnik, America reacted by expanding its development of nuclear-powered rockets.A terrifying realisation is taking hold in the United States: the country is lagging behind the Soviets in terms of innovation.John F. Kennedy was chosen President of the United States in 1960, as the Soviets appeared to have a direct early advantage in the space race.

SPACE RACE

The Space Race was a twentieth-century contest between two Cold War foes, the Soviet Union and the United States, to accomplish predominant spaceflight ability. It had its beginnings in the long-range rocket-based atomic weapons contest between the two countries following World War II. The innovative benefit shown by spaceflight accomplishment was viewed as essential for public safety, and turned out to be important for the imagery and philosophy of the time. The Space Race brought spearheading dispatches of fake satellites, automated space tests to the Moon, Venus, and Mars, and human spaceflight in low Earth orbit and eventually to the Moon.

The opposition started decisively on August 2, 1955, when the Soviet Union reacted to the American declaration four days earlier of the purpose of sending off fake satellites for the International Geophysical Year by proclaiming they would likewise send off a satellite "soon". Long-distance rocket advancements made it possible to take the conflict between the two countries into space.This opposition acquired public consideration with the "Sputnik Shock," when the USSR accomplished the main effective counterfeit satellite send off on October 4, 1957, of Sputnik 1, and therefore, when the USSR sent the first human into space with the orbital trip of Yuri Gagarin on April 12, 1961. The USSR exhibited an early lead in the race with these and different firsts over the course of the following many years, arriving at the Moon interestingly with the Luna programme by utilizing automated missions.

US President John F. Kennedy raised the stakes by stating that the goal was to "handle a man on the Moon and return him safely to Earth."[4] The two nations chipped away at growing very weighty lift-off vehicles, with the US effectively conveying the Saturn V, which was big enough to send a three-man orbited and two-man lander to the Moon. Kennedy's moon landing goal was met in July 1969 with the journey of Apollo 11, a single accomplishment considered by Americans to outperform any combination of Soviet accomplishments that had been made. Nonetheless, such an assessment is, for the most part, debatable, with others attributing the first man in space to a far greater achievement.The USSR sought after two-run lunar projects, but didn't prevail with their N1 rocket to send off and arrive on the Moon before the US, and at last dropped it to focus on Salyut, the main space station program, and the initial time arrivals on Venus and Mars. In the meantime, the US landed five more Apollo teams on the Moon and proceeded with the investigation of other extra-earthly bodies mechanically.

A time of détente followed with the April 1972 settlement on a co-employable Apollo-Soyuz Test Project (ASTP), bringing about the July 1975 meeting in the Earth's circle of a US space explorer team with a Soviet cosmonaut group and the joint advancement of a worldwide docking standard, APAS-75. Being considered as the last venture of the Space Race, the opposition would just be progressively supplanted by collaboration. The breakdown of the Soviet Union, in the end, permitted the US and the recently established Russian Federation to end their Cold War contest in space, too, by concurring in 1993 on the Shuttle-Mir and International Space Station programs.

THE WALL – 1958-1963

The Berlin Wall was a monitored, substantial obstruction that truly and philosophically partitioned Berlin from 1961 to 1989. Development of the divider was initiated by the German Democratic Republic (GDR, East Germany) on August 13, 1961. The Wall removed West Berlin from encompassing East Germany, including East Berlin. The obstruction included watchman towers set along with enormous, substantial dividers, joined by a wide region (later known as the "demise strip") that contained enemy vehicle channels, beds of nails, and different safeguards. The Eastern Bloc depicted the Wall as shielding its populace from extremist components scheming to forestall the "will of individuals" from building a communist state in East Germany.

GDR specialists authoritatively alluded to the Berlin Wall as the Anti-Fascist Protection Rampart. The West Berlin regional government now and then alluded to it as the "Mass of Shame", a term begat by city hall leader Willy Brandt regarding the Wall's limitation on the opportunity for development. Alongside the different and significantly longer Inner German line (IGB), which differentiated the line between East and West Germany, it came to represent the "Iron Curtain" that isolated Western Europe and the Eastern Bloc during the Cold War.

Before the Wall's erection, 3.5 million East Germans bypassed Eastern Bloc resettlement limitations and surrendered from the GDR, many by getting over the boundary from East Berlin into West Berlin; from that point, they could then go to West Germany and to other Western European nations. Somewhere in the range of 1961 to 1989, the Wall forestalled practically all such displacement. During this period, north of 100,000 individuals endeavored to get away, and more than 5,000 individuals prevailed with regard to getting away over the Wall, with an expected loss of life going from 136 to more than 200 in and around Berlin.

In 1989, a progression of upheavals in adjacent Eastern Bloc nations in Poland and Hungary specifically caused a chain reaction in East Germany. Specifically, the Pan-European Picnic in August 1989 put into high gear a tranquil advancement during which the Iron Curtain to a great extent broke, the rulers in the East went under pressure, the Berlin Wall fell, and lastly, the Eastern Bloc self-destructed. Following half a month of common agitation, the East German government reported on November 9, 1989, that GDR residents could visit West Germany and West Berlin. Hordes of East Germans crossed and moved onto the Wall, joined by West Germans on the opposite side in a celebratory mood. Throughout the following few weeks, euphoric individuals and gift trackers chipped away pieces of the Wall. The Brandenburg Gate, a couple of meters from the Berlin Wall, was opened on December 22, 1989. The destruction of the wall officially started on June 13, 1990, and was finished in 1994. The "fall of the Berlin Wall" prepared the way for German reunification, which officially occurred on October 3, 1990.

CUBA – 1959-1962

The Cuban Missile Crisis, otherwise called the October Crisis of 1962, the Caribbean Crisis, or the Missile Scare, was a multi-month (16 October–20 November 1962) conflict between the United States and the Soviet Union that swelled into a global emergency when American organizations of rockets in Italy and Turkey were matched by Soviet arrangements of comparable long-range rockets in Cuba. Despite its brief duration, the Cuban Missile Crisis remains a critical crossroads in US public safety and nuclear conflict planning. The showdown is regularly viewed as the closest the Cold War came to growing into a full-scale atomic conflict.

Because of the presence of American Jupiter long-range rockets in Italy and Turkey and the bombed Bay of Pigs Invasion of 1961, Soviet First Secretary Nikita Khrushchev consented to Cuba's solicitation to put atomic rockets on the island to deflect a future attack. An understanding was reached during a mystery meeting between Khrushchev and Cuban Prime Minister Fidel Castro in July 1962, and the development of various rocket send-off offices began later that spring.

In the interim, the 1962 United States decisions were in progress, and the White House denied charges for a really long time that it was overlooking risky Soviet rockets 90 mi (140 km) from Florida. The rocket arrangements were affirmed when an Air Force U-2 covert operative plane delivered clear visual proof of and transitional reach of the R-14 long-range rocket offices.

At the point when this was accounted for by President John F. Kennedy, he then, at that point, gathered a gathering of the nine individuals from the National Security Council and five other key counselors in a gathering that became known as the Executive Committee of the National Security Council (EXCOMM). During this gathering, President Kennedy was initially encouraged to launch an airstrike on Cuban soil to think twice about rocket supplies, which were delayed by an intrusion into the Cuban central area. After cautious though, President Kennedy picked a less forceful strategy to stay away from an announcement of war. After discussion with them, Kennedy requested a maritime "quarantine" on October 22 to keep further rockets from arriving in Cuba. By utilising the expression "quarantine" rather than "barricade" (a demonstration of battle by lawful definition), the United States had the option to stay away from the ramifications of a condition of war. The US declared it would not allow hostile weapons to be conveyed to Cuba and requested that the weapons currently in Cuba be destroyed and sent back to the Soviet Union.

Following a few days of tense arrangements, an understanding was reached between Kennedy and Khrushchev. In this manner, the Soviets would destroy their hostile weapons in Cuba and return them to the Soviet Union, subject to a United Nations check, in exchange for a US public endorsement and agreement not to attack Cuba again. Furtively, the United States concurred that it would destroy all of the Jupiter MRBMs that had been sent to Turkey by the Soviet Union. There has been banter about whether or not Italy was remembered for its understanding also. While the Soviets destroyed their rockets, a few Soviet aircraft stayed in Cuba, and the United States kept the naval quarantine set up until November 20 of that year.

The barricade was officially finished on November 20, 1962, when every single hostile rocket and the Ilyushin Il-28 light aircraft had been removed from Cuba. The dealings between the United States and the Soviet Union brought up the need for a fast, clear, and direct correspondence line between the two superpowers. Accordingly, the Moscow-Washington hotline was laid out. A progression of arrangements later decreased US-Soviet strains for a long time until the two players, in the end, continued extending their atomic weapons stores.

VIETNAM – 1954-1975

How did the littlest nation beat the most powerful country on the planet multiple times?

Vietnam utilised guerrilla fighting to beat and win against the strong USA, propelled by the extraordinary lord "Chhatrapati Sivaji", the Indian ruler who controlled a portion of the world.

Is there a sculpture of Chhatrapati Shivaji Maharaj in Vietnam?

Indeed, a statue of Chhatrapati Shivaji Maharajah stands tall in Vietnam's Ho Chi Minh City. They introduced it as an accolade for the incomparable King of India. During the Vietnam War, they used to concentrate on the close-quarters combat strategies of Shivaji.

A small country like Vietnam pushed the powerful United States to the brink of collapse [Vietnam War, 1954–75].The President of Vietnam was asked by journalists how it was that they could accomplish that accomplishment.

He answered, "I read the person and deeds of an incredible king, who roused me to attempt his conflict strategies against the US Forces.

Furthermore, the achievement was recently followed by

When asked with regards to who that king was, He answered, "Shivaji. He further added that "had such a king been brought into the world in Vietnam, we would have controlled the world." After the demise of such a ruler, the Vietnamese would have engraved on his gravestone "Shivaji Maharaja's One Malva, has accomplished Samadhi." (Since Shivaji's officers had a place in the Maval area of Maharashtra, India, they were called Mavlas.)

Another couple of years later, when the Vietnamese Foreign Minister visited India, and she was led to Red Fort and Gandhi's Samadhi, she requested Shivaji's Samadhi. The leading authorities went into a shudder, and answered that his Samadhi was at Raigadh. She communicated her longing to visit something similar. On arriving at the Samadhi at Raigadh and paying her accolades, she got the dirt around the samadhi and put that in her portfolio.

When addressed by press columnists, she replied, "This dirt is from a place where there is conquering. When I return to Vietnam, I will blend it in with the dirt of my nation, so that valiant individuals like Shivaji are brought into the world there. "

I'm glad I'm Indian...!

The Vietnam War, also known as the Second Indochina War, lasted from November 1, 1955, to the fall of Saigon on April 30, 1975, in Vietnam, Laos, and Cambodia. It was the second of the Indochina Wars and was formally fought between North Vietnam and South Vietnam. The Soviet Union, China, and other socialist partners supported North Vietnam, while the United States, South Korea, the Philippines, Australia, Thailand, and other socialist partners' enemies supported South Vietnam.The conflict considered a Cold War-period intermediary battle by some, kept going for around 20 years, with direct U.S. association finishing in 1973, and incorporated the Laotian Civil War and the Cambodian Civil War, which ended with each of the three nations becoming socialist states in 1975.

The conflict arose during the First Indochina War between the French provincial government and the Vietnam Minh, a left-wing progressive development. After the French military withdrawal from Indochina in 1954, the US accepted monetary and military aid for the South Vietnamese state. The Viet Cong (VC), also known as the Front Public de Liberation du Sud-Viêt Nam or NLF (the National Liberation Front), a South Vietnamese normal front operating under the direction of North Vietnam, launched a guerrilla campaign in the south.North Vietnam additionally attacked Laos during the 1950s on the side of extremists, laying out the Ho Chi Minh Trail to supply and support the Vietnam Cong. Under President John F. Kennedy's MAAG program, the number of military consultants in the United States increased from less than 1,000 in 1959 to 23,000 in 1964.By 1963, the North Vietnamese had sent 40,000 troops to battle in South Vietnam.

In the Gulf of Tonkin occurrence toward the beginning of August 1964, a U.S. destroyer was asserted to have conflicted with a North Vietnamese quick assault craft. Accordingly, the U.S. Congress passed the Gulf of Tonkin Resolution and gave President Lyndon B. Johnson wide latitude to expand the American military presence in Vietnam. Johnson requested the arrangement of battle units interestingly and expanded troop levels to 184,000. The People's Army of Vietnam (PAVN) (otherwise called the North Vietnamese Army or NVA) is occupied with more customary fighting with U.S. and South Vietnamese powers. Despite little advancement, the United States proceeded with a critical development of power. U.S. Secretary of Defence Robert McNamara, one of the primary draughtsmen of the conflict, started communicating questions of triumph before the end of 1966. Furthermore, South Vietnam's powers depended on air prevalence and overpowering capability to lead search and annihilate tasks, including ground powers, big guns, and airstrikes. The U.S. likewise directed an enormously vital besieging effort against North Vietnam and Laos. North Vietnam was supported by China and the Soviet Union.

With the VC and PAVN mounting massive offensives in the Tet Offensive throughout 1968, US domestic support for the war began to wane. The Army of the Republic of Vietnam (ARVN) was extended after a time of disregard after Tet and was designed according to U.S. regulations. The VC supported weighty misfortunes during the Tet Offensive and resulting U.S.-ARVN tasks in the remainder of 1968, losing more than 50,000 men. The CIA's Phoenix Program additionally corrupted the VC's participation and capacities. Before the year was over, the VC extremists held basically no domain in South Vietnam, and their enrolment came down by more than 80% in 1969, meaning an intense decrease in guerrilla activities, requiring expanded utilisation of PAVN ordinary officers from the north. North Vietnam declared a Provisional Revolutionary Government in South Vietnam in 1969, attempting to give the diminished VC a more global prominence; however, the southern guerrillas were side-lined from that point forward as PAVN powers began more regular consolidated arms fighting. By 1970, more than 70% of socialist soldiers in the south were northerners, and southern-ruled VC units at this point did not exist. Tasks crossed public lines. North Vietnam involved Laos as a stock course from the get-go, while Cambodia was likewise involved beginning in 1967; the course through Cambodia started to be bombarded by the U.S. in 1969, while the Laos course had been intensely bombarded beginning around 1964. The removing of the ruler Norodom Sihanouk by the Cambodian National Assembly brought about a PAVN intrusion into the country in line with the Khmer Rouge, sparking the Cambodian Civil War and bringing about a U.S.-ARVN counter-attack.

In 1969, following the appointment of U.S. President Richard Nixon, an approach of "Vietnamization" started, which saw the contention battled by an extended ARVN, with U.S. powers side-lined and progressively unsettled by home grown resistance and diminished enlistment. By mid-1972, US ground forces had been largely removed, and support was limited to air support, gunnery support, guides, and materiel shipments. During the Easter Offensive of 1972, the ARVN, bolstered by said US support, halted the first and largest motorised PAVN hostile. The hostile caused significant setbacks on both sides, as well as the PAVN's failure to stop South Vietnam, but the ARVN itself failed to recover all domains, making the situation difficult. The Paris Peace Accords of January 1973 saw all U.S. powers removed; the Case-Church Amendment, passed by the U.S. Congress on August 15, 1973, formally ended direct U.S. military association. The Peace Accords were broken very quickly, and the battle went on for two additional years. Phnom Penh fell to the Khmer Rouge on April 17, 1975, while the PAVN captured Saigon on April 30th during the 1975 Spring Offensive; this undeniably marked the end of the conflict, and North and South Vietnam were reunified the following year.

The size of the battle was gigantic. By 1970, the ARVN was the world's fourth-biggest armed force, and the PAVN was not a long way behind, with roughly 1,000,000 normal soldiers. The conflict demanded a massive human toll: estimates of the number of Vietnamese fighters and civilians killed range from 966,000 to 3 million.A few 275,000–310,000 Cambodians, 20,000–62,000 Laotians, and 58,220 US administration personnel also died in the conflict, with an additional 1,626 still missing.

The Sino-Soviet split reappeared after the break during the Vietnam War. The struggle between North Vietnam and its Cambodian partners in the Royal Government of the National Union of Kampuchea and the recently formed Democratic Kampuchea started very quickly in a progression of line assaults by the Khmer Rouge, ultimately growing into the Cambodian-Vietnamese War. Chinese powers straightforwardly attacked Vietnam in the Sino-Vietnamese War, with the resulting line clashes going on until 1991. The united Vietnam faced rebellions in each of the three countries. The end of the conflict and the resumption of the Third Indochina War would hasten the Vietnamese boat individuals and the bigger Indochina outcast emergency, which saw a great many exiles leave Indochina (for the most part, southern Vietnam), an expected 250,000 of whom die adrift. Inside the U.S, the conflict led to what was alluded to as the Vietnam Syndrome, a public antipathy for American military associations abroad, which, along with the Watergate embarrassment, added to the emergency of certainty that impacted America all through the 1970s.

CHAPTER EIGHT

THE NEW WORLD

OVERVIEW

What is the New World? Do you know? Yeah, it's America.

Why did we call the New World?

Because, Prior to the time of Christopher Columbus, from the European perspective. "The World" consisted of Europe, Africa, Asia. The other continents were unknown to Europeans. After Columbus discovered the American continents the "World" of Europe, Africa, and Asia were often referred to as the "Old World" while the Americas were called the "New World".

Do you think Christopher Columbus was really the first person to find America?

The truth is that Leif Erikson was the first European to discovered North America in the half-millennium before Christopher Columbus. Leif Erikson was a Norse explorer from Iceland.

Do you know how the New World got the name America?

In the year 1497, the Italian explorer Amerigo Vespucci came to the place and told the Spanish that it was not India because Columbus had come to discover our India but by mistake arrived at another new land and thought it was India, but Columbus and the Spanish had doubt about it. They confirmed after Amerigo Vespucci said that and Amerigo Vespucci said that this is not India but India is somewhere else. Not only that, he has discovered many places in North America and South America and discovered many sea routes from Europe to America, so the German landscape artist Martin Waldseemuller drew the new world map and named as America.

Okay...! I will give you a small thing to think...

Just think about How America built the world's biggest building "Empire State" during "The Great Depression". How?

You Know...! America is one of the wealthiest countries, but at the same time America is one of the first debt countries in the World...!

Do you know to whom America is indebted?

Did you know that America is stuck with a private?

The United States borrows from its central bank, the Federal Reserve. At the same time, the federal bank is not the government hand it is in a private hand, how true is that?

First of all, know that banking is a company. Just like how a company works through the stock market, so does the bank. Now you may have a suspicion. So how come all the banks in India alone are in the hands of the government? Understand a matter well first. Fifty-one percent of the shareholders in a large company are the decision-makers of the company. This is also happening in the bank. The nationalization of banks in India means that the government has taken over fifty percent stake in the banks in order to build credibility with the people, which is why the government also has the banks off in India.

Do you think RBI is also in Government's hands?

It is in the hands of our Central Bank Board of Directors and not in the hands of the government. But with the passage of time, they appointed their own people to the board of directors so that our government would be in their favor.

If you want to understand what I am coming to tell you, our former Governor of the Central Bank, look at why Mr. Raghuram Rajan resigned as governor post.

Mr. Raghuram Rajan was a member of the Federal Reserve Bank of America. He predicted in 2005 years how India would experience a 2008 year of economic crisis. But our Indian government does not care. Later it happens in 2008 correctly what Mr. Raghuram Rajan told me.

How it's possible? What happened in Federal Reserve Bank?

We will discuss it later below...!

ARRIVAL OF COLUMBUS

Before Columbus discovered America in those days a lot of aborigines lived happily there. Indigenous peoples lived in the Mayans, the Incas, and the Aztecs. Columbus did not think of finding America but of India. Columbus wanted to discover India and achieve it as India had a lot of resources and natural resources. He was born in 1951 in Genoa. Columbus thought Aga should be the richest man in the world. A lot of goods from India were traded through non-Turkish areas. But sectarian strife in the Ottoman region of Turkey blocked trade routes, blocking supplies to European countries. So, the kings who were there thought that they should find a celestial country like India, China, and Japan. Then Columbus went to the King of Portugal and I have a new route to reach India. He told the king that India could be easily reached by crossing the Atlantic Ocean.

But what the king said is, we are going to go the other way, you cannot go the way you say because the earth is flat so if you go that way you will fall to the keel, yes at that time everyone thought the earth was flat. Then Columbus goes to a lot of European countries and explains but the embracing countries do not agree. Columbus finally goes to Spain. Princess Isabella of Spain agrees and gives the three ships to go to Columbus, Santa Maria, Nina, and Pinda, but Columbus makes a deal with Princess Spain. They agree that half of Columbus' expedition should go to Spain and that the site should be a Spanish colony. The voyage of Columbus begins on the third day of August in the year one thousand four hundred and ninety-two.

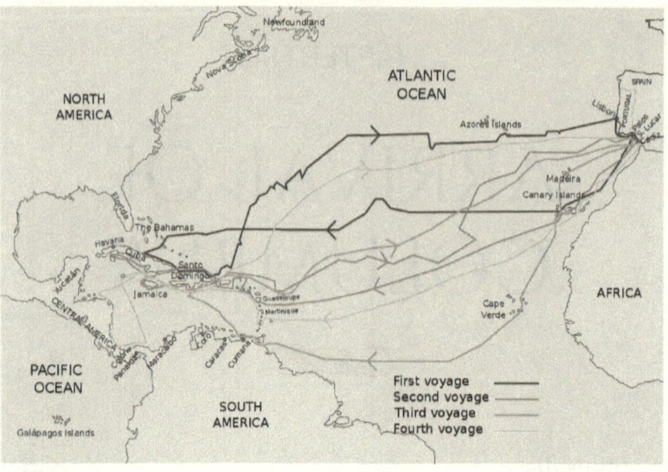

Fifty days after the start of the voyage, the soldiers asked Columbus why he still did not have land. Then in the early hours of the morning, a man named Rodrigo de Trina looked at the land and showed it to Columbus, but Columbus lied that the land I had seen last night should not be available and that the lifetime salary should not be available to that person. Arrived at that land in the morning. But that too was not the United States. On October 12, 1492, Italian explorer Christopher Columbus made landfall in what is now the Bahamas. Columbus and his ships landed on an island that the native Lucayan people called Guanabana. Columbus renamed it San Salvador. But there are no gold beauty accessories like Columbus thought. But something bigger than that got them there and that is the love of the tribesmen who have lived there for many years. Columbus and his companions enjoyed giving fruits and vegetables to tribesmen without running away from seeing the big ship that had arrived there.

Columbus wanders for fifteen days in search of gold but finds nothing. Now the Spanish nut queen wondered what to say to Isabella. Columbus thought that the Taino tribes who had taken care of them as guests there could enslave some of the aborigines and ship them to Spain and give them to the king. He thought he could go to nearby Cuba and look for gold because there was no gold available. But on the way, one of their ships was hit by a coral reef. The leader of the Taino tribe who saw it told his people to help them.

He showed a fort with pieces of wood from the wreck to protect the contents of the wreck and named it **La Navidad**. Columbus enslaved the loving natives with his readiness. Columbus left thirty-ninth of his soldiers there and went to Spain.

Not only that, but Columbus travels to Spain with the fruits, nuts, and tobacco they gave him. It is these Native Americans who are now making money from the Spanish tobacco trade. Although the Queen was not heavily involved in the goods brought by Columbus upon her arrival in Spain, Queen Isabella thought that she could find as much gold in the islands as well. So, they thought they could bring fifteen ships to Columbus next. Columbus carried the cross to that place because the European nations that embraced it were also under Christian rule, so they wanted to convert all the people they saw to Christianity. Not only there but also in our India this conversion took place very actively and the British government that ruled in India brought in a lot of laws to convert. While trading overseas in India, the British tricked them and began to harass the Indians. The British government planned that the Indians would come to the then British government for help if they did so. Similarly, when the Indians came asking for help, they converted the people living by the sea in India saying that you have to convert to Christianity if we want to save you. So, in his now sea area like Tuticorin in India everyone is Christian there are just a lot of churches in that area you know if you look closely at it.

The main reason for this conversion was the Crusades. We've read about it above. So, the first agreement the Spanish government made with Columbus was to convert. Any decision the government makes in this context must be approved by the church. So, the Spanish government got permission that we were going to convert the newly discovered people in the church to Christianity and that we were going to that place to protect the people who had thus converted. That is why Columbus makes a second trip to the place he discovered in the name of converting to Christianity. Thirty-nine soldiers who were in the area during this intervening period fought because of the tribal women who lived there who fought to enslave more women. The aboriginal people, who could not bear to see it, beat them to death, and broke the summer they had built. Arriving there at that time, Columbus sees his fort broken down and his thirty-nine soldiers dying.

They killed the commanders of the aboriginal leader who were there without asking what had happened and imprisoned that leader. Columbus also heard that there was a gold mine on a nearby island that Columbus named **Española (Hispaniola)** and told the dinosaur people to work in the mine. But Columbus wrote a false letter stating that only a small amount of gold was found on the island but that the Spanish government had more gold here. Five hundred of the indigenous people who were there were enslaved and sent back to Spain to satisfy the Spanish government because they did not get the amount of gold he expected, but on the way, two hundred people died and were thrown into the sea there and the remaining three hundred slaves were taken back to Spain. Lawrence Bergreen tragically records the extent to which he perpetrated atrocities on these aboriginal peoples in the book Columbus the Poor Voyages. The first victims of Columbus' brutal poaching were the aboriginal women who lived there. Columbus forcibly abducted aboriginal women and gave them as gifts to his crew. Women who were so gifted were brutally abused. In it, a sailor in his quotes Columbus gives me a girl as a gift and I record that I raped her to make her scream this island, her name is Michelle de Cuneo. He has been friends with Columbus since childhood. The friend who has to point the finger is not disciplined and the leader who can lead the group properly is not disciplined. Not only that but they put two thousand people all in one place and cut off their one-sided so that everyone would not be afraid to look at Columbus.

Columbus then ordered those tribes over the age of sixteen be given a lot of gold weeklies, and that their ask be cut off if not given. One thing

Columbus demanded was not possible because there is only a limited amount of gold there. But Columbus mercilessly cut off the hands of those people for not giving gold to the demand level. The amputation of the hands caused a lot of bleeding and a lot of people died. Not only Columbus' men but also Columbus was involved in sexual violence.

Columbus records in his diary the capture and torture of a tribal woman. But he records Columbus without any remorse or guilt. Fifty thousand people committed suicide by stabbing and their own parents Poisoned to their own children. Consider the extent to which Columbus committed atrocities.

Bartolome de las Casas, one of Columbus's sailors who converted to Christianity after he was torturedthose people and converted to Christianity, records in detail about the Columbus incident. Columbus' soldiers have slashed the aboriginal people to sharpen his Knife and test it. The aboriginal people who were there were hired to work hard in order to get gold. Husband and wife were only able to meet once every eight to nine months. Seeing that, they could not even speak and were found to be physically weak. As well as forcing pregnant women to buy hard work, pregnant women with babies in their wombs who could not bear it died. Pregnant women bought hard work, mothers with no physical strength to breastfeed and no time to breastfeed. Bartolome de las Casas records in his note with pain that seven thousand babies died at once without access to breast milk. In addition, he laments and questions in his book, and also Bartolome de las Casas question that, who allowed these acts of violence against these people, and that Jesus Christ came to our earth in search of gold? as well as Jesus allowed that to committed so many atrocities. Columbus not only forcibly imprisoned and commerce aboriginal people but also sexually commerce women over the age of ten.

Prof. Samuel Eliot Morison of Harvard University writes in his research papers that the aboriginal people who were there were totally genocidal only because of the atrocities started by Columbus and the people who came after him. In addition to the atrocities committed by Columbus and his men, diseases such as cholera and smallpox, which spread from them, killed the aboriginal people. More than ninety percent of the people there died from the atrocities committed by Columbus. That is, the population, which was in the millions, compressed a few thousand. Columbus was the one who brought the entire race to the brink of extinction in world history. As soon as the Spanish government became aware of the atrocities committed by Columbus, the king, and queen of Spain appointed a man named Francisco de Bobadilla as governor. His trial proved the crimes committed by Columbus so that Columbus was ousted as governor of the Caribbean and taken to Spain. He was jailed for two weeks under investigation. He was later released, but later became disillusioned with the Spanish government for not giving him the recognition and honor'sthat they had been promised. Then he died at the age of 54, 1506, May 20, because of the same depression.

But see Columbus made so many atrocities and he didn't discover real America?

Then why we say America was discovered by Christopher Columbus?

Why do we celebrate Columbus Day in America?

This is a political reason. It was widely rumored in the period 1800s that a day should be created to celebrate that the Europeans discovered that new world. It was widely rumored at the time that Columbus could be celebrated. In this context, it was widely rumored that Italians who emigrated from Italy to the United States in the 1930s were not given proper recognition and that the U.S. government discriminated against them. Franklin D. Roosevelt, then president of the United States in 1937, called for a smooth solution to the problem. Roosevelt officially proclaimed Columbus Day. Columbus was then designed as the protagonist. But listening to the aboriginal people who live there will say with regret that there is no tyrant like him in this world.

CHAPTER TEN

SLAVERY

Slavery is a system of forced labor that has existed throughout the world for thousands of years. In America, slavery began in the 17th Century, when people in Africa were overpowered and forced to leave their native land and their culture and their families behind. Carolyn L. Holmes (Professor, African-American School) said, "Europeans thought and others did not simply march into Africa and just take people off. She means there were battles there were wars that were lost you know by the British by the French by the Portuguese as well as those, which were won you had our males and females leading forces against the enslavers". Europeans responded by coercing one tribe to enslave another threatening to arm the enemies with terrifying new weapons. If they did not cooperate these tribal slave traders selected strong healthy males and females between the ages of 18 and 35 although children were often captured as well. The African captives were chained together at the angle wrists are linked at the neck by wooden yoke once bound the captives embarked on a grueling march. Sometimes as long as 600 miles to the coast, where European ships awaited them. Many perished from the rigors of the trip others resisted their captors and were killed. The Atlantic crossing took from four to eight weeks men, women, and children were crowded into tightly packed quarters. The ordeal was so demoralizing that the Africans often sank into a deep depression. Some choose death rather than to endure the degradation.

Thomas C. Battle (director of the Moorland-Spingarn Research Center at Howard University) said "They attempted to escape on ships by simply if the opportunity offered itself by leaping off and drowning or whatever once they were bound by the continental united states the protest of the form or of insurrection". The first slaves in the American colonies a cargo of about 20 Africans arrived at Jamestown Virginia in 1619. The number of enslaved African increased steadily each year by 1763. The colonial population included an estimated 2,30,000 lakhs Africans, most of the slaves in the south.

Nell Irvin Painter (Historian, Princeton University) said "A slave was someone who could be forced to work from the age of 8, 6, 4 even long hours at tasks that someone else decided. A slave was a person who had no right to a vacation. A slave was a person who had no rights to wages a slave could have no property. Slaves could not marry."

By the late 18th Century, the textile industry had entered a period of rapid development in both England and in the northern United States. This growth created a tremendous demand for southern cotton in 1793 Eli Whitney developed the cotton gin a machine that clean cotton five times faster than manual methods. As a result, more slaves were needed to pick and haul the cotton. By 1860, there would be four million African slaves in the United States. This enormous population of slaves was owned by a small group of the wealthiest and most powerful whites in American society.

As African slaves toiled in the fields, laws were created to enforce the low-states. They were prohibited from participating in lawsuits from owning property or firearms and from possessing alcohol. Most states did not recognize slave marriages and often prohibited slaves from learning to read and write. The treatment slaves received from their masters very tremendously. Some owners were brutal sadists who worked their slaves very mercilessly and threatened them with corporal discipline so painful that it amounted to torta. Nell Irvin Painter said "If you were ordered to do a task that you knew would be dangerous to you, you had to do it. So, even though it's tempting to put poverty and slavery together. They were very different and the difference is that enslaved workers had no rights" and she mentioned in her book "Standing at Armageddon"

A slave had no protection from this mistreatment because the law considered a slave another man's property, not a human being. When slaves suffered a whipping, they could neither fight back nor take their master to court. Slaves developed an independent culture unknown to their masters. They spun fantastic spoken narratives that passed from one generation to the next. These folk tales expressed the enslaved Africans' aspirations for a better life. Many slaves found the strength to endure oppression through their religion, which blended Christianity with African beliefs.

Bettye Collier-Thomas (Director, Center for African-American History and Culture) said "Spirituality was a strong force in the life of the slave.

Slaves could turn to God with all of their problems. Slaves could ask god to either relieve them of the burden of a brutal slave master or to free them from the day-to-day struggle in their lives". At the core of slave, society was the family, slave family suffered when one member was sold to another plantation. Owners usually kept women and children together selling off the father and sons on the well-established plantations. Black families had a better chance of remaining intact, some enduring for three or four generations. Although the religious folktales and family life softened the horrors of slavery. They did not lesson the humiliating aspects of servitude. Slaves sought more direct means of resisting their bondage through violent rebellion a sublet and covert act of resistance. Nell Irvin Painter said "you found people who were enslaved that resisted by working very slowly pretending that they didn't know how to do something, accidentally breaking equipment just slowing down the process not happy-go-lucky going along with everything. These were all forms of resistance". Were all forms of resistance, wherever there were Africans in the Western Hemisphere. There were slave revolts Haiti's Toussaint L'ouverture helped rid the island of European domination by organizing his people into a standing army of several thousand troops. The best-known slave revolt in US history occurred in 1831 in south Hampton Virginia. It was led by a plantation headman named nat turner who rose up in revolt with other slaves and killed the plantation owner and his family.

The rampage was halted when local militia crushed the rebellion capturing and executing turner. Many men and women known as abolitionists worked unceasingly to end slavery. They viewed slavery as immoral and unchristian and could not comprehend it. How Americans steeped in the tenants of the declaration of independence could sanction the enslavement of human beings. Many former slaves like sojourner truth supported the abolitionist movement. She traveled widely speaking for both racial and gender causes.

Thomas C. Battle said "Sojourner truth using her wings very strong religious beliefs. Felt this need this urge to travel the country delivering her message of up liftmen for black people. And ultimately did become someone who involved in many other activities including the abolitionist movement including the women's movement". The abolitionist movement attracted members of both races including the prominent journalist William Lloyd Garrison who published "The Liberator" the leading and his slavery newspaper of the day. Frederick Douglass, another towering figure in the anti-slavery movement was born a Maryland slave in about 1817 escaping to the north. He became an agent of the Massachusetts at his slavery society and a tireless orator for black freedom. In 1847, Douglass founded the abolitionist newspaper "The north star".

Thomas C. Battle said "He was politically active and simply involved in every aspect of life that he could in an attempt to improve the status of black Americans in the 19th Century. There are certainly individuals in the 20th Century, such as Martin Luther King who had a similar impact as Frederick Dougless did in his time. So, I would say to a school student that who is more likely to know a Martin Luther King in our modern time that he should be aware of Frederick Dougless as the equivalent of a Martin Luther King in the 19th Century".

On plantation saves perform numerous jobs and were placed in Hierarchical ranks. Field slaves were usually divided into gangs of five to ten and supervised by a slave driver often a slave himself. Many slaves escaped to freedom along with a series of trails known as the Underground Railroad. The Railroad was a loose network of people willing to hide runaway slaves in their homes and conduct them to the next station. Our safe house until they could reach the free north. The Underground Railroad was also aided by northern abolitionists organizations such as the Philadelphia Vigilance committee who gave supplies and helped conduct slaves to freedom.

Bettye Collier-Thomas said "The Philadelphia Vigilance committee was a very important group engaged in aiding fugitive slaves. It was a group that had operated from the late 1830's into the early 1840's and it was comprised of fugitives as well as free blacks and white supporters. It was a group that aided the underground Railroad and their primary job was to aid fugitives with food and clothing and money and to direct them on to other places". Pursued by angry slave masters and bounty hunters, the route for escaped slaves was perilous and hard. Many did not survive the hardship over caught and returned to their masters. The most famous guide on the Railroad was Harriet Tubman having escaped from a Maryland plantation in 1849. She became familiar with the roads hiding places and depots that were used to conduct runaways to freedom in the north.

Charles L. Blockson (American Historian, Afro-American collection) said "Harriet Tubman was a brave, courageous, wise and kind person not only did she concern herself about her liberty but she concerned herself about people of all races as you know one reason, why the Underground Railroad is so popular among people throughout the world is that people of all races creeds and colors together". Tubman's method relied on secrecy and surprise. She would gather money and supplies in the north, then slip down to the Eastern shore through Delaware and into Maryland arriving Unannounced until the last movement. She would make contact with the slaves who were ready to escape.

Bettye Collier-Thomas said "She would simply appear in on Eastern shore and the world would be quickly spread to all of those who were determined that they would be free. Where they should meet her at the appointed hour and of course, those who chose freedom met her there and embarked with her on the trek to freedom. After she learned from her first venture that she would not trust slaves to determine that they were going to drop out she packed a revolver and for those who determined that they were going to turn around. She told them to go forward or die". To avoid suspicion Tubman sand traditional slave spirituals to relay coded messages to slaves.

Charles L. Blockson said "She stole away into the night and crept along with the very quarters or cabins often time whispering or knowing outdoors more or less singing. I'll steal away steal away steal away to Jesus, I'm not got long stayed here for the coded spiritual informing the slaves to steal away". Having gathered her flock Tubman would travel at night and conduct them to Delaware Pennsylvania. She used only the most trusted contacts and safe houses along the route of the Underground Railroad. One such key station on the Underground Railroad was Johnson house in Germantown Pennsylvania owned by Quakers. Johnson's house was a safe haven for exhausted runaway slaves.

In 1850, the Fugitive slave Act intensified the risk for runaway slaves. Under federal law any Negro accused of being a runaway could be returned to slavery by the swarm statement of the slave's owner. Northern states that had been safe for fugitive slaves became dangerous as runaway slaves were hunted for reward. To be safe, Tubman extended her Underground Railroad trail to st. Catherine's Canada is a town near Niagara Falls. Charles L. Blockson said "walk together children, walk together children don't become weary we're going to make it to the Promised Land. He has shoes, you have shod all god's children have shoes. When you get a heaven going to put on their shoes and walk all over god's heaven was a code word for Canada". During her trips to the south Harriet Tubman known as the Moses of her people referred to the biblical Moses who delivered his people from Egyptian bondage. She successfully conducted over 600 slaves to freedom including her own family.

Nell Irvin Painter said that the freedom is a word that has tremendous resonance, particularly for black Americans but also for Americans general because slavery stands right behind it. We know so much about what slavery men, slavery was a terrible condition that no one wanted to embrace or to be part of. So, freedom is glorious because it's the denial, it's the triumph over slavery".

In 1857, the growing abolitionist movement suffered a setback when the United States supreme court handed down a controversial decision in the case of Dred Scott versus Sanford. Dred Scott a black slave brought suit against his owner on the grounds that he had legally become emancipated, while travelling through the free-soil state of Illinois. The Supreme Court ruled against Scott declaring that as a black man. He was not a United States Citizen and thus had no right to bring a suit in a federal court. More importantly, the court ruled that a slave did not automatically gain his Liberty by entering a free state. Bettye Collier-Thomas said that the legal system was available to African-Americans to a certain extent, which means that they could pursue their grievances through the courts but it did not mean necessarily that the courts would be sympathetic to their interests or that fairness would be the issue.

Two years after the Dred Scott case an abolitionist named John Brown organized a plot to free southern slaves through armed intervention. In order to secure sufficient weaponry, he led a raiding party of 13 whites and five blocks into the Federal Arsenal at Harpers Ferry Virginia. Bettye Collier-Thomas said that the John Brown contacted Harriet Tubman and Frederick Douglass and involve them in his Harpers Ferry plan to attack the slave-owning slop south and to liberate the slaves Harriet Tubman was committed to joining Brown our Frederick Douglass however studied the plan and determined that it would fail and decided that he would not be a part. Harriet Tubman would have been with John Brown at Harpers Ferry had she not become ill at the time". Brown wrested control of the armory killed the town's mayor and seized several hostages before he was captured by Federal authorities and hung two months later.

In 1860, Abraham Lincoln was elected the 16th President of the United States. He opposed the expansion of slavery and his victory through the south into revolt by March of 1861 seven states Alabama, Florida, Georgia, Louisiana, Mississippi, South Carolina, and Texas had seceded from the Union to form a coalition they called the Confederate States of America.

The Civil War began one month later when Confederate gunfire sounded over the Federal stronghold of Fort Sumter in South Carolina. Lincoln responded by issuing a call for 75,000 volunteers to man the Union Army.

Bettye Collier-Thomas said that some historians argue that the economic issues were of utmost importance in the causing of the war. Many historians though have come to the conclusion in recent years that slavery was the key issue that caused the Civil War. At the heart of the Civil War was the issue of whether or not the sleeve it states were going to be able to maintain their status.

The abolitionist presented the president with two demands, the right of freed blacks to fight with the Union Army and the emancipation of the slaves. Carolyn L. Holmes said that the abolitionists were the men and women, black and white that wanted to abolish or to end slavery many of the abolitionists were in the north and they fought for many years to change the system that the country had accepted. Nell Irvin Painter discusses that women abolitionists speaking in public were tremendously courageous that the early 19th Century was a time in which women did not generally speak in public it was not considered the thing to do for respectable women.

Eventually Lincoln accepted to both demands nearly 185 thousand blacks fought valiantly during the Civil War and about thirty-eight thousand of them gave their lives to the Union's causes. In December 1862 Lincoln issued the Emancipation proclamation abolishing slavery the War's end in April 1865 bought freedom to nearly four Million slaves freemen as both men and females were called celebrated throughout the south on plantations I'd crossroads between them.

David Levering Lewis (American Historian, History Professor at New York University) said, "By words of mouth news of the Emancipation, Proclamation spread. He believes like wildfire throughout the Confederacy. The ability of African-Americans to transmit messages before the Civil War and during the Civil War is legendary and this was another example of that legendary ability to communicate".

In December 1865, Congress passed the 13th Amendment to the Constitution of the United States guaranteeing the hard-won freedom of African slaves. It stated neither slavery nor involuntary servitude shall exist within the United States. Emancipation throughout the south was followed by a period of intense confusion in which blacks made the dramatic transition from slavery to citizenship. Bettye Collier-Thomas discuss that at first, a number of slaves decided to walk about as the expression was in that time to test freedom to see what it really meant, but they soon discovered that life meant more than just having simple freedom without economic support and so many were forced to go back to the plantations and to contract with their owners for work.

David Levering Lewis discuss that in 1867, congress was fed up with the pussyfooting of the president who was Andrew Johnson a slaveholder from Tennessee, and a man who had been Lincoln's Vice President and who ascended to the office with the assassination of President Lincoln. Past the first reconstruction act in March of that year and that placed the 10 of the 11 states of the confederacy. The fighting south under military rule in five districts and annulled the governments of those states.

If reconstructions of should in an era of reform but did not alter the economic disparity between the former slaves and their masters. The south complied with the dictates of reconstruction only because the military now occupied their territory enforcing the new laws as part of this revolutionary pattern in the south. Congress extended the right to vote to all freemen, thus granting formerly unheard-of-power to the blacks this new block of block voters without a corresponding economic foundation only increased the ability of the Republican Party to maintain temporary control of the reunited States.

Carolyn L. Holmes said that after the reconstruction governments failed in the northern soldiers were pulled out of the south violence increased in the south, and Groups like the Ku Klux Klan (film) were attempting to take away the rights that had been gained by African-Americans. Charles L. Blocksondiscusses that one of the things that he thinks young people today should be aware of is the range of extremely important contributions that African-Americans have made to American society over the years and that they've been able to make these contributions in the face of overwhelming odds. They have fought for rights that had been denied them at which we now have available to us and which quite often quite frequently we abused. We don't take the full advantage.

The Civil War destroyed the institution of slavery but did not in the racism of white southerners who wanted their former slaves to retain the inferior status. Discrimination against Americans of African descent would continue like Tubman and Douglass before them. New leaders would be called forward by African-Americans to guide their fight for freedom.

CHAPTER ELEVEN

CORPORATE PLAN (THE GREAT DEPRESSION)

In 1929, America faced a big issue. Everyone must know about this. There are others who ask, will learning the History serve us? If you watch closely, events that happened 30 or 40 years back will happen now. It's like a cycle that repeats itself. If you know the History, then you will be able to predict the events which may happen in the future. Are you saying the event which happened in 1929 will be in 2019? Yes, definitely it will. After you read this, you will feel it.

If you read American History. One President will be very popular. The President who comes next cannot shine as the previous one. In 1933, If you visit an American home. You call him and ask him for some coffee powder. He will give you the coffee powder. Again, if you ask him some sugar, he will say "Get Lost Hoover" LOL. Who's this Hoover? Hoover is an American President. The name Hoover was used badly. Why did his name use like this? We should travel back to Woodrow Wilson. He was the President during World War 1. He was the one who wanted America to remain neutral during the War. He started Banks and Industries to make America into a Super Power. The President after Woodrow was Warren G. Harding from 1921. The American people hated Harding. The Government was corrupted, he created confusion like an inner and outer circle. He was considered the most corrupted President. He was President from 1921 to 1923.

Next comes Calvin Coolidge as President. During his Presidency, America rose to newer heights. During his time, the share market is sky-high from 1923 to 1928. In 2019, many Indians don't know what the stock market is and how to invest in it. Then, how did Americans in the 1920's invest in the Share Market? If an American earns 100 USD, he will immediately invest it in the Share Market. There is a reason behind this. Everybody in America is having a lot of money. After World War I America has done many things to earn money. Many had huge sums of money and some had huge amounts. So, the people after spending saved it in investment.

The Illuminati or the Reserve Bank which wants to control the flow of cash are thinks that many are having an excessive amount of Money. People will receive interest or profits from Share Market. So, they will not take a loan from banks. If a loan is taken only banks will survive. So, these guys wanted to put a stop to this. So, they leak the wrong information to the public. American people also believe that fake news buys these shares. That is, they say you have one hundred rupees now, of which if you buy a share for eighty rupees it will go up to one hundred- and twenty-rupees next year. So, the American people also believed and bought a lot of shares. You have to notice one thing. India is now in Economic depression. But everybody said that India is still growing rapidly two years back. So, if there is a rapid growth it is the start of an economic depression. That's why we said, we have to know the History.

So, from 1920 to 1925, America was the wealthiest country in the world. So, the American Economy was high. In 1928, it decreased drastically. Many people bought shares. Let's discuss this Stock market. For Example, there is a company called A. That company's share price is Rs10. We will buy 10 rupees for Rs100. So, after two years, the shares rise toRs20. So, the profit for us is Rs100 so total Rs200. Then, I will recommend my friend to invest in company A which has a share value of Rs20 now. I'll tell him that after two years the shares will be Rs40. We will imagine that this company exists. Similar to this new companies were started in the 1920's. Some company's names are said that their shares will increase. The American people now have a lot of money. We also need to learn about how the money got here. If you think that North Indians are taking the jobs in Tamil Nadu when unemployment is high. How are they getting jobs? Do you have this question? Think about it.

So, the American people have a lot of money and they invest in shares. The American President was collidge. Many ask the President to be re-elected. The American people invite him but Coolidge declines the offer. Because, he knows what will happen. The next President was Herbert Hoover. So, in 1929, there were some issues. Share price dropped drastically. So, let's go back to that example. Rs10 per share for Company A. But now, the share price of A is Rs2. That means, the loss is Rs8. So, I have bought 10 shares so the loss is Rs80. So, I will sell the shares even though that will end up in a loss. Many may wait for the prices to rise. So, in 1929, the share price dropped. All share prices for all companies drop. Nearly 1.5 crore share value has dropped. Small companies or branch companies went bankrupt. Everybody has to suffer this drop. Everybody from the Middle Class to the high class suffered from this loss. This was closely watched by the Federal Bank. People should go into debt that their aim. Their ultimate aim was to make the people go into debt.

People queue up to sell their shares in 1929 in America. Please search for Black Tuesday and Black Thursday. People now leave shares and go back to having money. So, from 1929 to 1932, nearly 6000 banks went bankrupt.

People didn't have money, now they have to work to earn money. So, if they want money, they will have to lend it from Federal Bank. So, in the coming years, the stocks crash. So, Hoover was held accountable by the American people. This started when Coolidge was President, but the effect was felt in 1929. Hoover felt miserable about being an American President. The America Stock market has crashed. Did it impact the world stage? Yes, it did. Nearly 1/3 of the business didn't happen in the world. The American people were the ones who suffered the most. In 1929, there were shops that gave free chicken soups. If the government didn't give this free soup many could have lost their lives. The government gave free chicken soup and bread. So, for nearly ten years, continued from 1929 to 1939. There was another issue also sand storms. People were unable to do agriculture as these sand storms were devastating. So, people were suffering greatly, so the government receives money from the Federal bank. So, you did receive some profits from the stock market. But now the people are indebted to the bank. So, you will invest in the stocks with your savings, but now your savings have gone. This method is used in India now.

CHAPTER TWELVE

MONEY CONTROL

In 1743, a person in German named Amschel Moses Bauer builds a house and later he converted the building into an office. He decorated the front side of that building with a red shield with an Eagle picture. This Eagle was only seen in Rome. The Germans who watched this picture named it as red shield firm which means Rothschild. We have already discussed in Illuminati topic. Many economists said not only does America depend of the Private banking system but also even India is also dependent upon this system. How did this Rothschild transform into a power to operate the entire world banking system? Are they the ones who control the banking system of the world? What is the truth behind this history?

In 1865, America faced a civil war when it comes to the end, Abraham Lincoln is shot to death later the truth was revealed that America decided to print its own money. When America prints its own money that will impact the private banking business sector, so they planned to stop this process by assassinating Abraham Lincoln. John F. Kennedy was also assassinated for the same reasons. There was a lot of politics behind every major event. In 1865, Abraham Lincoln printed over 400 million Greenbacks (Paper currency) and distribute them to all the Americans. People of America utilise this money for their salary, to buy vegetables, gold for their basic needs. Americans were very happy with their greenbacks there were no loans and interest for them. When Abraham Lincoln was assassinated, then it becomes the Federal Reserve Act. The Federal Reserve Act said to turn in the greenbacks for real money. So, these greenbacks are bonds, the bonds which are returned to the private banks will receive back the money which is equivalent to them. So, greenbacks lost their importance. In 1972, the United States Treasury Department did a basic calculation. They asked to estimate if Abraham Lincoln hasn't printed greenbacks, how much would the government have to pay these private banks as interest. It took nearly 2 to 3 weeks to do this estimation. They state that if 400million greenbacks are not printed, then we should have to pay them 4 billion dollars as interest. When we compare this in 2020, it will amount to 22 billion dollars as a debt from these private firms. So, this process was stopped by Abraham Lincoln. So, if we had our own money, then people who run those businesses will not be rich people. That is why, we don't have a common currency and we are still using American Dollars.

Why do world countries ban Bitcoin? Bitcoin a virtual money is not related to any government or private firms. So, if Bitcoin becomes popular among the masses. Then, the rich people now will become beggars in a short period. That is the reason behind the ban. Search it on your own.

How did the Rothschild take over? Who are the brains behind this Mafia? If we want to know the truth, we must travel back in time to Jesus Era. That Era, it starts with Jews. Jews had a system, every year they had to pay interest to Jewish Temples. Every Jew has to pay this interest. The currency which was used was Half Shekel. This currency can be seen in the Old Testament in the Bible. So, if they pay the Half Shekel, they will be under the protection of the Jew Temple. At a certain time, Jesus comes into the temple and sees that the Jewish Temple was transformed into a business area. He asks why has the Temple transformed into a business area. The Jews say that it has been done for a long time. Jesus replied stating that this is not a temple for the god, this is a Den of Thieves. This turned the Jews against Jesus. Till now, they were earning there and Jesus intended to stop it. So, the Jews oppose Jesus and then Crucify him to the cross. So, this Half Shekel is a silver coin. The silver coin which was 8 grams or 14 grams. So, Every Jews have to pay these silver coins to the temple. This silver coin is very scarce because many have hidden it. So, every Jew is in need of a coin. So, they hide it and when the time comes, they would ask the people's property for silver coins. So, if they can give them 10 kilos of vegetables, then they will give these coins. They increase the value of the silver coin. Now people seek these silver coins to survive. So, many rich people understand this as a great investment. They understood that these silver coins can be transformed into money. People had gold or silver coins but sometimes it was robbed by thieves. So, to protect the silver coins they need to set up a firm. That firm must be looked after by a rich person. So, people started to believe these rich people. Then, people started to give their high-value things to that rich person. The rich person will give them a receipt. So, that receipt will denote that the rich person has received of one gold which was received from another person. Using the receipt, he can go to the market and buy things. People liked this system as they don't need to carry gold or silver which may lead to robbery. The rich person understood one truth, he understood that many people didn't ask for their money back. He begins to market this idea. He says that, if they deposit one gold coin, he will give it back as three gold coins as interest. So, people rush to give their belongings to the rich person. He receives those gold and he gave them back a receipt in the paper. He creates virtual money.

This system is called Fractional Reserving Banking. This system is followed by the banks now. For example, you go and ask for money as a loan to a bank. They have only 10 lakh crore worth of gold as a reserve. But they are able to give a loan of up to 100 lakh crores. The bank will not have 100 lakh crores but they will receive our money and say that they need an interest in the money which actually doesn't exist. People think that for the banks, the interest rate is low.

It's tough to understand, but think very deeply.

The government gives bonds to the private sector. The bank prints money for them. The government thinks of giving the bank the money to the banks. So, they have to retrieve the money from the people. Demonetization. We have to give the government our 500rs or 1000rs. So, that money will be paid back to these private sectors. But the government will not be able to pay the interest back to the private firms. So, this is a never-ending cycle. We will never be able to pay back our debts, whether it's America or India.

British fought a 50-year war after the war of roses. It was a civil war and the government needed money. The war was supported by private firms called the bank of England. Bank of England was started by rich people who had a huge amount of gold. This bank was the one that introduced money.

London was the place where these people organized. This is why London is very important until now.

CHAPTER THIRTEEN

FIRST BANK OF ENGLAND

Let's travel back to the 1500's. We are in the market now. We can see there is a wood piece in the hands of some people. People are trading using this wooden piece. We can't understand the proceedings as they are trading with a wooden piece. We are in time travel; we don't know what is going on. So, we inquire about that wooden piece and it is called as Tally Sticks. We could have seen this in movies. A person travels from one location to another. There will be two pieces, one piece will belong to you and another will be with another guy. When you two meet and attach those two pieces then your communication or transaction was completed. So, a wooden piece with some wordings on it will be created and broke into two parts. For example, In Britain, there was a king. One half will be with the king and the other one will be given to people. People can use it for buying goods. This method did have any interests or loans. In this method, no one is a slave to anyone. So, based on people's work and these tally sticks were given to them. Some rich people saw this and were not happy. Money has to come into existence and it should be in control by us.

So, we must travel to the 1600's now. The year is 1694. Some say that they are going to build a bank. The bank's name is Bank of England. So, when they said about starting a bank. The king nor the government opposed it. How was that possible? The answer to that question was hidden in the year 1642. In 1642, there was a huge crisis. Many kings were assassinated. The most important king was king Charles. He was killed by Oliver Cromwell.

Oliver Cromwell, then becomes king. He was the one who received a lot of money as debts. He was the main reason behind the creation of the Bank of England.

In 1642, the foundation for the Bank of England was laid there. The government then stopped producing the Tally Sticks. People were still using Tally Sticks, So the Bank of England was created in 1694 and the shares were distributed among private sectors. All the private sectors combined and started a Bank of England. They all invest to buy these Tally Sticks. They informed people that they have printed money and its return of Tally Sticks, money will be given. They also advise the public to not use tally sticks and they receive all the tally sticks.

After that, a law has been passed stating nobody can use tally sticks. De-Monetization existed in those days. People who had tally sticks were unable to use them anymore. This happened in 1694.

Now we have to see how much debt did the England government have at that time? How much debt did it have in 1698?

If you have answers to these questions, then you will know how money has enslaved the masses.

The total debts of England in 1694 were 1,250,000 Euros. In 1698, the debts raised to 16,000,000 Euros. How did the debts raise this much within 4 years? They bought in a system. When the Bank of England was started in 1694, they gave away debts both to the government and the masses.

Suppose, if a bank says to you that you can receive money for 1% as interest. Will we receive the loan or not? Definitely, we will receive the loan.

Now the politics will play a role.

When we receive that loan, a multinational company will say that there is an offer for their products, only for ten days. So, we will receive that money from the bank and use it to buy products from the Multinational company. So, all together we will be a debtor to the bank. Have we purchased products that are useful to us? Nope.

This is a masterstroke.

The bank will lend money, MNC will give you an offer and we become slaves of that system.

This is how they transformed England into Debt Country.

In the 1700's England GDP was very high but its debts were also equal to high. During that time, there was a feud between England and America. There was a conspiracy behind this feud. To understand that conspiracy, we need to learn about Franklin. Now let's assume it is 1710 and England's debt is Ten crore Euros. It started at one lakh Euros, then after 4 years it went to one crore Euros and within 10 years it become Ten crore Euros. Franklin was just scared that all this debt was given by the Bank of England. Within a short period, some business people have taken control of the country. The bank is still asking for interest. So, now England issues new taxes to its colonies to pay their debts. So, if you are drinking a coffee, you should pay the tax. America was one of the important colonies of Britain. Britain was unable to receive money in huge numbers from the colony. Now Franklin starts to think that they have given so much money and their debt was still in place. So, Franklin stopped receiving money from the Bank of England and began to printing colony money. That colony money was called Colonial Scripts or Green Backs. We have already discussed Greenbacks.

So, they create Colonial Scripts and distribute it to the American people. Now People from the Bank of England visit the colony to find out why America was not receiving money from them. In 1763, they visit America to meet Benjamin Franklin. They find out that America has printed its own money. We have printed Colonial Scripts and people are using it as money. People are using it and they are happy. England officers appreciate to Franklin and return to England. Next year they bring in a law that forbids colonies from making paper money. If people are found using that paper money, then they will be put to death. This law was passed by England's Parliament. The order was directly from the Bank of England. Who owns the Bank of England? There is a twist here.

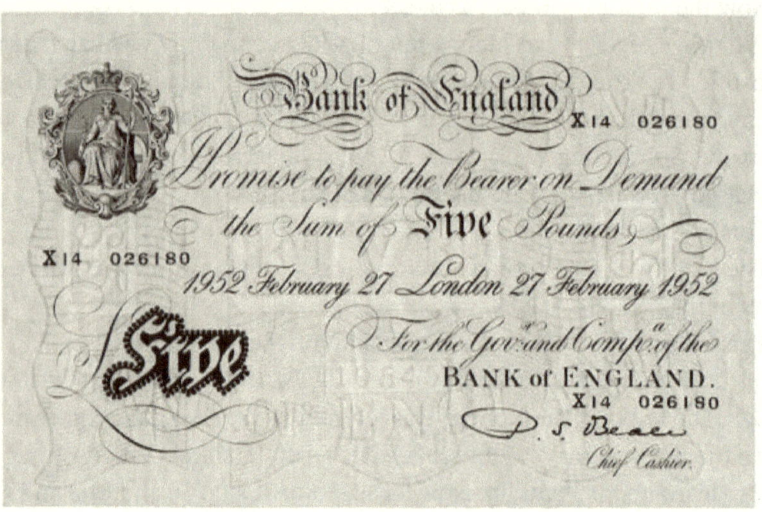

FEDERAL RESERVE BANK (POLITICS BEHIND)

JP Morgan is a familiar name. Many could have read about him. People who studied Illuminati, Edison, Tesla, American History, and Banks History should have read about this man. JP Morgan is one of the world's important wealthy men. Still now JP Morgan is number 6th in the leading banks in the world. After World War 2 was over, everybody around the world had a doubt. Who will be the richest person on the planet? Because, World War 2 was devastating for many countries. When people asked this question, many replied as JP Morgan. After his death, there was a request for an estimation of his wealth. When people started to analyse his movable and non-movable assets, a truth comes out. JP Morgan was no wealthy man. He was a Benami. He was a Benami to the Rothschilds. JP Morgan was a person who took care of 19% of the total wealth of the Rothschilds. The remaining 81% is directly owned by the Rothschild family. Imagine the wealth of the Rothschilds.

Money has taken a huge toll on our lives. Abraham Lincoln, who saw the corruption of the banks, thought that these banks were enslaving the people with money. He was the first and last person to think about this. So, Abraham Lincoln thought that money should not belong to the private, it should be controlled by the government. In return, the United States created its own money, the government. Cash bosses killed him within days of creating it. They changed it to say that he died just because slavery sounded to cover it up. To understand this first we need to look at events that took place before the year 1910. How did money originate in the United States then? Why do we talk about America? Do you think we can talk about India? Because only if you look at the United States do you know what is happening in our India.

There were many small banks in the United States before 1910, but even before the monarchy, the king of that city gave gold in cash. Only by keeping it will a man be determined to what extent he is rich. Because the world knows that gold is a precious commodity. There was a civil war in the 19th century over Abraham Lincoln's sounding American slavery. Abraham Lincoln then asked the banks for loans because the government needed the money. Banks then said they would pay 26 percent interest. On hearing this Abraham Lincoln thought of the atrocities the bank would inflict on the people. He is doing further research on this. Then, he feels that money is running here only for some money bosses then and for bank bosses. People who were there also started to understand this a little bit. Because when this bank goes to a country there is discrimination between rich and poor.

After the end of the Civil War, the US government printed money for itself. Within days of the money being released into the public domain, Abraham was shot dead. Within days of his shooting, all the money he had printed was gone. Once again, the government is stuck with private banks, which is still happening in the United States today. During the 1910s the bank lent to the people at high interest rates.

It began to understand the pranks they were doing to the people there and at the beginning of the 20th century people began to speak out against the Banks. The six largest banks there at the time drafted a massive bill to convince the public. That is the Federal Reserve Act. Together those six banks started this big bank. They also said that the Federal Reserve would print the money and give it to the people. But the US government and people do not accept it. So, in order to convince the people, those six banks joined hands with the people and told them not to trust Federal Bank. Then people trusted the Federal Reserve because people told these six banks not to trust the Federal Reserve. This is a tricky game to convince people. But people do not know that these six banks started the Federal Reserve together. At the same time, they have bought the government. Then in 1913, the Federal Reserve introduced the bill with government assistance. They started with the Federal Reserve and printed money based on gold. But after some years they started printing money without relying on gold.

What has this got to do with what is happening in India? India also printed money based on gold at that time. Not only India but all countries printed money based on gold. But with the advent of the Federal Reserve, we now see the US dollar as the net for gold. Money in India is printed on the basis of how much the US dollar is with India, keeping only a little gold in India now. Not only India but all the countries in the world are printing their money on a dollar basis. The thing is that Russia and China thought that the US would take all the power. So, again they printed money based on gold. But within a few years, Russia had switched to the dollar.

If we look at how this thing affects our lives, first understand one thing is how India prints money based on dollars, for example, if India now exports goods to the US, they will give dollars to India. Then we will keep the dollar in a FOREX (Foreign Exchange Market) and print the Indian currency equivalent to the dollar value by RBI. FOREX is controlled by RBI Bank. For example, if the US prints $ 100 now, India will have $ 20,then India will print currency depending on the value of 20 dollars. Now maybe if the value of a dollar is 75 Indian rupees, then we will print 1500 Indian currency. Suppose, if the Federal Reserve prints $200 the value of the dollar will fall in the world market. If the dollar depreciates in India, there will be an economic downturn. This is very difficult to understand. To illustrate this point, an incident occurred in 2008 around the world. It also had a huge economic impact on India.

CHAPTER FIFTEEN

ABRAHAM LINCOLN DEATH

In 1860, Abraham Lincoln becomes President of the United States. Forty percent of the population supported Abraham Lincoln. At that time, the United States was made up of 13 states. It splits into two parts, North America and South America. There are factory and cash bosses in North America. South America has a farming and slave population. Those in the South were the ones who opposed the Abraham Lincoln. North America is called Union and South America is called Confederation. On the same day that Abraham Lincoln assumes office, 7 out of 13 provinces divide that they want slavery. 4 months after those 4 more provinces split that they want slavery. Then the civil war broke out there. The war, which began in 1861, lasted for three to four years. 620,000 people are being killed in this war alone. They think more than this could have been killed. Because the statistic of how many persons were enslaved there, is not known. Then Abraham Lincoln needed money to deal with that civil war. Money is in the United States. Because that's where the banks are. This is what we already saw in the above topic.

When Abraham Lincoln asked banks for loans, they said they would charge 26 percent interest. Abraham Lincoln was then assisted by US Army soldier Dick Taylor. Dick Taylor suggested to Abraham Lincoln that the idea of printing dollars could alleviate the civil war a little. The dollar is a bond or currency printed by the US government. This means that if you give this bond to the banks, they will pay for the value they have on it. But the US government has no credibility in this document. Suppose, if banks say they can't afford the equivalent of that bond, it becomes an invalid bond. Not only that but a lot of counterfeiting was generated by keeping it.

Again, Dick Taylor called on the US government to abolish the dollar and again issue a new bond. But Dick Taylor said to show the people that the US government has credibility behind that bond. Abraham Lincoln likes the idea that Dick Taylor said. Because there was no money to buy weapons for war and to feed the soldiers. Then Abraham Lincoln gives a notice and shows the people the paper he printed saying, "People, do not be afraid. You can use your own money to pay off your debt. Here is your own picture." People called it greenbacks because this paper is green. People used to call the dollar Confederate bond as Greybacks. This greenback has been printed for nearly 450 million copies. This greenback is given to every person in the United States for free without any interest or debt. So, all people buy into this. Because, the US government has credibility behind that bond.

The United States has said it will use cash to replace the bond within six months of the end of the civil war. So, now they can buy anything like vegetables or paying the debt, This greenback is beginning to rule the United States. Bank bosses in the United States are angry that the United States has printed and used it on its own. But in countries like Britain and London, the press opposed Abraham Lincoln and said that Abraham Lincoln was doing something wrong.

Then think of how banks are enslaving people.

Many in the North were outraged that the American people were living without debt and took a lot of action against Abraham Lincoln. Abraham Lincoln, who was watching all this, makes a great announcement in 1863. It's the law that makes slavery no more in this United States. The announcement was reached up to in the UK. So, after hearing this announcement, the people of Britain are supporting Abraham Lincoln. There is nothing that the British government can do about it. Abraham Lincoln kept these Greenback and won this civil war. All the provinces together. The Civil War ended in 1865, and Abraham Lincoln was killed on the fifth day after the end of the Civil War. Although there was a lot of cause for his death. But the main reason was the bank bosses killed him only if America brought money for them. After Lincoln's death, they did an invalid of the greenback. After that, they formulate the National Banking Policy. Abraham Lincoln has assassinated by, John Wilkes Booth.

CHAPTER SIXTEEN

2008 PREDICTION

In 2005, Raghuram Rajan said the monetary framework was in danger "of a devastating implosion." After spells at the I.M.F. what's more India's national bank, he sees another possible emergency and he offers an answer. IMF boss Christine Lagarde today said not paying attention to his forecast of the 2008 credit emergency was a serious mix-up of the multilateral financing organization.

Rajan, presently the Reserve Bank Governor, was the Chief Economist and Research Director at the IMF during 2003-2006. He is credited with accurately gauging in 2005 an approaching worldwide monetary emergency at the yearly gathering of conspicuous financial specialists and brokers at Jackson Hole, US.

What happened in 2008?

Following the 2001 downturn and the World Trade Center assaults of 9/11/2001, the U.S. Central bank pushed loan costs to the least levels seen up to that time in the post-Bretton Woods time trying to keep up with financial solidness. The Fed held low loan fees through mid-2004. Joined with a government strategy to empower house buying, these low loan costs helped flash a precarious blast in land and monetary business sectors and an emotional extension of the volume of the absolute home loan obligation. Monetary advancements, for example, new kinds of subprime and customizable home loans permitted borrowers, who in any case probably won't have qualified in any case, to get liberal home credits in view of assumptions that financing costs would stay low and home costs would keep on rising endlessly.

In any case, from 2004 through 2006, the Federal Reserve consistently expanded loan costs trying to keep up with stable paces of expansion in the economy. As market loan fees rose accordingly, the progression of new credit through customary financial channels into land directed. Maybe more truly, the rates on existing movable home loans and surprisingly more outlandish advances started to reset at a lot higher rates than numerous borrowers expected or were directed to anticipate. The outcome was the blasting of what was later generally perceived to be a lodging bubble.

During the American lodging blast of the mid-2000s, monetary establishments had started advertising contract that upheld protections and complex subsidiary items at extraordinary levels. At the point when the housing market fell in 2007, these protections declined steeply in esteem. The credit showcases that had financed the lodging bubble, immediately followed lodging costs into a slump as a credit emergency started unfurling in 2007. The dissolvability of over-utilized banks and monetary organizations came to a limit starting with the breakdown of Bear Stearns in March 2008.

Things reached a critical stage sometime thereafter with the chapter 11 of Lehman Brothers, the country's fourth-biggest speculation bank, in September 2008. The infection immediately spread to different economies all over the planet, most outstandingly in Europe. Because of the Great Recession, the United States alone shed more than 8.7 million positions, as indicated by the U.S. Agency of Labor Statistics, causing the joblessness rate to twofold. Further, American families lost generally $19 trillion of total assets because of the financial exchange plunge, as indicated by the U.S Department of the Treasury. The Great Recession's true end date was June 2009.

Understanding the Crisis

The term The Great Recession is a play on the term The Great Depression. The last option happened during the 1930s and included a (GDP) decay of over 10% and a joblessness rate that at one point came to 25%. While no express standards exist to separate a downturn from a serious downturn, there is a close to an agreement among business analysts that the slump of the last part of the 2000s, during which U.S. Gross domestic product declined by 0.3% in 2008 and 2.8% in 2009 and joblessness momentarily came to 10%, didn't arrive at sorrow status. Be that as it may, the occasion is verifiably the most exceedingly terrible monetary decline in the interceding years.

For instance, in the event that I have no cash now, the Federal Reserve will loan me one percent premium. Then, at that point, I will purchase the stuffed stuff for myself. In the end, I just paid a one percent premium.

Causes of the Crisis

As per a 2011 report by the Financial Crisis Inquiry Commission, the Great Recession was avoidable. The deputies, which included six Democrats and four Republicans, referred to a few key contributing variables that they asserted prompted the slump.

In the first place, the report recognized disappointment concerning the public authority to manage the monetary business. This inability to manage incorporated the Fed's failure to control harmful home loan loaning.

Then, there were such a large number of monetary firms taking on an excess of hazard. The shadow banking framework, which included trading companies, was developed to match the safe financial framework however was not under a similar examination or guideline. Whenever the shadow banking framework fizzled, the result impacted the progression of credit to shoppers and organizations.

Different causes recognized in the report included extreme getting by shoppers and companies and officials who couldn't completely comprehend the falling monetary framework.

Response to the Crisis

The forceful financial strategies of the Federal Reserve and other national banks in response to the Great Recession, albeit broadly attributed with forestalling much more noteworthy harm to the worldwide economy, have likewise been censured for expanding the time it took the general economy to recuperate and laying the foundation for later downturns.

The Dodd-Frank Act

Not exclusively did the public authority bring improvement bundles into the monetary framework, however, new monetary guideline was additionally established. As per a few financial experts, the cancelation of the Glass-Steagall Act-the downturn time guideline during the 1990s helped cause the downturn. The nullification of the guideline permitted a portion of the United States' bigger banks to consolidate and structure bigger foundations. In 2010, President Barack Obama marked the Dodd-Frank Act to give the public authority extended administrative control over the monetary area.

The demonstration permitted the public authority some command over monetary foundations that were considered on the cusp of falling flat and to help set up shopper insurances against savage loaning.

Nonetheless, pundits of Dodd-Frank note that the monetary area players and foundations that effectively drove and benefitted from ruthless loaning and related works on during the lodging and monetary air pockets were likewise profoundly associated with both the drafting of the new regulation and the Obama organization offices accused of its execution.

CHAPTER SEVENTEEN

OSAMA BIN LADEN (POLITICS BEHIND)

Comrade Osama bin Laden. Whose friend? Friend of America? Friend of the Arab country? Pakistan's friend? In an interview, Julian Assange says that the CIA of the United States created the terrorist organization ISIS. Why should these people create ISIS extremists? Julian Assange gives conclusive evidence for this. Gives nearly 30 lakh documents to the public domain. This caused fear from Hillary Clinton to Obama. These 30 lakh documents contained the history of the major wars, including the Iran War, the Afghanistan War, and the Iraq War. It also contained information on how these wars originated and by whom. The US government imprisoned Julian Assange for this. Julian Assange was not the only one to say this information. Fidel Castro claims that Osama bin Laden was created by the United States. Fidel Castro says Osama bin Laden should be there if the United States wants to seize a country or the Al-Qaeda organization will be there.

Where the history of ISIS begins, it begins with the Mujahideen. Along with that came the Al Qaeda and the Taliban. ISIS is an organization that broke away from Al Qaeda. ISIS is an Islamic organization, so its leader must be an Islamist. But no, the leader of the ISIS organization is a Jewish person. Abu Bakr al-Baghdadi is the person who has the evidence for this, who he is belongs to the Mossad organization in Israel but a lot of people will say this is a lie. A journalist asks Julias Assange what he thinks should change in this world. To which he says that if I had the greatest authority in this world now, I would put the year 1979of zero years in the calendar.

We know our Calendar, right? Before Jesus and After Jesus.

But Julias Assange said that it would be before 1979 and After 1979.

What is the reason for that?

Because, it's all based on the ISIS organization terrorist issues.

The United States says there must be democracy in every country in the world. Whichever country the US goes to, that is, countries like Iran, Iraq, and North Korea, where the tyrannical rule is taking place, where the US says the democratic rule should flourish. why not Saudi Arabia. Yet in Saudi Arabia, the king monarchy is running itself.

Now you may have doubts.

It all started in 1979. Afghanistan is occupied by the Soviet Union. These Arabs have nothing to do with Islam. The Arabs are a different Muslim people, the ones in Iran are a different Muslim people, as well as the Muslim people in Egypt, are another, understand well, first of all, their history will all change. If the Soviet Union wants to invade Afghanistan, it is because Afghanistan has a lot of resources.

But the United States now thought that World War III would break out if it opposed Russia. And so, the United States undertook the crosshairs. This is because the Palestine -Israeli civil war was raging after World War II. At that time, the United States have been supporting the country, Isreal. At this time the United States was unable to defend Afghanistan against Russia. So, the US told Saudi Arabia to save Afghanistan from Russia. The United States went to the King of Saudi Arabia and said that if Russia conquered Afghanistan, communism would spread throughout the world and that your regime would continue, and that the United States would not bother you. So, the United States told Saudi Arabia that you and the organization are giving money to help the Mujahideen. The United States has said it will provide cash assistance through Pakistan, not directly. Only then will the eyes of the nations of the world go on Pakistan, and the United States says we can both escape. But when Saudi Arabia asked the United States that why Afghanistan wanted for, the United States said, "Afghanistan is the oilcenter of resources. If we capture Afghanistan, we can rule the world, and we can divide our profits. Saudi Arabia gives lakhs and lakhs of money to Pakistan, after the deal between Saudi and America.

After that, the biggest unrest in Afghanistan took place. The United States wanted one hero to took the leadership of mujahideen in Afghanistan in its favor. They thought he had to be a millionaire and he had to be an Islamist. Because the United States thought that a rich man was fighting for us, people in Afghanistan will should fight too, and that we should create a religious frenzy. The United States thought that by doing so, Islam would be introduced there as well. One of the protagonists created for this is Osama bin Laden.

A few sources have asserted that the Central Intelligence Agency (CIA) had attached with Osama bin Laden's al-Qaeda and its "Afghan Arab" contenders when it furnished Mujahideen gatherings to battle the Soviet Union during the Soviet-Afghan War.

Regarding a similar time as the Soviet attack of Afghanistan, the United States started working together with Pakistan's Inter-Services Intelligence (ISI) to give a few hundred million dollars per year in helping to the Afghan Mujahideen radicals battling the Afghan favorable to Soviet government and the Soviet Army in Operation Cyclone. Alongside local Afghan mujahideen were Muslim volunteers from different nations, famously known as "Afghan Arabs". The most renowned of the Afghan Arabs were Osama container Laden, referred to at the time as an affluent and devout Saudi who gave his own cash and aided raise millions from other rich Gulf Arabs.

Whenever the conflict finished, container Laden coordinated the al-Qaeda association to continue outfitted jihad against different nations, fundamentally against the United States.

Various observers have depicted Al-Qaeda assaults as "blowback" or an unseen side-effect of American guide to the mujahideen. Accordingly, the United States government and American and Pakistani knowledge authorities engaged with the activity have denied this hypothesis. Numerous columnists including Peter Bergen have additionally disproved the case. They keep up with the guide was given out by the Pakistan government, that it went to Afghan not unfamiliar mujahideen, and that there was no contact between the Afghan Arabs (unfamiliar mujahideen) and the CIA and other American authorities, not to mention the outfitting, preparing, instructing or influence.

During the counter Soviet conflict, Bin Laden and his warriors got American and Saudi subsidizing. A few examiners accept Bin Laden himself had security preparing from the CIA.

Robin Cook, Foreign Secretary in the UK from 1997 to 2001, accepted the CIA had given arms to the Arab mujahideen, including Osama receptacle Laden, expressing, "Canister Laden was, however, a result of a stupendous error by western security organizations. All through the '80s he was outfitted by the CIA and supported by the Saudis to take up arms against the Russian control of Afghanistan."

In discussion with previous British Defence Secretary Michael Portillo, double-cross Prime Minister of Pakistan Benazir Bhutto said Osama receptacle Laden was at first favorable to American. Ruler Bandar canister Sultan of Saudi Arabia, has likewise expressed that receptacle Laden once communicated appreciation for the United States' assistance in Afghanistan. On CNN's Larry King program, he said:

Bandar receptacle Sultan: This is amusing. During the '80s, in the event that you recollect that, we and the United - Saudi Arabia and the United States were supporting the Mujahideen to free Afghanistan from the Soviets. He [Osama canister Laden] came to say thanks to me for my endeavors to bring the Americans, our companions, to help us against the nonbelievers, he said the socialists. Isn't it amusing?

Larry King: How unexpected. At the end of the day, he came to thank you for carrying America to help him.

Bandar receptacle Sultan: Right.

U.S. government authorities and various different gatherings keep up with that the U.S. upheld just the native Afghan mujahideen. They reject that the CIA or other American authorities had contact with Bin Laden, not to mention outfitted, prepared, instructed, or inculcated him. American researchers and correspondents have called the possibility of a CIA-upheld Al Qaeda "garbage", "sheer dream", and a "typical legend".

As per Peter Jouvenal, Americans couldn't prepare mujahideen since Pakistani authorities would not permit in excess of a small bunch of U.S. specialists to work in Pakistan and none in Afghanistan.

Al-Qaeda pioneer Ayman al-Zawahiri says a lot of exactly the same thing in his book "Knights Under the Prophet's Banner".

Canister Laden himself once said "The breakdown of the Soviet Union ... goes to God and the mujahideen in Afghanistan ... the US played no mentionable part," however "the breakdown made the US haughtier and more pompous."

In Ghost Wars (2004), Steve Coll related: "Container Laden moved inside Saudi insight's compartmented activities, outside of CIA vision. CIA files contain no record of any immediate contact between a CIA official and receptacle Laden during the 1980s." Yet Coll additionally archives that container Laden in some measure casually helped out the ISI during the 1980s and had close associations with CIA-supported mujahideen commandant Jalaluddin Haqqani; Milton Bearden, the CIA's Islamabad station boss from mid-1986 until mid-1989, took a respecting perspective on canister Laden at that point. Afghan resources related the zeal and prejudice of large numbers of the supposed "Afghan Arabs" to the CIA, yet the CIA limited these reports, rather thinking about direct help to the Arab volunteers assuming some pretense of a Spanish Civil War-enlivened "worldwide unit" an idea that never got off the paper.

As per Norwegian analyst Thomas Hegghammer, the book "Unholy Wars" by columnist John K. Cooley did the most to engender the view that the CIA prepared the Afghan Arabs. In this book, Cooley depicted "the focal job of the CIA's Muslim hired fighters, including as much as 2,000 Algerians, in the Afghanistan war". However, he didn't present any proof for his cases. What's more as per history specialist Odd Arne Westad his book is problematic. In light of data by Soviet deserter Vasili Mitrokhin, portions of the book "clearly begin in Soviet disinformation from the 1980s".

As per CNN columnist Peter Bergen, known for directing the principal TV meet with Osama container Laden in 1997, "Canister Laden had his own cash, he was hostile to American and he was working furtively and freely."

Bergen quotes Pakistani Brigadier Mohammad Yousaf, who ran the Inter-Services Intelligence (ISI) Afghan activity somewhere in the range of 1983 and 1987:

It was continuously rankling to the Americans, and I can comprehend their perspective, that in spite of the fact that they recognized the cold hard reality, they couldn't make a judgment call. The CIA upheld the mujahideen by spending the citizens' cash, billions of dollars of it throughout the long term, on purchasing arms, ammo, and hardware. It was their mystery arms acquisition branch that was kept occupied. It was, in any case, a cardinal decision of Pakistan's approach that no Americans at any point become associated with the circulation of assets or arms once they showed up in the country. No Americans at any point prepared or had direct contact with the mujahideen, and no American authority at any point went inside Afghanistan.

Marc Sageman, a Foreign Service Officer who was situated in Islamabad from 1987 to 1989, and worked intimately with Afghanistan's Mujahideen, expresses that no American cash went to the unfamiliar volunteers.

Sageman likewise says:

Contemporaneous records of the conflict don't make reference to [the Afghan Arabs]. Many were not kidding about the conflict. Not many were engaged with real battling. For the vast majority of the conflict, they were dispersed among the Afghan gatherings related to the four Afghan fundamentalist gatherings.

No U.S. official at any point interacted with the unfamiliar volunteers. They essentially went in various circles and never crossed U.S. radar screens. They had their own wellsprings of cash and their own contacts with the Pakistanis, official Saudis, and other Muslim allies, and they made their own arrangements with the different Afghan opposition pioneers."

Vincent Cannistraro, who drove the Reagan organization's Afghan Working Group from 1985 to 1987, puts it,

The CIA was exceptionally hesitant to be involved by any means. They figured it would wind up with them being accused, as in Guatemala." So, the Agency attempted to stay away from the direct association in the conflict, the touchy CIA, Cannistraro gauges, had under ten agents going about as America's eyes and ears in the district. Milton Bearden, the Agency's central field employable in the conflict exertion, has demanded that "The CIA didn't have anything to do with" receptacle Laden. Cannistraro says that when he composed Afghan strategy from Washington, he not even once heard container Laden's name.

Fox News journalist Richard Miniter composed that in interviews with the two men who "managed the dispensing for all American assets to the counter Soviet obstruction, Bill Peikney CIA station boss in Islamabad from 1984 to 1986 and Milt Bearden CIA station boss from 1986 to 1989 he found,

Both straight rejected that any CIA reserves at any point went to receptacle Laden. They felt so unequivocally concerning this point that they consented to go on the record, a surprising move by ordinarily hesitant insight officials. Mr.Peikney included an email to me: "I don't remember UBL [bin Laden] going over my screen when I was there.

Different reasons progressed for an absence of a CIA-Afghan Arab association of "urgent significance," (or even any association whatsoever), which was that the Afghan Arabs themselves were not significant in the conflict but rather were an "inquisitive sideshow to the genuine battling."

One gauge of the quantity of warriors in the conflict is that 250,000 Afghans battled 125,000 Soviet soldiers, however, just 2000 Arab Afghans battled "at any one time".

As per Bearden, the CIA didn't enlist Arabs since there were a huge number of Afghans generally very ready to battle. The Arab Afghans were pointless as well as "troublesome," enraging neighborhood Afghans with their more-Muslim-than-thou disposition, as indicated by Peter Juvenal.

Veteran Afghan cameraman Peter Juvenal quotes an Afghan mujahideen as saying "at whatever point we definitely disliked one of them [foreign mujahideen], we just shot them. They thought they were rulers."

Numerous who went to Afghanistan, including Olivier Roy and Peter Jouvenal, announced of the Arab Afghans' instinctive antagonism toward Westerners in Afghanistan to help Afghans or report on their predicament. BBC columnist John Simpson recounts the account of running into Osama container Laden in 1989, and with neither knowing who the difference was, receptacle Laden endeavoring to pay off Simpson's Afghan driver $500 a huge total in a helpless country to kill the unbeliever, Simpson. Whenever the driver declined, Bin Laden resigned to his "camp bed" and sobbed "in disappointment."

Sir Martin Ewan's expressed that the Afghan Arabs "benefited by implication from the CIA's financing, through the ISI and obstruction associations," and that "it has been figured that upwards of 35,000 'Middle Easterner Afghans' might have gotten military preparation in Pakistan at an expected expense of $800 million in the years up to and including 1988."

A portion of the CIA's most prominent Afghan recipients were Arabist authorities, for example, Haqqani and Gulbuddin Hekmatyar who were key partners of Bin Laden over numerous years. Haqqani one of Bin Laden's nearest relates during the 1980s got immediate money installments from CIA specialists, without the intervention of the ISI. This free wellspring of financing gave Haqqani a lopsided impact over the mujahideen, and assisted Bin Laden with fostering his base.

Sheik Omar Abdel Rahman, a partner of Bin Laden's, was given visas to enter the US on four events by the CIA. Rahman was enrolling Arabs to battle in the Soviet-Afghan conflict, and Egyptian authorities affirmed that the CIA effectively helped him. Rahman was a co-plotter of the 1993 World Trade Center bombarding.

One claim not denied by the US government is that the U.S. Armed force joined up and prepared a previous Egyptian warrior named Ali Mohamed, and that it realized Ali periodically went on outings to Afghanistan, where he professed to battle Russians. As per writer Lawrence Wright, who talked with U.S. authorities about Ali, the Egyptian told his Army bosses he was battling in Afghanistan, yet didn't let them know he was preparing other Afghan Arabs or composing a manual from what he had gained from the US Army Special Forces. Wright likewise reports that the CIA neglected to illuminate different US offices that it had learned Ali, who was an individual from Egyptian Islamic Jihad, was an enemy of an American government agent.

Why Osama Bin Laden against the US

The September 11, 2001 fear monger assaults in the United States were done by 19 criminals of the assailant Islamist psychological oppressor association al-Qaeda. Intentions were expressed when the assaults were in a few sources. Furthermore, al-Qaeda pioneer Osama container Laden announced a sacred conflict against the United States, and two fatwā were delivered by receptacle Laden and others in 1996 and 1998.

In receptacle Laden's November 2002 "Letter to America", he said that al-Qaeda's intentions in the assaults included Western help for assaulting Muslims in Somalia, supporting Russian monstrosities against Muslims in Chechnya, supporting the Indian persecution against Muslims in Kashmir, support for Israel in Lebanon, the presence of US troops in Saudi Arabia, US backing of Israel, and authorizations against Iraq.

The U.S. government took the situation, as regularly rehashed by the Bush Administration, that psychological oppressors assaulted the United States since "they disdain us for our opportunities." For instance, President George W. Hedge in a discourse to Congress nine days after the assaults said: "They disdain right what we find in this chamber- - an equitably chosen government. Their chiefs are self-designated. They disdain our opportunities - our opportunity of religion, our right to speak freely, our opportunity to cast a ballot and collect and can't help contradicting one another."

Source

Before the assaults, Al-Qaeda gave declarations that give understanding into the inspirations to the assaults: one was the fatwā of August 1996, and a second was a more limited fatwa in February 1998. The two records showed up at first in the Arabic-language London paper Al-Quds Al-Arabi. Three years before the September 11 assaults, Al-Qaeda delivered a Fatwa, expressing "We with God's assistance approach each Muslim who has faith in God and wishes to be compensated to conform to God's structure to kill the Americans and loot their cash any place and at whatever point they track down it. We likewise approach Muslim ulema, pioneers, young people, and fighters to send off the attack on Satan's U.S. troops and Satan's allies aligning with them, and to dislodge the people who are behind them so they might gain proficiency with an illustration." The Fatwa likewise gripes against the presence of the US in Saudi Arabia and backing for Israel. After the assaults, receptacle Laden and al-Zawahiri have distributed many video tapes and sound tapes, many portraying the inspirations for the assaults. Two especially significant distributions were canister Laden's 2002 "Letter to America", and a 2004 video tape by receptacle Laden. Notwithstanding immediate declarations by receptacle Laden and Al-Qaeda, various political experts have hypothesized inspirations for the assaults.

CHAPTER EIGHTEEN

CORONAVIRUS AND EVENT 201

Corona virus, a virus that has sunk the world, a virus that has killed millions of people in the world, a virus that has changed the economies of all the countries in the world. We thought that this world will end due to nuclear weapons or Natural disasters. But there is a high probability that due to this virus. The world may come to an end. Corona virus clearly shows that it is a possibility. Now we are affected by one of the families in Corona virus. Yes, there are six types already we faced in this world. Now we are facingthe seventh type of virus. Researchers say the virus is 10,000 years old. So far six types of viruses have been identified. The most recent common ancestor (MRCA) of all coronaviruses is estimated to have existed as recently as 8000 BCE, although some models place the common ancestor as far back as 55 million years or more, implying long term co evolution with bat and avian species. Scientists say it affects not only humans but also animals. They are said to attack mammals in particular. Yes, we are a mammal. The virus is now newly discovered and hence the name Novel Corona. The first case of the virus was reported in China, and at the same time the first case was filed in Indonesia, Thailand, United States, in the corner of the world. How is this possible? How will affect these countries instead of between other countries?

Did you think, how China controls the coronavirus from their country? Only nearby one lakh cases were filed, but the origin of the corona virus was China, we know that.

Wuhan is the place; the virus originated and made its first attack. How did it originate from Wuhan? Why did it come? From whom did it spread from? In Wuhan, there is a huge fish market and meat market. They said, there is a possibility it would have spread from the market.

Is the Corona virus a manmade virus? Can we believe this or not? Is it possible that some corporations are building a virus like that? How can Corona affect our lives? Two years before in 2019, many cautioned world governments that this virus will affect people. Is the news true or not? We will give answers to these questions.

In 2004, the SARS virus somehow escapes from China. From 2002 to 2003 Chinese government said that it has quarantined the SARS virus. How did it escape from Quarantine? The International community asked this question to China. The Chinese government said that they were learning about the SARS virus, due to a leak from the laboratory the SARS virus escaped the lab. The International community was frightened, many companies thought of leaving China. The Chinese government said that we will build the most advanced lab within 2015 and nobody has to worry. The lab was built and called as Wuhan Institute of virology. This lab is present only 30 kilometers from the Huanan Seafood Market. This is where the Corona virus started its attack. In 2015, this lab was built and safety is being checked now. This lab was open within 2 years. The lab is the first-ever lab to meet biosafety level 4 standard – meaning it has the capacity to handle the most dangerous pathogens. Similar to this lab, there is a total of 54 BSL Standard labs in the world. SARS virus belongs to the BS3 level virus. The BS3 level says, how strong the virus is and how it spreads, this will determine which level the virus will belong to. Wuhan Institute of virology belongs to a BS4 level lab. This NCOV2019 also belongs to the BS4 level virus.

EVENT 201

What is this Event 201?

Before the day of the Twin Towers attack in the United States, September 11, this event, the Event 201, demonstrated the extent of the damage if the Twin Towers were attacked. This is how the attack took place on the same day. No one there knew that Osama bin Laden was going to attack the Twin Towers.

We can see there is a two types NPRS (No Problem Reaction Solution) and PRS (Problem Reaction Solution). For example, I would say that Saddam Hussein has a nuclear weapon. My goal is for me to start a war on that country. People will question why you attacked Saddam Hussein if he was hit at an unexpected time. So I'm trying to convince people that the news is a hoax. I'm going to tell people that the only solution is to kill Saddam Hussein.In the second type, I will create a problem myself. I will make people yearn that no one will save us. After that, I will give the solution for it myself. Through it all, I will accomplish what I want.

In 2019, in America, Eric Toner, Bill Gates (Microsoft), and Melinda Gates sponsor research. That research was to contain a virus called CAPS. Which is organized from Pig meat which may come from the Brazil meat market. This research was a simulation of how they will protect the world. The simulation results, they were unable to contain the virus even after one year those were the results. The result also showed that the virus will kill nearly 6.5 crore people in the world. This research was held in October 2019. But the first virus case file in December 2019. Just think about it.

Why did Bill Gates sponsor this stimulation? Who is Eric Toner? The answer will not available. Because, the information from many websites is deleted now. They simply say that the simulation was a warning to the world, if a virus attacks. In 2015, there was another simulation that happened. After the simulation H1N1, the Nipah virus attacked the people. After the 2019, Simulation NCOV2019 has attacked the people. We think that there is a connection here. But if we say that they will easily consider this as a conspiracy theory or they would say fake news.

Don't believe someone said, research by yourself.

The Wuhan Institute of virology has been studying coronavirus since at least 2016. The Chinese government has said America is responsible for spreading the virus. Did the virus originate from Sea food, snakes? Nearly 29 Chinese researchers have sent a report to the British Medical Journal called Lancet. In January 2020, the report was uploaded to their website. In the report, the first person to be affected was discovered in December. But that person has no connection with the market or the Seafood. The report clearly says that the first 13 affected patients had no connection to the market. But somehow the virus will spread. In Japan, a person will be affected by the Coronavirus, but he has no connection with China. So, this virus is strong and spreads rapidly. Who spreads this virus? Many said the virus spread through meat and Seafood. But now, they have altered their answer and say that the origins are from somewhere else. This virus may have originated from a bird or some other meat. But the Wuhan market scenario is considered a false statement.

The Simulation which Bill Gates sponsored. The results say that the stock market price will fall down to 20% to 40%. There will be a loss of shares. Many countries will cancel their flights. Nearly 120 countries will be affected. It also says that 6.5 crore people will perish.

Now China is placed 120th rank between other countries on Coronavirus. How is this possible?

Is there a similarity between the simulation reports and the current happenings? Hong Kong shares are gone down by nearly 3%. Chinese stocks are closed right now. Many flights from other countries are cancelled. They have also advised not to fly to China or nearby countries. They have also said that the virus will be active for nearly one year. But now the situation was different. There is a Swiss Pharmaceutical company its name is Novartis AG. The chief executive of Novartis has said that it will take 12 months to find a new vaccine for the corona virus. After the interview, their shares have skyrocketed. What does Hong Kong say? They say that they have found a cure. But first, they have to test it on animals. So, for the cure to come into the market, it will take nearly one year. So, the simulation results are happening right now. What conclusion has the World Health Organisation come to? BSL level 4 labs are funded by World Health Organisation. To check SARS, Corona World Health Organisation is funding. Is there proof? Yes, from 2013 to 2014, there was a BSL level 4 lab built in Pune by India. That lab was funded by World Health Organisation.

What is happening here? Is there any Bio-war conducted by any other?

Now, nearly 40 crore people were affected by Coronavirus, nearly 60 lakh people were dead and nearly 31.5 crore people were recovered.

CHAPTER NINETEEN

COMMUNISM

ABOUT

Socialism, a political and monetary precept that intends to supplant private property and a benefit-based economy with public possession and collective control of at minimum the significant method for creation (e.g., mines, plants, and production lines) and the normal assets of a general public. Socialism is consequently a type of communism a higher and further developed structure, as per its supporters. Precisely the way that socialism contrasts from communism have for some time involved discussion, however, the differentiation lays generally on the socialists' adherence to the progressive communism of Karl Marx.

Like most scholars of the nineteenth century, Marx would, in general, utilize the terms socialism and communism conversely. In his Critique of the Gotha Program (1875), in any case, Marx recognized two periods of socialism that would follow the anticipated defeat of private enterprise: the primary would be a momentary framework where the middle class would control the public authority and economy yet still track down it important to pay individuals as indicated by how long, hard, or well they worked, and the second would be completely acknowledged socialism a general public without class divisions or government, wherein the creation and appropriation of merchandise would be founded on the guideline "From each as per his capacity, to each as per his necessities." Marx's supporters, particularly the Russian progressive Vladimir Ilich Lenin, took up this differentiation.

Present-day socialist philosophy started to create during the French Revolution, and its original lot, Karl Marx and Friedrich Engels' "Socialist

Manifesto," was distributed in 1848. That leaflet dismissed the Christian tenor of past socialist ways of thinking, spreading out a realist and its advocates guarantee logical examination of the set of experiences and future direction of human culture. "The historical backdrop of all until now existing society," Marx and Engels stated, "is the historical backdrop of class battles."

The Communist Manifesto introduced the French Revolution as a significant chronicled defining moment, when the "bourgeoisie", the shipper class that was currently solidifying command over the "method for creation" upset the primitive power structure and introduced the cutting edge, industrialist time. That upheaval supplanted the archaic class battle, which set the honourability in opposition to the serfs, with the advanced one setting the average proprietors of capital in opposition to the "working class," the common who sell their work for compensation.

In the Communist Manifesto and later works, Marx, Engels, and their devotees upheld (and anticipated as generally inescapable) a worldwide common unrest, which would introduce an initial a time of communism, then, at that point, of socialism. This last phase of human advancement would check the finish of class battle and subsequently of history: all individuals would live in friendly balance, without class differentiations, family designs, religion, or property. The state, as well, would "shrink away." The economy would work, as a famous Marxist trademark puts it, "from each as per his capacity, to each as indicated by his requirements."

CHAPTER TWENTY

KARL MARX (FATHER OF COMMUNISM)

BBC Radio conducted a poll with its Internet users in September at a time when the world was looking forward to the New Year at the end of the 1999. The question asked there is who is the greatest thinker of the last thousand years. Edward de Bono, a scholar in many fields, chose and nominated William James, an American philosopher and psychologist, and St. Thomas Aquinas, a Catholic priest. But the opinion of the BBC co-readers who responded to the poll from around the world was different. They chose Karl Marx as the foremost thinker of the last thousand years. Albert Einstein, Sir Isaac Newton, Charles Darwin, Thomas Aquinas, Stephen Hawking, Emmanuel Kant, Rene Descartes, Jams Clerk Maxwell, Friedrich Nietzsche, all of the world's greatest thinkers were named after Karl Marx. Who is this Marx, whose name was born in a city somewhere in Germany, is still ringing around the world today? Despite attempts to suppress him as a German or a Jew, the world-class celebrates him as its ideal hero, at dawn.

In a sense, Marx's name is still the talk of the world today. Who is this, Marx? What has he done like that? Karl Heinrich Marx was born on May 5, 1818, in Trier, Germany to a middle-class family. The aftershocks of the French Revolution of the late eighteenth century were similar to those of Marx at the time of Marx's birth. Karl Marx's father and lawyer, Heinrich Marx, was somewhat influenced and progressive. Marx's mother's name was Henriet Presberg. Heinrich converted to Christianity with his Marx family. Marx, who joined the school in the 1930s, was under the progressive influence. Interested in studying, Marx studied German, Latin, Greek, and French, and majored in mathematics, history, physics, and geography.

Karl was immersed in a similar church in 1824, at 6 years old. Karl went to a Lutheran grade school however later turned into an agnostic and realist, dismissing both the Christian and Jewish religions. It was he who begat the maxim "Religion is the opium of individuals," a cardinal standard in present-day socialism.

Karl went to the Friedrich Wilhelm Gymnasium in Trier for quite some time, graduating in 1835, at 17 years old. The exercise room educational plan was the standard traditional one-history, science, writing, and dialects, especially Greek and Latin. Karl became capable in French and Latin, the two of which he figured out how to peruse and compose easily. In later years he showed himself different dialects, so exceptionally that as a full-grown researcher he could likewise understand Spanish, Italian, Dutch, Scandinavian, Russian, and English. As his articles in the New York Daily Tribune show, he came to deal with the English language amazingly (he cherished Shakespeare, whose works he knew forwards and backward), in spite of the fact that he never lost his weighty Teutonic inflection in talking.

In October 1835 Marx registered in Bonn University, where he went to courses principally in statute, as it was his dad's fervent desire that he become an attorney. Marx, notwithstanding, was more inspired by theory and writing than in regulation. He needed to be a writer and playwright, and in his understudy days, he composed a lot of verse its vast majority protected which in his adult years he properly perceived as imitative and unremarkable. He spent a year at Bonn, concentrating on close to nothing yet roistering and drinking. He went through a day in prison for upsetting the harmony and battled one duel, where he was injured in the right eye. He likewise stacked up weighty obligations.

Marx's overwhelmed father removed him from Bonn and had him enter the University of Berlin, then, at that point, a center of scholarly mature. In Berlin, a universe of splendid scholars was testing existing foundations and thoughts, including religion, theory, morals, and governmental issues. The soul of the incredible thinker G. W. F. Hegel was as yet unmistakable there. A gathering is known as the Young Hegelians, which included educators like Bruno Bauer and brilliant, logically arranged understudies, met habitually to discuss and decipher the inconspicuous thoughts of the expert. Youthful Marx before long turned into an individual from the Young Hegelian circle and was profoundly impacted by its overall thoughts.

Marx spent over 4 years in Berlin, finishing his investigations there in March 1841. He had surrendered statute and dedicated himself essentially to reasoning. On April 15, 1841, the University of Jena granted "Carolo Henrico Marx" the level of specialist of reasoning on the strength of his recondite and learned exposition, Difference among Democritean and Epicurean Natural Philosophy, which depended on Greek-language sources.

His Exile

Marx's expectations of showing reasoning at Bonn University were baffled by the traditionalist approach of the Prussian government. He then, at that point, went to composing and news-casting for his job. In 1842 he became manager of the liberal Cologne paper Rheinische Zeitung, yet it was stifled by the Berlin government the next year. Marx then, at that point, moved to Paris. There he initially interacted with the common laborers, surrendered his way of thinking as an all-consuming purpose, and attempted his genuine investigation of financial matters.

In January 1845 Marx was removed from France "at the incitement of the Prussian government," as he said. He moved to Brussels, where he resided until 1848 and where he established the German Workers' party and was dynamic in the Communist League. It was for the last option that he, with his companion and partner Friedrich Engels, distributed, in 1848, the renowned Manifesto of the Communist Party (known as the Communist Manifesto). Ousted by the Belgian government for his radicalism, Marx moved back to Cologne, where he became editorial manager of the Neue Rheinische Zeitung in June 1848. Under a year after the fact, in May 1849, the paper was smothered by the Prussian government, and Marx himself was banished. He got back to Paris, however, in September, the French government ousted him once more. Dogged from the Continent, Marx at long last gotten comfortable London, where he resided as a stateless exile (Britain denied him citizenship and Prussia declined to denaturalize him) for the remainder of his life.

In London, Marx's only method for help was reporting. He composed for both German and English-language distributions. From August 1852 to March 1862, he was a journalist for the New York Daily Tribune, contributing an aggregate of around 355 articles, a considerable lot of which were utilized by that paper as driving (unsigned) publications. News-casting, be that as it may, paid wretchedly (£2 per article); Marx was in a real sense saved from starvation by the persistent monetary help of Engels. In 1864 Marx served to establish in London the International Workingmen's Association (known as the First International), for which he composed the debut address. In 1872 he broke down the International, to keep it from falling under the control of the rebels under the authority of Mikhail Bakunin. From there on, Marx's political exercises were bound for the most part to correspondence with extremists in Europe and America, offering guidance and assisting with forming the communist and work developments.

Appearance and Personal Life

Marx was short and stocky, with a ragged head of hair and glimmering eyes. His skin was dark, so his loved ones called him Mohr in German, or Moor in English. He, at the end of the day, took on the epithet and utilized it with lingerie. His physical make-up gave an impression of energy, notwithstanding the way that he was an inert tubercular (four of his more youthful kin passed on from tuberculosis). A man of huge learning and sharp scholarly power, Marx, regularly fretful and bad-tempered, alienated individuals by his cynical mind, gruffness, and unyieldingness, which verged on pomposity. His adversaries were an army. However, notwithstanding his merited standing as a hard and unpalatable individual, he had a weakness for kids; he profoundly cherished his own little girls, who, thusly, revered him.

Marx was hitched to his youth darling, Jenny von West Phalen, who was known as the "most excellent young lady in Trier," on June 19, 1843. She was completely committed to him. She passed on from disease on December 2, 1881, at 67 years old. For Marx, it was a blow from which he won't ever recuperate.

The Marx's had seven kids, four of whom passed on in early stages or adolescence. Of the three enduring little girls Jenny (1844-1883), Laura (1845-1911), and Eleanor (1855-1898) two wedded Frenchmen: Jenny, Charles Longuet; Laura, Paul Lafargue. Both of Marx's children in-regulation became conspicuous French communists and individuals from Parliament. Eleanor lived with Edward Aveling and was dynamic as a British work coordinator. Both Laura and Eleanor ended it all.

Marx invested a large portion of his functioning energy in the British Museum, doing investigate both for his paper articles and his books. He was a most upright researcher, forever discontent with handed down data yet following raw numbers to their unique sources. In anticipation of Das Kapital, he read for all intents and purposes each accessible work in monetary and monetary hypothesis and practice in the significant dialects of Europe.

At home, Marx regularly kept awake till four AM, perusing and making voluminous notes in his tight penmanship, which was so crabbed as to be practically muddled. He was a weighty smoker of lines and stogies, spending amounts of matches all the while. His workroom was thickly smoke-filled. "Das Kapital," he told his child in-regulation, Paul Lafargue, "won't pay for the stogie's I smoked composing it."

Marx's unreasonable smoking, wine drinking, and utilization of vigorously flavored food sources might have been contributory causes to his sicknesses, the majority of which would have all the earmarks of being, in the radiance of present-day information, hypersensitive and psychosomatic. Over the most recent twenty years of his life, he was tortured by a mounting progression of afflictions that would have attempted the persistence of Job. He experienced inherited liver insanity (of which, he asserted, his dad kicked the bucket); successive flare-ups of carbuncles and furuncles on his neck, chest, back, and backside (frequently he was unable to sit); toothaches; eye irritations; lung abscesses; haemorrhoids; pleurisy; and constant migraines and hacks that made rest unthinkable without drugs. In the last dozen or so long periods of his life, he could never again do any supported scholarly work. He passed on in his easy chair in London on March 14, 1883, around two months before his sixty-fifth birthday celebration. He lies covered in London's Highgate Cemetery, where the grave is set apart by a bust of him.

His Work

Marx's works fall into two general classes, the polemical-philosophical and the financial-political. The originally mirrored his Hegelian-optimistic period; the second, his progressive political interests.

Marx composed many articles, pamphlets, and reports yet a couple of books in that capacity. He distributed just five books during his lifetime. Two of them were polemical, and three were political-monetary. The main, The Holy Family (1845), written in a joint effort with Engels, was a question against Marx's previous educator and Young Hegelian savant Bruno Bauer. The second was Misère de la philosophie (The Poverty of Philosophy), composed by Marx himself in French and distributed in Paris and Brussels in 1847. As its caption demonstrates, this polemical work was "An Answer to the Philosophy of Poverty by M. Proudhon."

Marx's third book, The Eighteenth Brumaire of Louis Bonaparte, distributed sequentially in a German distribution in New York City in 1852, is a splendid authentic political examination of the ascent and interests of the Bonaparte who became Napoleon III. The excess two books, both on financial aspects, are the ones on which Marx's overall standing rests: Critique of Political Economy and, all the more especially, Das Kapital (Capital).

Scrutinize was distributed in 1859, after around 14 years of discontinuous exploration. Marx thought of it as simply a first portion, hoping to draw out extra volumes, however, he rejected his arrangement for another methodology. The outcome was Das Kapital, captioned Critique of Political Economy, of which just the main volume showed up, in 1867, in the course of Marx's life. After his demise, two different volumes were brought out by Engels based on the materials Marx left behind. Volumes 2 (1885) and 3 (1894) can be appropriately viewed as works by Marx and Engels, rather than by Marx himself. For sure, without Engels, as Marx conceded, the entire fantastic venture probably won't have been delivered by any stretch of the imagination. The evening of August 16, 1867, when Marx finished rectifying the evidence sheets of volume 1, he kept in touch with Engels in Manchester: "I have you alone to thank that this has been made conceivable. Without your penances, for me, I would never perhaps have accomplished the huge work for the three volumes. I embrace you, loaded with much obliged!"

The fourth volume of Das Kapital was united by Karl Kautsky after Engels' demise. It depended on Marx's notes and materials from Critique of Political Economy and was distributed in three sections, under the title Theories of Surplus Value, somewhere in the range of 1905 and 1910. A Russian version, additionally in three sections, emerged somewhere in the range of 1954 and 1961, and an English interpretation in 1968.

Two of Marx's books were distributed post mortem. The Class Struggles in France, 1848-1850, written in 1871, showed up in 1895. It was, Engels wrote in his presentation, "Marx's first endeavor, with the guide of his realist origination, to clarify a part of contemporary history from the given financial circumstance." The second after-death work, The German Ideology, which Marx wrote as a team with Engels in 1845-1846, was not distributed in full until 1932. The book is an assault on the scholars Ludwig Andreas Feuerbach and Max Sterner and on the purported genuine communists.

The other's distributions, generally printed post mortem, comprise of pamphlets. Herr Vogt (1860) is an incensed questioning against a man named Karl Vogt, whom Marx blamed for being a police spy. Wage-Labour and Capital (1884) is are reproduction of paper articles. Scrutinize of the Gotha Program (1891) comprises of notes which Marx shipped off the German Socialist faction congress in 1875. Wages, Price, and Profit (1898) is a location that Marx conveyed at the General Council of the International in 1865.

His ideas

Marx's real significance doesn't lie in his financial framework, which, as pundits call attention to, was not unique but rather was gotten from the old-style market analysts Adam Smith and David Ricardo. Das Kapital, for sure, isn't principally a specialized work on financial aspects however one that utilizes monetary materials to layout a moral-philosophical-humanistic construction. Marx's widespread allure lies in his ethical way to deal with social-monetary issues, in his bits of knowledge into the connections among establishments and values, and in his origination of the salvation of humanity. Thus, Marx is best perceived if one examination, not his financial aspects, but rather his hypothesis of history and governmental issues.

The focal thought in Marx's thinking is the materialistic origination of history. This includes two fundamental thoughts: that the financial framework at some random time decides the overarching thoughts; and that set of experiences is a continuous cycle controlled foreordained by the monetary establishments which develop in ordinary stages.

The principal idea flipped around Hegel. In Hegel's view, not entirely settled by the general thought (God), which shapes common organizations. Marx formed the opposite: that organizations shape thoughts. This is known as the materialistic translation of history. Marx's subsequent thought, that of authentic development, is associated with his idea of rationalizations. He found in history a proceeding with a rationalistic cycle, each progressive phase being the result of the proposal, direct opposite, and blend.

Accordingly, postulation compares to the antiquated, pre-capitalist period, when there were no classes or double-dealing. Absolute opposite compares to the time of free enterprise and works double-dealing. Union is the eventual outcome of socialism, under which capital would be possessed in like manner and there would be no double-dealing.

To Marx, free enterprise is the last phase of recorded advancement before socialism. The low class, created by private enterprise, is the last recorded class. The two are destined to be in the struggle the class battle, which Marx broadcasted so articulately in the Communist Manifesto until the low class is definitely triumphant and lays out a temporary request, the lowly fascism, a political framework which Marx didn't intricate or clarify. The lowly autocracy, thus, advances into socialism, or the tactless society, the last phase of verifiable turn of events, when there are no classes, no abuse, and no imbalances. The consistent ramifications is that with the last foundation of socialism, history reaches an unexpected conclusion. The rationalistic cycle then, at that point, probably stops, and there are not any more recorded developments or social battles. This Marxist understanding of history, with its last idealistic prophetically catastrophic vision, has been condemned in the non-communist world as generally erroneous, experimentally unsound, and intelligently ludicrous.

All things considered, Marx's message of a natural heaven has furnished millions with trust and new significance of life. Starting here of view, one might concur with the Austrian financial expert Joseph A. Schumpeter that "Communism is a religion" and Marx is its "prophet."

His Death

In his last years, Karl Marx was in imaginative and actual decay. He invested energy at wellbeing spas and was profoundly bothered by the demise of his better half, in 1881, and one of his little girls. He kicked the bucket on 14 March 1883 and was covered at Highgate Cemetery in London.

CHAPTER TWENTY-ONE

VLADIMIR LENIN

Dear Comrades, you have overthrown the tyrannical king by your heroism. However, this success cannot be considered complete. Tsar's power is taken over by the bosses and the peasants. They support the exploitation of the poor by the rich. They will continue to wage war with the intention of plundering other nations. They must be removed from power and working people come to power. Socialism is the only solution. Keep moving forward. The Russian workers' revolution aimed at overthrowing the Tsar had brought employers and peasants to power. Lenin then came to Russia immediately from abroad. The revolutionary speech addressed to the millions of workers and people who had gathered in his former city of Petrograd. These are the words that laid the foundation for an epoch-making revolution that revolutionized the long-term rules of the globe. Basically, the history of human society is full of armed revolutions and paper revolutions. The revolution that took place in Russia was the shattering of the norms that had been the norm for the revolution for so long. The practice of mobilizing the army as a revolution to fight and win against the state changed then. Workers and peasants took up arms and overthrew the state. The world's first socialist state was formed. Vladimir Lenin was the driving force behind this revolution. The socialist, who has been seen as a parasite for centuries, after disappeared.

Vladimir Ilich Ulyanov was brought into the world on April 10, 1870, Simbirsk, Russia-kicked the bucket January 21, 1924, Gorki [later Gorki Leninskiye], close to Moscow), author of the Russian Communist Party (Bolsheviks), inspirer and head of the Bolshevik Revolution (1917), and the draftsman, developer, and first head (1917-24) of the Soviet state. He was the author of the association known as Comintern (Communist International) and the after-death wellspring of "Leninism," the teaching systematized and conjoined with Karl Marx's works by Lenin's replacements to shape Marxism-Leninism, which turned into the Communist perspective.

Revolution

The distinctions among Lenin and the Mensheviks became more honed in the Revolution of 1905 and its fallout, when Lenin moved to a particularly unique view on two issues: class arrangements in the unrest and the personality of the post-progressive system.

The flare-up of the upheaval, in January 1905, tracked down Lenin abroad in Switzerland, and he didn't get back to Russia until November. Promptly Lenin put down a clever methodology. The two wings of the RSDWP, Bolshevik and Menshevik, stuck to Plekhanov's perspective on the upheaval in two phases: initial, an average transformation; second, a lowly unrest. In any case, the Mensheviks contended that the common transformation should be driven by the bourgeoisie, with whom the working class should align itself to make the vote-based upset. This would carry the liberal bourgeoisie to full power, whereupon the RSDWP would go about as the party of resistance. Lenin's resistant dismissed this sort of coalition and post-progressive system. Until recently he had talked about the requirement for the low class to win "authority" in the vote-based transformation. Presently he straight announced that the low class was the main impetus of the upset and that its just dependable partner was the proletariat. The bourgeoisie he marked as miserably traditionalist and too apprehensive to even consider making its own upset. Subsequently, dissimilar to the Mensheviks, Lenin consequently bets on a partnership that would lay out a "progressive popularity-based tyranny of the working class and the proletariat."

Nor would the upset fundamentally stop at the primary stage, the middle-class upheaval. Assuming that the Russian insurgency ought to motivate the western European working class to make the Socialist upheaval, for which modern Europe was ready, the Russian upset may well ignore straightforwardly to the subsequent stage, the Socialist transformation. Then, at that point, the Russian working class, upheld by the rustic working class and semi-working class at home and helped by the victorious modern working class of the West, which had laid out its "autocracy of the low class," could stop the life expectancy of Russian private enterprise.

After the loss of the Revolution of 1905, the issue among Lenin and the Mensheviks was more obviously drawn than any time in recent memory, regardless of endeavours at the get-together. However, constrained again in banishment from 1907 to 1917, Lenin found genuine difficulties to his approaches from the Mensheviks as well as inside his own group also. The blend of constraint and the unassuming change affected by the tsarist system prompted a decrease of party participation. Bafflement and hopelessness in the possibilities of effective insurgency cleared the dwindled party positions, lease by debates over strategies and reasoning. Endeavors to join the Bolshevik and Menshevik groups failed miserably, all breaking on Lenin's die-hard demand that his circumstances for reunification be embraced. As one Menshevik adversary portrayed Lenin: "There could be no other man who is consumed by the upset 24 hours per day, who has no different musings except for the prospect of insurgency, and who in any event, when he does, fantasies about only transformation." Placing upheaval above party solidarity, Lenin would acknowledge no solidarity compromise assuming that he figured it may delay, not speed up, unrest.

Frantically battling to keep up with the union of the Bolsheviks against inside contrasts and the Mensheviks' becoming stronger at home, Lenin gathered the Bolshevik Party Conference at Prague, in 1912, which split the RSDWP for eternity. Lenin declared that the Bolsheviks were the RSDWP and that the Mensheviks were schismatics. From there on, every group kept up with its different focal board of trustees, party contraption, and press.

Whenever war broke out, in August 1914, Socialist factions all through Europe mobilized behind their legislatures in spite of the goals of pre war congresses of the Second International obliging them to oppose or even defeat their individual state-run administrations assuming that they dove their nations into a radical conflict.

After Lenin recuperated from his underlying incredulity in this "disloyalty" of the International, he broadcasted an arrangement whose daringness dazed his own Bolshevik friends. He condemned the favourable to war Socialists as "social-chauvinists" who had deceived the worldwide common reason by the help of a conflict that was a settler on the two sides. He articulated the Second International as dead and pursued for the production of a new, Third International made out of truly progressive Socialist factions. All the more promptly, progressive Socialists should attempt to "change the radical conflict into common conflict." The genuine adversary of the laborer was not the specialist in the contrary channel but rather the industrialist at home. Laborers and fighters ought to accordingly turn their firearms on their rulers and annihilate the framework that had dived them into colonialist savagery.

Lenin's approach tracked down a couple of supporters in Russia or somewhere else in the principal months of the conflict. Without a doubt, in the primary flush of devoted enthusiasm, not a couple of Bolsheviks upheld the conflict exertion. Lenin and his nearest confidants were left a disconnected band going against the flow.

Lenin prevailed with regards to arriving at unbiased Switzerland in September 1914, there joining a little gathering of against war Bolshevik and Menshevik émigrés. The conflict essentially cut them off from all contact with Russia and with similar Socialists in different nations. By the by, in 1915 and 1916, against war Socialists in different nations figured out how to hold two enemies of war meetings in Zimmerwald and Kienthal, Switzerland. Lenin fizzled at the two gatherings to convince his companions to embrace his trademark: "change the radical conflict into common conflict!" They took on rather the safer recipe: "A quick harmony without additions or repayments and the right of the people groups to self-assurance." Lenin thusly tracked down his party a minority inside the gathering of against war Socialists, who, thusly, established a little minority of the global Socialist development contrasted and the supportive of war Socialists.

Unflinching, Lenin kept on pounding home his perspectives on the conflict, sure that in the long run, he would win definitive help. In his Imperialism, the Highest Stage of Capitalism (1917), he set off to clarify, first, the genuine reasons for the conflict; second, why Socialists had deserted internationalism for positive energy and upheld the conflict; and third, why unrest alone could achieve an equitable, vote based harmony.

War ejected, he composed, due to the voracious, expansionist person of colonialism, itself a result of restraining infrastructure finance free enterprise. Toward the finish of the nineteenth century, a small bunch of banks had come to overwhelm the high-level nations, which, by 1914, had in their individual realms brought otherworld under their immediate or circuitous controls. Accumulating tremendous amounts of "excess" capital, the goliath banks observed they could collect super profits on interests in states and semi-provinces, and this strengthened the race for realm among the incredible powers. By 1914, disappointed with the manner in which the world had been shared out, rival alliances of colonialists sent off the conflict to achieve a division of the world to the detriment of the other alliance. The conflict was consequently settler in its starting points and points and merited the judgment of veritable Socialists.

Communist Party and worker's organization chiefs had energized to help their separate settler legislatures since they addressed the "work nobility," the better-paid laborers who got a little portion of the provincial "super profits" the colonialists proffered them. "Paid off" by the settlers, the "work privileged" took the side of their paymasters in the radical conflict and sold out the most taken advantage of laborers at home and the super-taken advantage of in the states. The colonialists, Lenin fought, driven by an annexationist dynamic, couldn't close an equitable, enduring harmony. Future conflicts were unavoidable inasmuch as government existed; colonialism was inescapable insofar as free enterprise existed; just the defeat of free enterprise wherever could end the settler war and forestall such conflicts later on. First distributed in Russia in 1917, Imperialism right up 'til the present time gives the instrument that Communists wherever utilize to assess significant patterns in the non-Communist world.

Leadership in the Russian Revolution

By 1917 Lenin couldn't help thinking that the conflict could continue forever and that the possibility of unrest was quickly subsiding. Yet, in the seven days stretch of March 8-15, the destitute, freezing, war-exhausted specialists and troopers of Petrograd (until 1914, St. Petersburg) prevailed with regards to dismissing the Tsar. Lenin and his nearest lieutenants rushed home after the German specialists consented to allow their section through Germany to impartial Sweden. Berlin trusted that the arrival of hostile to war Socialists to Russia would sabotage the Russian conflict exertion.

Lenin showed up in Petrograd on April 16, 1917, one month after the Tsar had been compelled to surrender. Out of the insurgency was conceived the Provisional Government, framed by a gathering of heads of the average liberal gatherings. This present government's increase to drive was made conceivable simply by the consent of the Petrograd Soviet, a chamber of laborers' appointees chose in the manufacturing plants of the capital. Comparative soviets of laborers' delegates jumped up in every one of the significant urban areas and towns all through the nation, as did soviets of fighters' agents and of workers' appointees. Albeit the Petrograd Soviet had been the sole political power perceived by the progressive laborers and fighters in March 1917, its chiefs had quickly surrendered full capacity to the Provisional Government. The Petrograd Soviet was going by a larger part made out of Menshevik and Socialist Revolutionary (SR), or worker party, pioneers who respected the March (February, O.S.) Revolution as common; henceforth, they accepted that the new system ought to be going by heads of the average gatherings.

On his re-visitation of Russia, Lenin zapped his own confidants, the greater part of whom acknowledged the power of the Provisional Government. Lenin called this administration, regardless of its vote-based assumptions, completely settler and undeserving of help by Socialists. It was unequipped for fulfilling the most significant cravings of the specialists, officers, and laborers for guaranteed harmony and division of landed domains among the workers.

Just a soviet government that is, immediate rule by laborers, fighters, and workers could satisfy these requests. Thusly, he raised the call to war, "All capacity to the Soviets!" albeit the Bolsheviks actually comprised a minority inside the soviets and regardless of the manifest reluctance of the Menshevik-SR greater part to exercise such power. This presented what Lenin called the time of "double power." Under the initiative of "entrepreneur" Socialists, the soviets, the genuine power, had surrendered capacity to the Provisional Government, the ostensible power in the land. The Bolsheviks, Lenin admonished, should convince the specialists, workers, and warriors, briefly deluded by the "entrepreneurs," to recover state power for the Soviets from the Provisional Government. This would comprise a subsequent upheaval. Be that as it may, inasmuch as the public authority didn't stifle the progressive gatherings, this insurgency could be accomplished calmly, since the Provisional Government existed simply by the fortitude of the soviets.

At first, Lenin's kindred Bolsheviks felt that he was briefly muddled by the intricacy of the circumstance; moderate Socialists thought him frantic. It required half a month of diligent influence by Lenin before he won the Bolshevik Party Central Committee to his view. The April Party Conference embraced his program: the party should keep support from the Provisional Government and win a greater part in the soviets for soviet power. A soviet government, once settled, should start prompt arrangements for an overall tranquillity on all fronts. The soviets should forthwith take property managers' homes without pay, nationalize all land, and split it between the laborers. Also, the public authority ought to lay out close powers over the exclusive industry to the advantage of work.

From March to September 1917, the Bolsheviks stayed a minority in the soviets. By harvest time, nonetheless, the Provisional Government had lost famous help. Expanding war exhaustion and the breakdown of the economy overburdened the tolerance of the specialists, laborers, and troopers, who requested quick and central change. Lenin profited by the developing frustration of individuals with Kerensky's capacity and eagerness to finish the transformation. Kerensky, thusly, guaranteed that main an unreservedly chosen constituent get together would have the ability to choose Russia's political future yet that should anticipate the arrival of request. In the interim, Lenin and the party requested harmony, land, and bread quickly, immediately. The Bolshevik line won expanding support among the laborers, officers, and workers. By September they casted a ballot in a Bolshevik greater part in the Petrograd Soviet and in the soviets of the significant urban areas and towns all through the country.

Lenin, who had gone underground in July after he had been denounced as a "German specialist" by Kerensky's administration, presently concluded that that was the ideal opportunity to hold onto power. The party should quickly start arrangements for an equipped uprising to oust the Provisional Government and move state capacity to the soviets, presently headed by a Bolshevik greater part.

Lenin's choice to layout soviet power got from his conviction that the ordinary insurgency should crush the current state hardware and present a "fascism of the working class"; that is, immediate rule by the furnished laborers and laborers which would ultimately "shrink away" into a non-coercive, boorish, stateless, Communist society. He clarified this view most sharply in his leaflet The State and Revolution, composed while he was still sequestered from everything. The pamphlet, however never finished and frequently excused as Lenin's most "Idealistic" work, all things considered filled in as Lenin's doctrinal springboard to control.

Until 1917 all progressive Socialists properly accepted, Lenin composed, that a parliamentary republic could serve a Socialist framework as well as an industrialist. In any case, the Russian Revolution had delivered a novel, new thing, the soviets. Made by laborers, officers, and workers and barring the propertied classes, the soviets boundlessly outperformed the fairest of parliaments in vote-based system, since parliaments wherever practically avoided laborers and workers. The decision before Russia toward the beginning of September 1917, from Lenin's perspective, was either a soviet republic a tyranny of the propertyless larger part or a parliamentary republic from his perspective, an autocracy of the propertied minority.

Lenin thusly raised the trademark, "All capacity to the Soviets!", despite the fact that he had enthusiastically yielded in the spring of 1917 that progressive Russia was the "freest of the multitude of aggressive nations." To Lenin, nonetheless, the Provisional Government was simply a "tyranny of the bourgeoisie" that kept Russia in the radical conflict. Likewise, it had turned transparently traditionalist in the long stretch of July when it blamed the Bolshevik chiefs for injustice.

From late September, Lenin, a criminal in Finland, sent a flood of articles and letters to Petrograd hotly urging the Party Central Committee to put together an equipped uprising immediately. The lucky second may be lost. Be that as it may, for almost a month Lenin's intense urgings from a far distance were ineffective. As in April, Lenin again ended up in the party minority. He turned to a frantic trick.

Around October 20, Lenin, in mask and at impressive individual danger, slipped into Petrograd and went to a mystery meeting of the Bolshevik Central Committee hung on the evening of October 23. Not until following a warmed 10-hour banter did he at long last win a greater part for setting up a furnished takeover. Presently steps to enroll the help of fighters and mariners and to prepare the Red Guards, the Bolshevik-drove laborers' state army, for an outfitted takeover continued straightforwardly all the while intending to mislead and misdirect. However, arrangements moved slowly, in light of the fact that genuine resistance to the pivotal choice endured in the Central Committee. Energetically as per Lenin on the idealness of a furnished uprising, Trotsky drove its readiness from his essential situation as recently chose director of the Petrograd Soviet. Lenin, presently stowing away in Petrograd and unfortunate of additional lingering, frantically squeezed the Central Committee to fix an early date for the uprising. On the evening of November 6, he composed a letter to the individuals from the Central Committee urging them to continue that very evening to capture the individuals from the Provisional Government. To postpone would be "lethal." The Second All-Russian Congress of Soviets, booked to gather the following evening, ought to be put before a done deal.

On November 7 and 8, the Bolshevik-drove Red Guards and progressive officers and mariners, meeting just slight obstruction, removed the Provisional Government and declared that state power had passed under the control of the Soviets. At this point, the Bolsheviks, with their partners among the Left SR's (protesters who broke with the favourable to Kerensky SR pioneers), comprised a flat-out larger part of the Second All-Russian Congress of Soviets. The representatives consequently casted a ballot predominantly to acknowledge full power and chose Lenin as an executive of the Council of People's Commissars, the new Soviet Government, and endorsed his Peace Decree and Land Decree. Short-term, Lenin had vaulted from his safe-house as a criminal to head the Revolutionary administration of the biggest country on the planet. Since his childhood he had gone through his time on earth assembling a party that would win such a triumph, and presently at 47 years old he and his party had won. "It blows one's mind," he admitted. Be that as it may, power neither inebriated nor terrified Lenin; it cleared his head. Calmly, he controlled the Soviet government toward the union of its power and exchanges for harmony.

In the two circles, Lenin was tormented by breaks inside the positions of Bolshevik pioneers. He hesitantly concurred with the conservatives that it would be alluring to remember the Menshevik and Right SR parties for an alliance government however based on Lenin's conditions. They should most importantly acknowledge the soviet type of government, not a parliamentary one; they rejected it. Just the Left SRs concurred, and a few were remembered for the Soviet government. Similarly, when the uninhibitedly chosen Constituent Assembly met in January 1918, the Mensheviks and Right SR greater part straight dismissed sovietism. Lenin without a second thought arranged the dispersal of the Constituent Assembly.

The Allies would not perceive the Soviet government; thusly it entered alone into harmonious dealings with the Central Powers (Germany and her partners Austro-Hungary and Turkey) at the town of Brest-Litovsk. They forced ruinous circumstances that would strip away from Soviet Russia the western level of non-Russian countries of the old Russian Empire. Left Communists fanatically went against acknowledgment and lectured a progressive conflict, regardless of whether it endangered the Soviet government. Lenin demanded that the terms, but ruinous and embarrassing, should be acknowledged or he would leave the public authority. He detected that harmony was the most profound longing of individuals; regardless, the broke armed force couldn't raise viable protection from the trespasser. At last, in March 1918, after a still bigger part had been cut out of old Russia by the foe, Lenin prevailed with regards to winning the Central Committee's acknowledgment of the Treaty of Brest-Litovsk. Finally, Russia found a sense of contentment.

Yet, Brest-Litovsk just heightened the assurance of traditionalist powers and the Allies who upheld them to achieve the defeat of the Soviet government. That assurance solidified when, in 1918, Lenin's administration disavowed reimbursements of all unfamiliar credits acquired by the tsarist and Provisional states and nationalized unfamiliar properties in Russia without remuneration. From 1918 to 1920 Russia was torn by a Civil War, which cost a huge number of lives and untold annihilation. Perhaps the earliest casualty was Lenin himself. In August 1918 a professional killer shot two slugs into Lenin as he left an industrial facility in which he had recently conveyed a discourse. On account of his vigorous constitution, he recuperated quickly.

The Soviet government confronted colossal chances. The counter Soviet powers, or Whites, headed mostly by previous tsarist officers and naval commanders, battled frantically to topple the red system. Besides, the Whites were richly provided by the Allies with materiel, cash, and backing troops that got White bases. However, the Whites fizzled.

It was generally a direct result of Lenin's roused authority that the Soviet government figured out how to get by against such military chances. He caused the development and directed the system of the Workers' and Peasants' Red Army, told by Trotsky. Albeit the economy had imploded, he figured out how to assemble adequate assets to support the Red Army and the modern laborers. In any case, overall, it was his political initiative that made all the difference for the Soviets. By declaring the right of the people groups to self-assurance, including the right to severance, he won the dynamic compassion, or if nothing else the altruistic non-partisanship, of the non-Russian identities inside Russia, on the grounds that the Whites didn't perceive that right. For sure, his keen, talented arrangement on the public inquiry empowered Soviet Russia to stay away from absolute deterioration and to stay an immense global state. By making the modern laborers the new advantaged class, inclined toward in the conveyance of proportions, lodging, and political power, he held the devotion of the working class. His advocating of the workers' interest that they take all the land from the upper class, church, and crown without remuneration prevailed upon the laborers, without whose help the public authority couldn't get by.

Due to the breakdown of the economy, in any case, Lenin took on an arrangement toward the laborer that took steps to annihilate the Soviet government. Lacking assets or merchandise to trade against grain expected to take care of the Red Army and the towns, Lenin established a procedure for demanding grain overflows without pay. Numerous laborers opposed essentially until they encountered White "freedom." On the domains that the Whites won, they re-established landed property to the past proprietors and viciously rebuffed the workers who had tried to hold onto the land. Regardless of the workers' loathing of the Soviet's grain demand, the laborers, when compelled to pick either Reds or Whites, picked the Reds.

After the loss of the Whites, the laborers no longer needed to settle on that decision. They currently completely wouldn't give up their grain to the public authority. Undermined by mass worker disobedience, Lenin called a retreat. In March 1921 the public authority presented the New Economic Policy, which finished the arrangement of grain demanding and allowed the laborer to sell his collection on an open market. This established a halfway retreat to private enterprise.

From the second Lenin came to drive, his standing points in worldwide relations were twofold: to forestall the arrangement of a settler joined front against Soviet Russia; be that as it may, considerably more significant, to animate common upsets abroad.

In his first point, he to a great extent succeeded. In 1924, soon after his demise, Soviet Russia had won by law acknowledgment of the relative multitude of significant world powers with the exception of the United States. In any case, his more prominent any desire for the development of a world republic of soviets neglected to emerge, and Soviet Russia was left detached in antagonistic entrepreneur enclosure.

Formation of the Third International

To break this encompassing, he had approached progressives to frame Communist coalitions that would copy the case of the Bolshevik Revolution in all nations. Sensationalizing his break with the reformist Second International, in 1918 he had changed the name of the RSDWP to the Russian Communist Party (Bolsheviks), and in March 1919 he established the Communist, or Third, International. This International acknowledged the association just of gatherings that acknowledged its choices as restricting, forced iron discipline, and made a total separation with the Second International. In total, Lenin presently held up the Russian Communist Party, the main party that had made an effective upset, as the model for Communist factions in all nations. One consequence of this arrangement was to cause a split on the planet work development between the followers of the two internationals.

The Communist International scored its most prominent achievement in the provincial world. By advocating the privileges of the people groups in the provinces and semi-settlements to self-assurance and autonomy, the International won extensive compassion toward Communism. Lenin's approach in this question actually resounds through this present reality. Furthermore, it offers one more illustration of Lenin's special capacity to find partners where progressives had not tracked down them previously. By taking the side of the public freedom developments, Lenin could guarantee that by far most of the total populace, then, at that point, living under the colonialist rule, as well as the European low class, were the regular partners of the Bolshevik Revolution.

In this way, Lenin's progressive virtuoso was not bound to his capacity to partition his foes; more significant was his ability in tracking down partners and companions for the exiguous low class of Russia. To begin with, he won the Russian laborers to the side of the working class. Second, while he didn't win the laborers to make effective Communist upsets in the West, they constrained their legislatures to reduce outfitted mediation against the Bolshevik Revolution. Third, while the Asian transformations scarcely blended in the course of his life, they reinforced the Soviet Communists in the conviction that they were in good company in a threatening world.

By 1921 Lenin's administration hosted squashed all resistance gatherings because they had gone against or neglected to help adequately the Soviet reason in the Civil War. Since harmony had come, Lenin accepted that their resistance was more hazardous than any time in recent memory, since the proletariat and surprisingly an enormous segment of the middle class had become offended with the Soviet system. To subdue adversaries of Bolshevism, Lenin requested the most extreme measures, including "show" preliminaries and continuous hotel to capital punishment. In addition, he demanded significantly more tight command over contradict inside the party. Lenin's emphasis on pitiless obliteration of the resistance to the Bolshevik fascism in this manner drove numerous spectators to reason that Lenin, however actually went against to one-man rule, by the by accidentally got the way for the ascent free from Joseph Stalin's tyranny.

By 1922 Lenin had become definitely mindful that degeneration of the Soviet framework and party was the most serious risk to the reason for Socialism in Russia. He observed the party and Soviet state mechanical assembly horrendously caught informality and ineptitude. Indeed, even the office headed by Stalin that was answerable for smoothing out organization was, truth be told, less proficient than the remainder of the public authority. The Soviets of Workers' and Peasants' Deputies had been depleted of all power, which had streamed to the middle. Most upsetting was the Great Russian haughtiness that driving Bolsheviks appeared toward the non-Russian ethnicities in the redesign of the state wherein Stalin was assuming a key part. Also, in April 1922 Stalin won an arrangement as broad secretary of the party, in which post he was quickly packing gigantic power in his grasp. Soviet Russia in Lenin's last years could never have been additional remote from the image of Socialism he had depicted in State and Revolution. Lenin stressed each nerve to switch these patterns, which he viewed as contradictory to Socialism, and to supplant Stalin.

His Death

In the spring of 1922, be that as it may, Lenin fell truly sick. In April his PCPs extricated from his neck one of the projectiles he had gotten from the professional killer's weapon in August 1918. He recuperated quickly from the activity, however after a month he became sick, to some degree incapacitated and unfit to talk. In June he made an incomplete recuperation and hurled himself entirely into the development of the Union of Soviet Socialist Republics, the government arrangement of rearrangement he inclined toward against Stalin's unitary plan. Be that as it may, in December he was again crippled by semi paralysis. Albeit as of now not the dynamic head of the state and party, he gathered the solidarity to direct a few perceptive articles and what is called his political "Confirmation," directed to his secretary between December 23, 1922, and January 4, 1923, in which he communicated an incredible dread for the strength of the party under the initiative of divergent, powerful characters like Stalin and Trotsky. On March 10, 1923, another stroke denied him of discourse. His political movement reached a conclusion. He endured one more stroke on the morning of Jan. 21, 1924, and kicked the bucket that evening in the town of Gorki (presently known as Gorki Leninskiye).

The last year of Lenin's political life, when he battled to destroy maltreatments of his Socialist goals and the defilement of force, may well have been his most noteworthy. Regardless of whether the historical backdrop of the Soviet Union would have been on a very basic level different had he made due past his 54th birthday celebration, nobody can say with assurance.

CHAPTER TWENTY-TWO

JOSEPH STALIN

Who contributed to the victory of the Allies in World War II? Hitler, the world's most condemned man, has run away. Who made Russia self-sufficient in education, medicine, and the economy? Who killed communists for claiming to be artisans? The story of a dictator named Stalin.

Stalin enters the Arbor Squad surrounded by colleagues. The crowd applauds when they see Stalin. Stalin sits with a thin smile and shakes his hand in a dictatorial pose. The crowd calms down. Children line up praising Lenin and Stalin. Among them was Engelsina Markizova, who stood in the evening meeting that day and wondered about Stalin as a child. After listening to Markizova, Stalin hugs her and kisses her. The next day the newspaper published a photo of baby Markizova Stalin all over and portrayed her as a heroine to the people of Russia. Sculptures of Stalin Markizova are placed all over Russia. This happiness did not last even a few days for that child. Markizova's family is falling apart. The reason was that Stalin had ordered the arrest of Markizova's father as a spy. If the little Markizova senile dies in that agony without finally seeing his father's face.

In 1941, houses in Mexico are bombed next to the room of the old man who is writing an article for the next day's newspaper. The bewildered family is huddled in a corner of the room, lifeless. The man who thought he had killed the old man fled the scene. Regardless of the joy of survival, the old man sits back in his chair and continues to write the next day's article. The article was published. The man who wondered how the article of the old man, who thought he had been killed was published, this time descends on the old man who can trust the axe, not the gun. The man strikes the old man on the head with an axe and moves slowly from there into the darkness.

Who is Stalin? How did he become a dictator? We will see her timeline...!

1879

He is brought into the world on 18 December 1879 in Gori, Georgia in the Russian domain. He is first named Iosif (Joseph) Vissarionovich Dzhugashvili. Joseph experiences childhood in neediness. His mom is a washerwoman and his dad is a shoemaker. He gets little pox matured seven and is left with a scarred face and a marginally twisted left arm. He is harassed by different youngsters and feels a constant need to substantiate himself. His dad is a heavy drinker who arrangements out ordinary beatings. As youthful Joseph grows up, Georgia's heartfelt fables and against Russian practices catch his creative mind.

1899

Joseph's strict mother needs him to be a cleric and in 1895 sends him to study in Tiflis, the Georgian capital. Be that as it may, Joseph rebels and on second thought of concentrating on sacred text he peruses the mysterious works of Karl Marx and joins a neighbourhood communist gathering. He dedicates quite a bit of his chance to the progressive development against the Russian government and loses interest in his investigations. Conflicting with his mom's desires, Joseph turns into an agnostic and as often as possible contends with the ministers. In 1899 he is at long last tossed out of the theological college subsequent to neglecting to go up to his tests.

1901

While functioning as a representative at the Meteorological Observatory, Joseph continues with his progressive exercises, sorting out strikes and fights. His exercises become known to the Tsarist mystery police and he is compelled to go underground. He joins the Bolshevik party and directs close-quarters combat without precedent for the 1905 Russian Revolution. His first gathering with Lenin, the Bolshevik chief, is at a party meeting in Finland. Lenin is dazzled by this 'savage underground administrator'. In 1907 Joseph takes 250,000 rubbles (roughly $3.4m in US dollars) in a bank burglary in Tiflis to assist with subsidizing the reason.

1907

Joseph weds his first spouse KetevanSvanidze in 1906. She comes from a helpless group of minor honourabilities. Ketevan brings forth their child Yakov Dzhugashvili the next year. After the Tiflis bank burglary, Joseph and his family get away from Tsarist powers by venturing out to Baku in Azerbaijan. Whenever Ketevan passes on from typhus in 1907, Joseph is wracked with pain. He passes on his child to be really focused on by his in-laws and hurls himself entirely into his progressive work. He embraces the name 'Stalin' which signifies 'steel' in Russian. He is captured on various events and banished to Siberia in 1910.

1917

Lenin sorts out the Russian Revolution and guarantees "harmony, land, and bread". Stalin assumes a vital part by running Pravda, the Bolshevik paper. He is hailed as a legend when he assists Lenin with getting away from the Tsar's military into Finland and is delegated to the internal circle of the Bolshevik party. At the point when the Tsar has overturned the nation drops into common conflict. Stalin, as other the hardliners inside the party, orders the public execution of weaklings and rebels. Whenever Lenin takes power, he chooses Stalin to be General Secretary of the Communist Party. Stalin acquires new abilities filling in as a go-between for authorities all through the party.

1929

After Lenin's demise in 1924, Stalin starts heartlessly advancing himself as his political beneficiary. Numerous in the party anticipates that Red Army pioneer Leon Trotsky should be Lenin's regular replacement, yet his thoughts are excessively optimistic for most of the Communist Party. Stalin, nonetheless, fosters his own nationalistic image of Marxism - "Communism in One Country" - focusing on fortifying the Soviet Union rather than world insurgency. Whenever Trotsky condemns his arrangements, Stalin has him banished. Stalin's thoughts are famous with the party and by the last part of the 1920s he becomes a tyrant of the Soviet Union.

1928-1938

In the last part of the 1920s Stalin induces a progression of five-year intends to transform the Soviet Union into an advanced industrialized country. He is worried about the possibility that in the event that the Soviet Union doesn't modernize then Communism will fizzle and the nation will be annihilated by its entrepreneur neighbours. He accomplishes tremendous expansions in coal, oil, and steel efficiency and the nation sees huge monetary development. His arrangements are savagely authorized - plants are given severe targets which numerous specialists find difficult to satisfy. The people who fizzle are scapegoated by a lot of people as wreckers and saboteurs and detained or executed as adversaries of the state.

1928-1940

At the point when Stalin takes power, Soviet horticulture is as yet overwhelmed by little landowners and cursed by starvations and failure. Stalin modernizes agribusiness by prompting collectivisation - the gathering of homesteads to be claimed by the state. It is gone against by a great many customary ranchers who resort to killing domesticated animals and furtively storing grain. Around 5,000,000 kicks the bucket in a progression of starvations. By the by, Stalin accepts the end legitimizes the means and a great many little holders are killed or detained. By the last part of the 1930s cultivating is completely collectivized and efficiency increments.

1934-1939

Stalin advances a picture of himself as an incredibly considerate pioneer and saint of the Soviet Union. However, he is progressively distrustful and cleanses the Communist coalition and Army of any individual who may go against him. 93 of the 139 Central Committee individuals are killed and 81 of the 103 officers and chiefs of naval operations are executed. The mystery police rigorously authorize Stalinism and individuals are urged to illuminate on each other. 3,000,000 individuals are blamed for restricting Communism and shipped off the gulag, an arrangement of work camps in Siberia. Around 750,000 individuals are immediately killed.

1932-1943

In 1919 Stalin weds his second spouse Nadezhda Alliluyeva and they have two kids - Svetlana and Vassily. He manhandles Nadezhda and she at last commits suicide in 1932. He ensures her passing is authoritatively announced as being brought about by a ruptured appendix. Yakov, his child from his first spouse, is a warrior in the Red Army and is caught right off the bat in WW2. At the point when the Germans propose to free him in a detainee trade, Stalin declines as he accepts his child gave up will fully, Yakov kicks the bucket in a Nazi inhumane imprisonment in 1943.

1939

Stalin signs a peace settlement with Adolf Hitler and they consent to cut up Eastern Europe between them. At the point when Hitler's militaries effectively routed France and Britain withdraws, Stalin disregards alerts from his commanders and is totally not ready for the Nazi Blitzkrieg assault of June 1941, which tears through Poland and into the Soviet Union. The Soviet Army experience immense misfortunes. Stalin is brilliant with rage at Hitler's selling out and withdraws to his office incapable to settle on any choices. Soviet Russia is incapacitated for quite some time as the Nazi conflict machine rolls on towards Moscow.

1943

With the fate of the Soviet Union in limbo, Stalin is ready to forfeit millions to accomplish triumph over the Nazis. German powers clear the nation over and by December 1941 have nearly arrived at Moscow. Stalin won't leave the city, concluding triumph should be succeeded at any expense. The Battle of Stalingrad is the defining moment of the conflict. Hitler assaults the city bearing Stalin's name to embarrass him, yet Stalin tells his military "Not a stage in reverse". They experience more than 1,000,000 losses however figure out how to overcome the Nazis in 1943. The Soviet Army starts the long opposition into Germany and the whole way to Berlin.

1946

Stalin assumes an unequivocal part in Germany's loss and extraordinary wraps of Eastern Europe are involved by Soviet powers including East Berlin. Stalin is inflexible these nations will be satellite conditions of the Soviet Union. His previous partners America and Britain currently become his opponents and Churchill expresses that an "iron shade" is falling over Europe. In a battle for control of the capital, Stalin blocks passage to partnered involved West Berlin. The US reacts with an 11-month long carrier of provisions to individuals caught in that area of the city. On 29 August 1949, the Soviet Union tests its first nuclear bomb. The Cold War starts decisively.

1953

In Stalin's last years he turns out to be progressively dubious, and keeps on directing cleanses against his foes inside the Party. Following an evening of weighty drinking Stalin passes on from a stroke on 5 March 1953. Numerous in the Soviet Union grieves the deficiency of this extraordinary pioneer who changed the Soviet Union from a primitive economy to a modern power and assumed an urgent part in overcoming Hitler. However, the large numbers detained cheer at the end of one of the most dangerous despots ever. Stalin's replacement Khrushchev decries the dead tyrant and starts a flood of "destalinization."

CHAPTER TWENTY-THREE

UNKNOWN WORLD RESOURCES

THE AFRICA RESOURCES

Africa, the second-biggest mainland, is limited by the Mediterranean Sea, the Red Sea, the Indian Ocean, and the Atlantic Ocean. It is separated in half similarly by the Equator. Africa's actual topography, climate and assets, and human geology can be thought about independently. The beginning of the name "Africa" is significantly questioned by researchers. Most accept it comes from words utilized by the Phoenicians, Greeks, and Romans. Significant words incorporate the Egyptian word Afru-ika, signifying "Homeland"; the Greek word aphrike, signifying "without cold"; and the Latin word aprica, signifying "bright."

Various variables impact Africa's radiant environment. The Equator almost divides the mainland into halves. Climatic zones lie on one or the other side of this line as though it were a mirror, with tropical wet environments nearer to the Equator and more parched circumstances nearer to the jungles.

This climatic balance is upset, nonetheless, by Africa's inconsistent shape. The mainland's tight southern segment is definitely more impacted by maritime variables than the swelling northern area. Africa's northern half is drier and more sizzling, while its southern end is more sticky and cooler.

Climate and Agriculture

Climatic factors extraordinarily impact Africa's agribusiness, which is viewed as the landmass' single most significant monetary movement.

Farming utilizes 66% of the mainland's functioning populace and contributes 20 to 60 percent of each nation's (GDP). Gross domestic product is the absolute worth of labour and products delivered in a country during one year.

Significant climatic locales of agribusiness incorporate tropical wet, savanna, desert, Mediterranean, and high country.

Tropical wet circumstances happen along the Equator, the Gulf of Guinea, and the east Madagascar coast. Temperatures stay close to 27° Celsius (80° Fahrenheit) all year. Yearly precipitation changes from 152 centimetres (60 inches) inland to 330 centimetres (130 inches) along the coasts. Significant harvests to Africa's tropical wet locales incorporate the plantain, pineapple, espresso, cocoa, and oil palms. (Oil from this palm tree is the essential cooking oil in Africa, as natural as olive oil or corn oil in North America.)

Savanna conditions happen in quite a bit of eastern and southern Africa. Temperatures here are cooler and have more variation than in tropical wet districts. Yearly precipitation is somewhere in the range of 50 and 152 centimeters (20 to 60 inches). The dry season in the savanna can keep going up to a half year. Significant savanna crops incorporate the cassava (connected with the potato), peanuts, peppers, okra, eggplant, cucumber, and watermelon. Africa's most significant grain harvests, millet and sorghum, are become here.

Desert conditions happen in northern Africa, particularly in the Sahara and the Sahel. Temperatures can go from 54° Celsius (130° F) on the most sizzling days to freezing on the coldest evenings. Yearly precipitation never surpasses 25 centimetres (10 inches), and a few regions do without downpour for a really long time. Significant desert crops incorporate date palms and cotton.

Mediterranean environment conditions happen along the super northern and southern shorelines of Africa. These districts have gentle temperatures, dry summers, and reasonably stormy winters. Significant harvests incorporate figs, olives, oranges, tomatoes, onions, and enormous vegetables, like cabbage and cauliflower.

Good country conditions happen in the most noteworthy rises of Africa, especially in the Ethiopian Highlands. Temperatures here are a lot colder than the encompassing marshes. Precipitation relies upon the direction of the mountain comparable to dampness-bearing breezes. Significant high-country crops incorporate hay, potatoes, and wheat.

Forestry and Fishing

Ranger service, the administration of trees and other vegetation in backwoods, is a significant financial movement in Africa. By and large, backwoods items represent 6% of Africa's total national output (GDP), more than some other landmass. This is an aftereffect of Africa's bountiful timberland cover, with 0.8 hectares (2 sections of land) per individual, contrasted and 0.6 hectares (1.5 sections of land) all around the world. In focal and western Africa, where backwoods cover is heaviest, the timberland area offers in excess of 60% of GDP.

The commodity of woodland items, particularly high-grade woods like mahogany and Okoume, acquires critical income. These woods are generally found in the nations of the Congo Basin Cameroon, Central African Republic, Republic of the Congo, the Democratic Republic of the Congo, Gabon, and Equatorial Guinea where there is a thick tropical jungle. Okoume, for instance, represents 90% of the trees signed in Gabon. These woods are by and large sent out to Japan, Israel, and the European Union. Mahogany and Okoume are utilized to make everything from homes to instruments to the lightweight airplane.

Africa's timberland area, in any case, experiences illicit logging and overharvesting of specific tree species. Numerous types of both mahogany and Okoume are imperiled. Specialists contend that overharvesting will ultimately obliterate woodland natural surroundings. Saplings planted to supplant the logged trees don't develop quickly to the point of being collected consistently, and the tropical jungle territory where these trees flourish is being annihilated for horticulture and improvement.

Today, Africa is conflicted between fostering its backwoods to their fullest monetary potential and shielding these regular scenes from over-improvement. For example, the Central African Forests Commission controls Africa's ranger service area and advances maintainable employments of the Congo Basin's tropical jungle items. The commission made the Sangha Tri-National Landscape, a save that covers more than 1 million hectares (2.4 million sections of land) of tropical jungle in Cameroon, the Central African Republic, and the Republic of the Congo.

Africa's fishing industry turns out revenue to in excess of 10 million individuals and has a yearly commodity worth of $2.7 billion. Africa has fisheries on the entirety of its marine coasts, as well as inland. The Great Lakes and Nile River, for example, support gigantic freshwater fisheries.

Marine fisheries are vital to numerous seaside nations in Africa. West Africa is one of the most monetarily significant fishing zones on the planet, creating 4.5 million tons of fish in 2000. Namibia and South Africa are additionally key partsof the marine fish market, trading somewhere in the range of 80 and 90 percent of their fish yearly. The Eastern African nations of Eritrea, Djibouti, Somalia, and Kenya have grounded fisheries in the Red Sea and the Indian Ocean. Little fish, for example, herring and sardines are the most well-known catch on the African shoreline. Nonetheless, bigger fish, like fish, cod, hake, and haddock, are the most productive.

Africa's broad inland fisheries contain in excess of 3,000 fish species and record for 66% of worldwide inland fish creation. Dissimilar to marine fisheries, the catch from Africa's inland fisheries isn't sent out. It is consumed primarily on the landmass, framing a significant wellspring of individuals' protein consumption.

Africa's Great Lakes support the biggest inland fisheries on the landmass. Lake Victoria is the most useful freshwater fishery on the planet, creating in excess of 500,000 tons of fish worth $600 million consistently. The Nile roost, a profoundly valued catch that can gauge in excess of 45 kilograms (100 pounds), and the Nile tilapia are Lake's Victoria's prevailing business fish species.

Similar as the ranger service area, Africa's fishing area experiences overharvesting. Thus, in the previous century, fish stocks have declined by up to half in a few beachfront zones. The Partnership for African Fisheries (PAF) is being executed to fortify Africa's fisheries area. PAF will zero in on stricter guidelines and ecological administration. These cycles will build fishery income and advance the manageable utilization of marine and inland fish assets.

Mining and Drilling

Africa is a significant maker of significant metals and minerals. Metals traded by African nations incorporate uranium, used to create thermal power; platinum, utilized in gems and modern applications; nickel, utilized in hardened steel, magnets, coins, and battery-powered batteries; bauxite, a principal aluminum metal; and cobalt, utilized in shading colors.

Africa's two most productive mineral assets are gold and precious stones. In 2008, Africa delivered around 483 tons of gold, or 22% of the world's complete creation. South Africa represents close to half of Africa's gold creation. Ghana, Guinea, Mali, and Tanzania are other significant makers of gold.

Africa overwhelms the worldwide jewel market. In 2008, the mainland created 55% of the world's jewels. Botswana, Angola, South Africa, the Democratic Republic of the Congo, and Namibia are Africa's biggest makers of precious stones.

Sadly, a few African contentions and common conflicts have been caused and supported by the precious stone industry. Precious stones that come from these locales are known as struggle jewels or blood jewels.

In 2002, the United Nations made the Kimberley Process Certification Scheme (KPCS) to guarantee jewels from sources that are liberated from the struggle. The KPCS additionally plans to keep precious stone deals from financing wars. Nations that don't meet KPCS necessities are not permitted to exchange with a significant part of the remainder of the world. The Republic of the Congo, the Democratic Republic of the Congo, and Côte d'Ivoire have all been removed sooner or later somewhat recently.

Africa is home to choose stores of oil and petroleum gas, which are penetrated for energy and fuel. In 2007, the mainland delivered 12.5 percent of the world's absolute oil creation and 6.45 percent of the world's complete gaseous petrol creation. Nigeria, Libya, Algeria, Egypt, and Angola rule Africa's oil industry. Oil investigation has altogether expanded on the mainland, and numerous nations are hoping to turn out to be first-time makers.

Oil and flammable gas creation have likewise been associated with a common clash. In Nigeria, guerrilla bunches have assaulted oil frameworks and taken oil from pipelines since the mid-1990s. These gatherings, fundamentally ethnic minorities, say unfamiliar oil organizations have taken advantage of their work while keeping the majority of the riches. They additionally charge that obsolete gear has seriously dirtied air, soil, and water assets. This contamination has prompted misfortunes in arable land and fish stocks. Notwithstanding, the serious activities of these guerrilla bunches have likewise expanded contamination as they have harmed hardware. The assaults have likewise diminished creation and neighborhood pay, as many organizations are compelled to close down.

The Built Environment

Africa's regular asset economy contributes incredibly to the landmass fabricated climate, or human-made structures and constructions. The biggest designing tasks and metropolitan regions are straightforwardly connected to the creation and exchange of assets like water, oil, and minerals. However similar to the asset economics depicted over, Africa's framework experiences helpless administration and wasteful unofficial law.

Africa is home to various designing wonders. The Aswan Dam, a complex of two dams in Aswan, Egypt, catches the world's longest stream, the Nile, on the planet's third-biggest supply, Lake Nasser. The Aswan High Dam, the more current and bigger of the two dams, creates in excess of 10 billion kilowatt-long periods of power consistently, enough power for around 15% of the country.

The Aswan Dam complex controls the flooding of the Nile and stores water for agribusiness. While farmland has expanded by 500% because of the dam, land richness has diminished. Supplement-rich sediment can't spread over the Nile valley since it is caught in Lake Nasser.

The Driefontein Gold Mine outside of Johannesburg, South Africa, is one of the biggest gold mines on the planet. The mine is comprised of eight shafts that arrive at profundities of up to 3,352 meters (11,000 feet) underground. One of the shafts is currently being developed to around 4,115 meters (13,500 feet), making it the most unimaginable mine on the planet. These outrageous profundities make mining tasks unimaginably risky at Driefontein, which has one of the most exceedingly terrible records of worker fatalities in the business.

Two metropolitan regions that show Africa's lopsided development are Lagos, Nigeria, and Johannesburg, South Africa. Both of these huge urban areas have particular monetary motors that make them great for development. Simultaneously, each deals with comparative issues because of this development.

Lagos is Africa's second most-crowded city, with a populace of around 10.2 million individuals. Lagos is growing multiple times quicker than New York City, New York, or Los Angeles, California, in the United States. The United Nations gauges that Lagos will be one of the biggest megacities on the planet by 2015.

Lagos is the business and modern center point of Nigeria, which has a total national output that is triple that of some other West African countries. Situated on the oil-rich Gulf of Guinea and neighboring the Niger Delta, Lagos is a focal point of oil extraction, refining, and commodity. The city is attached to the ascent and fall of oil costs, making patterns of outrageous riches and neediness.

Lagos' unregulated development has made a rambling and tumultuous metropolitan scene. Helpless settlers from rustic Nigeria have overflowed the city searching for financial open doors. Private zones are stuffed, averaging six individuals for every room. Ghetto people groups are developing quickly, taking over unsatisfactory regions like close by tidal ponds and lakes. Lagos experiences water deficiencies, helpless disinfection administrations, and weighty traffic. Government bodies and metropolitan designers are finding it hard to stay aware of Lagos' quick development.

Johannesburg is the biggest city in South Africa, with a metropolitan populace of in excess of 7 million. Johannesburg is additionally the world's biggest city not arranged on a stream, lake, or shoreline. The city was created around the gold and precious stone industry arranged on a mineral-rich mountain range.

While mining activities are steadily losing significance in Johannesburg, most mining organizations actually have their central command there. The riches and exchange of these organizations and other assembling businesses is upheld by Africa's biggest stock trade, the JSE (Johannesburg Stock Exchange). In that capacity, Johannesburg has turned into the monetary center point for the African landmass.

Similar to Lagos, Johannesburg's unregulated improvement has caused specific framework issues. During the most recent forty years, Johannesburg's ghetto of Hill brow has experienced a lack of foresight and an absence of venture. Hill brow is known for undeniable degrees of joblessness, neediness, and wrongdoing. Johannesburg authorities are attempting to take care of these issues by reinvesting in Hill brow's midtown organizations.

Inhabitants of Johannesburg compensate for the city's undeniable degree of joblessness by partaking in one of the world's biggest casual economies. A casual economy is now and then called a bootleg market. In a casual economy, labour and products are traded without charges, or cash going to the public authority. An enormous populace of Johannesburg, generally migrants, have become cash-just merchants who don't work for any authority element. These casual monetary exercises disapprove of work and trade guideline. Without realizing the number of individuals is utilized, how much cash they are making, or the way that they are making it, it is progressively hard to follow the city's monetary advancement.

NATURAL RESOURCES
Top minerals per country

The most abundant resource for each African country per tonne of production.

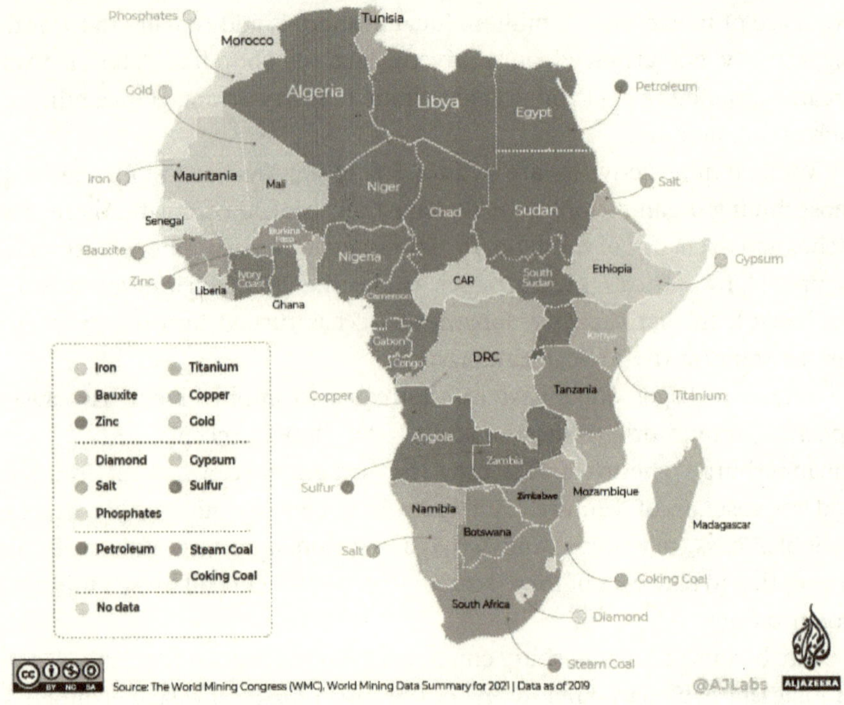

CHAPTER TWENTY-FOUR

BLACK PANTHER

Now those in the West have changed to respect blacks. The reason is that they are black or because they have no wealth or because they are enslaved without the wealth of their own. But the property value of a man who lived in Africa would not be equal to the dust of a quarter compared to the property value of the richest people in the world today.

A character in the Avengers movie that came out a few days ago would have portrayed that person as wealthier than the character of the other Avengers and his country as the richest. That character, as you now know, is a Black panther. Why show him like that. Who is the reason for the emergence of this character in the Western world where blacks are seen as slaves? None other than Mansa Musa, the prince of the empire of Mali. How much property he have like that? What is the reason why it took twelve years for his arrival in Egypt to bring their economy back to equilibrium there?

Mamoudou Gassama born in 1996, he is a Malian-French resident, living in France who, on 26 May 2018, climbed four stories on the outside of a square of pads in the eighteenth arrondissement of Paris (51 lament Marx-Dormoy) in 30 seconds to save a four-year-old kid who was dangling from an overhang. The kid's dad had obviously left the kid unattended to go out on the town to shop, and was hence accused of leaving his child solo.

Paris Mayor Anne Hidalgo referred to Gassama as "Insect Man of the eighteenth" regarding the city's eighteenth arrondissement (region) where the salvage occurred. On 28 May 2018, President Emmanuel Macron met Gassama at the Élysée Palace to say thanks to him by and by. He was granted the Médaille d'honneur pour acte de boldness et de dévouement and offered a job in the fire administration which he, therefore, took up; as of December 2018, he is working a multi month contract as an assistant. At the affectation of President Macron, Gassama was made a French resident in September 2018.

But do you really know who he is? He was a descendant of the great King Mansa Musa. But it has gone unnoticed by anyone.

What do you remember when you think of Africa with your eyes closed? Hunger, starvation, poverty are all scenes for you. But at one time Africa was a prosperous country in the world. May that country be celebrated as a treasure of the world. That is why many Western nations have colonized Africa and exploited its wealth. One of the richest men in the world came from this prosperous region of Africa. His name is Mansa Musa. Any quantity can be placed on being the richest man in the world. Money? No money is subject to change over time. A person's wealth is calculated by keeping the pleasure of the land during that period. After that gold was scaled. Because gold is common all over the world. Based on gold they calculated how much wealth a person has. This Mansa Musa is the one who bathed in gold like that. The Mali Empire was one of the three most important kingdoms in Africa at the time. The Mali Empire has founded in the year 1240 AD by the King Sundiata Keita. This king is praised in African oral literature as The Lion King. A lot of kings come to power after this monarch. After that, in the year 1300 AD, Mansa Abubakari Keita II came to power. What he has done is sail around the Atlantic Ocean to see how many more countries there are and how many more resources there will be. But the one who went did not come back. The Mali Empire was ready for the next king in the context of not knowing what he had become.

Mansa Musa is the next king of the Mali Empire. His nickname was Maghan Musa. In Mali, the Mansa is referred to as the emperor. After his inauguration, he was renamed as Mansa Musa. Mansa Musa, born in the year 1280 AD, was thirty-two years old when he became the king of the Mali Empire. The Mali Empire, which was prosperous during the reign of Mansa Musa, became super prosperous. Africa became a continental superpower. Knowing that there was still a large amount of gold on the border of the Mali Empire, Mansa Musa cut it too much. Not only that, but knowing that there is a lot of salt available there, Mansa Musa ingested more of it. He also heavily exported ivory during that period. Wealth from these three began to accumulate in large numbers in the Mali Empire. But it was not known to outside countries, only to neighbouring countries.

If only it had been known that the Mali Empire was so rich and that its king, Mansa Musa, was such a prosperous beastly king. That was when he started his journey to Mecca.

A lot of what has had some significant awareness of Musa comes from Arabic sources composed after his hajj, particularly the compositions of Al-Umari and Ibn Khaldun. While in Cairo during his hajj, Musa become friends with authorities, for example, Ibn Amir Hajib, who found out with regards to him and his country from him and later gave that data to antiquarians like Al-Umari. Extra data comes from two seventeenth century original copies written in Timbuktu, Oral practice, as performed by the jeliw otherwise called griots, incorporates generally little data about Musa contrasted with other pieces of the historical backdrop of Mali.

Traveling to Mecca

Musa was a sincere Muslim, and his journey to Mecca, otherwise called hajj, spread the word about him well across Northern Africa and the Middle East. To Musa, Islam was "a passage into the refined universe of the Eastern Mediterranean". He would have invested a lot of energy cultivating the development of the religion inside his domain.

Musa made his journey somewhere in the range of 1324 and 1325 crossing 2,700 miles. His parade allegedly included 60,000 men, all wearing brocade and Persian silk, including 12,000 slaves, who each conveyed 1.8 kg (4 lb) of gold bars, and messengers wearing silks, who bore gold staffs, coordinated ponies, and took care of packs. Musa gave all necessities to the parade, taking care of the whole organization of men and creatures. Those creatures included 80 camels which each conveyed 23-136 kg (50-300 lb) of gold residue. Musa gave the gold to the helpless he met along his course. Musa not just provided for the urban communities he gave the way to Mecca, including Cairo and Medina, yet additionally exchanged gold for trinkets. It was accounted for that he fabricated a mosque each Friday.

Musa's excursion was archived by a few observers along his course, who were in amazement of his riches and broad parade, and records exist in an assortment of sources, including diaries, oral records, and narratives. Musa is known to have visited the Mamluk ruler of Egypt, Al-Nasir Muhammad, in July 1324. Due to his tendency of giving, Musa's monstrous spending and liberal gifts made a gigantic long term gold downturn. In the urban areas of Cairo, Medina, and Mecca, the unexpected inundation of gold degraded the metal altogether. Costs of merchandise and products turned out to be significantly swelled. This slip-up became evident to Musa and coming back from Mecca, he acquired all of the gold he could convey from cash loan specialists in Cairo at an exorbitant premium. This is the main time recorded in history that one man straightforwardly controlled the cost of gold in the Mediterranean. A few history specialists accept the Hajj was less out of strict commitment than to earn worldwide consideration regarding the thriving territory of Mali. Al-Umari who visited Cairo soon after Musa's journey to Mecca, noticed that it was "a rich showcase of influence, abundance, and remarkable by its size and pomp". The making of a downturn of that greatness might have been deliberate. All things considered; Cairo was the main gold market at that point (where individuals went to buy a lot of gold). To migrate these business sectors to Timbuktu or Gao, Musa would need to initially influence Cairo's gold economy. Musa made a significant reason behind flaunting his country's abundance. His objective was to make a wave and he succeeded significantly in this, to such an extent that he landed himself and Mali on the Catalan Atlas of 1375.

During his long return venture from Mecca in 1325, Musa heard the news that his military had recovered Gao. Sagmandia, one of his officers, drove the undertaking. The city of Gao had been inside the realm since before Sakura's rule and was a significant however regularly insubordinate exchanging focus. Musa made a diversion and visited the city where he got, as prisoners, the two children of the Gao ruler, Ali Kolon, and Suleiman Nar. He got back to Niani with the two young men and later instructed them at his court. Whenever Mansa Musa returned, he brought back numerous Arabian researchers and draftsmen.

Constructions of Mansa Musa

Musa left on an enormous structure program, bringing mosques and madrasas up in Timbuktu and Gao. Most quiet, the antiquated focus of learning Sankore Madrasah (or University of Sankore) was developed during his rule.

In Niani, Musa assembled the Hall of Audience, a structure imparting by an inside way to the regal castle. It was "an excellent Monument", conquered by a vault and enhanced with arabesques of striking tones. The wooden window casings of an upper story were plated with silver foil; those of a lower story with gold. Like the Great Mosque, a contemporaneous and bombastic design in Timbuktu, the Hall was worked of cut stone.

During this period, there was a high-level degree of metropolitan living in the significant focuses of Mali. Sergio Domain, an Italian researcher of workmanship and design, composed of this period: "Hence was established the framework of a metropolitan development. At the stature of its power, Mali had somewhere around 400 urban areas, and the inside of the Niger

Delta was thickly populated.

It is recorded that Mansa Musa went through the urban communities of Timbuktu and Gao en route to Mecca, and made them a piece of his domain when he returned around 1325. He brought designers from Andalusia, a district in Spain, and Cairo to construct his fabulous royal residence in Timbuktu the incomparable Djinguereber Mosque that actually stands today.

Timbuktu before long turned into the focal point of exchange, culture, and Islam; markets got shippers from Hausaland, Egypt, and other African realms, a college was established in the city (as well as in the Malian urban areas of Djenné and Ségou), and Islam was spread through the business sectors and college, making Timbuktu another region for Islamic grant. Fresh insight about the Malian realm's city of abundance even gone across the Mediterranean to southern Europe, where brokers from Venice, Granada, and Genoa before long added Timbuktu to their guides to exchange fabricated products for gold.

The University of Sankore in Timbuktu was restaffed under Musa's rule with legal scholars, space experts, and mathematicians. The college turned into a focal point of learning and culture, drawing Muslim researchers from around Africa and the Middle East to Timbuktu.

In 1330, the realm of Mossi attacked and vanquished the city of Timbuktu. Gao had as of now been caught by Musa's general, and Musa immediately recovered Timbuktu, constructed a defense and stone fortress, and put a standing armed force to safeguard the city from future trespassers.

While Musa's castle has since disappeared, the college mosque actually stands in Timbuktu today.

Before the finish of Mansa Musa's rule, the Sankoré University had been changed over into a complete set up University with the biggest assortments of books in Africa since the Library of Alexandria. The Sankoré University has equipped for lodging 25,000 understudies and had perhaps the biggest library on the planet with around 1,000,000 compositions.

CHAPTER TWENTY-FIVE

EXPLOITATION OF AFRICA

Africa is a poor country, the people living in Africa are poor, Africa is a continent, this is what we have all heard. Why world politics is centered on this African country. In fact, the world powers are running on the other side of the African nation. African refugees or Asian refugees, i.e., refugees who arrived in Africa through war or natural disasters or if there were any refugees, should not go to Europe. Refugees in Mexico should not travel to the United States. But the United States or European countries can come to the refugee countries. Come there and do business for them or do the things they need. There is no barrier for them to this.

How is their world politics?

You should not come to our country but we will come to your country. If we want to come to your country, we need the right reason. I would call that reason extremism. The people of the world will trust and beg us to help them and suppress the extremism that is there, and through that, we will get there, says the United States. In addition, the US military is now stationed in about 35 countries in Africa.

I think you were just shocked?

Because you can see in the world map, Africa was shown as the smallest continent, then how you say 35 Countries? The World map is a Blindfold (Mercator projection). Africa is the second largest Continent in the World you know? With 54 Countries.

What we have to say about this Africa is that blacks are living in Africa, that poverty is rampant, there is famine, there is a hurricane. These media only show us negative news like this. We have seen in the media that hunger is high in Sudan, Libya, Egypt, and Somalia, especially in Somalia. Now if you go to the website and search for Africa a message will come up. They are showing that Africa is the poorest country in the world that the World Bank is going to lend five hundred and forty five million dollars to Africa. But if you look at the other side, US company claiming that the Trump's decisions have led to China's dominance on the African continent, with tens of thousands of Chinese companies' start-ups there, and the revenue available to China through those companies alone is about one hundred and eighty billion dollars.

The World Bank is going to lend five hundred and forty-five million dollars to such a country. We need to look at one more thing here, the countries of this African continent borrow fifty billion dollars every year from the World Bank. But at the same time, the nations of the world are making almost one point two trillion dollars using this continent of Africa. That is, they repay almost two hundred times more than they borrowed, and many of us are unaware of the fact that the African continent is repaying the world with interest, natural resources, and petrol. The World Bank claims that the countries on the African continent are the largest economies in the world in the year 2034. Because it is from these countries that all the petrol, diamonds, minerals, and metals in the world are stored in these African countries. The long-held dream of the United States is to seize these countries. Not only the United States but a lot of countries are thinking. China lends a lot to African countries and their companies start more there. One-third of the petrol available to China comes from this Africa. Exports from Africa to China have risen from $ 5 billion in ten years to $ 93 billion now.

Now imagine the extent to which the nations of the world are exploiting the resources that exist in Africa.

Africa has an enormous amount of normal assets, including jewels, sugar, salt, gold, iron, cobalt, uranium, copper, bauxite, silver, petrol, and cocoa beans, yet additionally tropical lumber and tropical organic product.

As of late found oil holds have expanded the significance of the item on African economies. Sudan and Nigeria are two of the fundamental oil makers. The United States and European nations took a large portion of the Democratic Republic of the Congo's (DRC) oil creation. Oil is given by both mainland and seaward creations. Sudan's oil trades in 2010 are assessed by the United States Department of State at US$9 billion.

Five nations rule Africa's upstream oil creation. Together they represent 85% of the landmass' oil creation and are, all together, from most noteworthy to least result: Nigeria, Libya, Algeria, Egypt, and Angola. Other African oil delivering nations are Gabon, the DRC, Cameroon, Tunisia, Equatorial Guinea, the Republic of the Congo, Ivory Coast, and all the more as of late, Ghana. The investigation is occurring in various different nations that mean to expand their result or become first-time makers. Remembered for this rundown are Chad, Sudan, Namibia, South Africa, and Madagascar, while Mozambique and Tanzania are potential oil makers.

Oil and Minerals

Africa has 30% of the excess mineral assets on the planet. 57% of Africa's product profit comes from hydrocarbons. From 1980 to 2012, demonstrated oil saves in Africa developed by 150%.

Metal assets in Africa are bountiful while different landmasses are starting to confront exhaustion of assets. The copper belt in Haut-Katanga Province, the jewel mines in Sierra Leone, Angola, and Botswana are notable for the wealth of mineral assets, yet with a negative standing emerging from the view of their businesses' association in degenerate practices, and connections to savage radical developments. The RUF (Revolutionary United Front) and the blood precious stones used to supply these radical groups with arms is one such model.

As of late, investigation exercises have filled in West Africa. In any case, absence of administrations turned into an issue for investigation organizations. In 2020, West Africa got the third bigger financial plan for investigation projects. From 2009 to 2019, West Africa accounted a significant accomplishment in gold disclosures. Investigation spending plans in Africa fell 10% in 2020, arriving at their lower levels over the most recent four years.

Non-African Exploitation

With a low populace thickness, Africa has been colonized by non-African countries from the sixteenth century, all taking advantage of African assets to changing degrees. A few financial analysts have contended this set of experiences of outside double-dealing exhibits the 'scourge of natural substances' concern. In the present circumstance, profoundly pursued, yet interesting, crude assets are available in a less-grown, less-strong substance. Such a circumstance puts serious tensions on the first "owners" of the assets. In African countries, these tensions, it is contended, have prompted wars and eased back improvement. While Western countries like the United States, Canada, Australia, France, and the United Kingdom, as well as arising financial forces to be reckoned with like China, keep on taking advantage of Africa's regular assets, the worth from the normal assets goes toward the West and East Asia, rather than Africa, worsening neediness in Africa, regardless of Africa's overflow of normal assets. A Guyanese history specialist, Walter Rodney, sets that unfamiliar responsibility for normal assets is the "most immediate way" those rich nations keep on ruling African states without officially colonizing them: "When residents of Europe own the land and the mines of Africa, this is the most immediate approach to sucking the African landmass."

In the name of American extremism, the United States says the Twin Tower terrorists here have blown up in the 2000s. So, they said we were going to invade Afghanistan and Iraq. During the invasion, there was a small uprising in the country of Libya, which overthrew the then president and established a puppet regime by the United States. It then implements a new configuration there, which is named U.S. AFRICOM (The United States Africa Command) i.e., the Africa-America constraint. The United States is ruling Africa as a whole with Libya as its center. If the American command in Libya wants to go to Africa, they will do a little bit of extremism there. After that, there will be a drone strike. From 2003 to 2019, various drone strikes were carried out in many countries, including Somalia, Sudan, and Nigeria. Eighty percent of those killed in this unmanned attack were common people in Africa. This is what global terrorism is all about. But the fact is that the people there do not understand these politics when so much is going on.

Why aren't the right leaders available in Africa yet? Why are the leaders there like an ignorant puppet? The political turmoil there is also one reason.

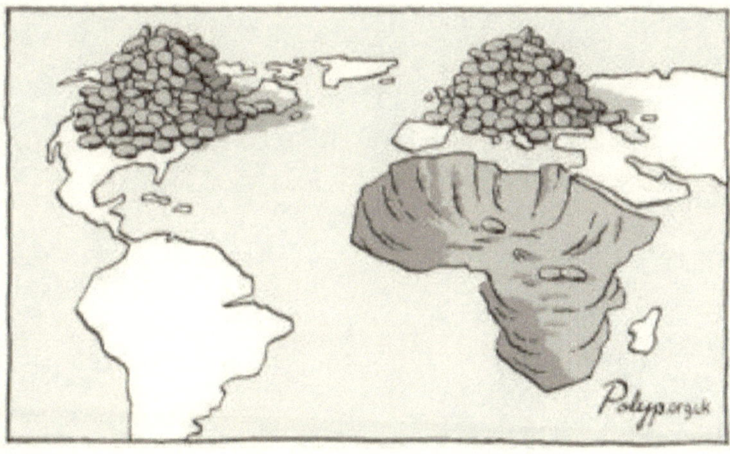

CHAPTER TWENTY-SIX

CRUDE OIL POLITICS

At the age of one thousand nine hundred and eighty-nine, i.e., 90's kids' period, a liter of petrol in India worked for just eight rupees. What is the reason for growing from just eight rupees to a hundred rupees? It has a great history of looking at the history of this gold that can be described as Liquid Gold. We need to know what petrol is before we can look at history, which is a mixture of surprise, wonder, blood, and sweat. This petrol is what we get by first refining the crude oil. This crude oil is a fossil fuel. That is to say, the creatures that have been buried in the earth for millions of years are the fossils of oil. Normally this oil comes out automatically from the bottom of the earth to the crust. After the heat of the sun evaporates oil too, they will call oil as an Asphalt or Bittu, who is the rest of the spirit. This was the first petroleum product used by man. This asphalt has been in use by humans for thousands of years. The ancients used this asphalt as a glue for building houses and making pottery. The Babylonians even used it to build their Ship. Mesopotamia made jewelry using similar oils four thousand years ago. This number was used by the Egyptians in the process of body processing from 1550 BC to 1070 AD. Not only that but this crude oil has been used in medicine as it has a lot of medicinal purposes.

The history of contemporary petroleum begins only in the nineteen-eighties, after a long hiatus. Strictly speaking, it was during the height of the Industrial Revolution in Europe and the United States that factories began to demand more energy.

Until then, oil was not considered an end in itself. I mean people in the US would be very upset if they came to me while building a house. But what will you do if you get oil now? Coal was then the world's largest source of energy, it was at that time, in the seventeenth century. In 1847, that the Scottish chemist James Young discovered oil in a coal mine in

Alfreton, in England. Taking it, he researched and found oil for lighting lamps and thick oil suitable for lubricating machines. The development of these oils and strong paraffin wax from coal framed the subject of his patent dated 17 October 1850. In 1850 Young and Meldrum and Edward William Binney went into the organization under the title of E.W. Binney and Co. at Bathgate in West Lothian and E. Meldrum and Co. at Glasgow; their works at Bathgate were finished in 1851 and turned into the primary really business oil-works and petroleum processing plant on the planet, utilizing oil removed from privately mined torbanite, shale, and bituminous coal to produce naphtha and greasing up oils; paraffin for fuel use and strong paraffin were not sold till 1856.

Kerosene

Abraham Pineo Gesner, a Canadian geologist fostered a cycle to refine a fluid fuel from coal, bitumen, and oil shale. His new revelation, which he named lamp fuel, consumed more neatly and was more affordable than contending items, for example, whale oil. In 1850, Gesner made the Kerosene Gaslight Company and started introducing lighting on the roads in Halifax and different urban areas. By 1854, he had extended to the United States where he made the North American Kerosene Gas Light Company at Long Island, New York. Request developed to where his organization's ability to create turned into an issue, however, the revelation of oil, from which lamp fuel could be all the more handily delivered, tackled the stock issue.

Ignacy Lukasiewicz further developed Gesner's strategy to foster a method for refining lamp fuel from the more promptly accessible "rock oil" ("petroleum") leaks, in 1852, and the primary stone oil mine was underlying Bóbrka, close to Krosno in focal European Galicia (Poland) in 1854. These disclosures quickly spread all over the planet, and Meerzoeff constructed the main present-day Russian processing plant in the developed oil fields at Baku in 1861. Around then Baku created around 90% of the world's oil.

Oil Wells

The topic of what comprised the primary business oil well is a troublesome one to reply. The accompanying synopsis draws from that in Vassiliou (2018). Edwin Drake's 1859 well close to Titusville, Pennsylvania, talked about more completely beneath, is prevalently viewed as the principal current well. Drake's well is likely singled out in light of the fact that it was bored, not burrowed; in light of the fact that it utilized a steam motor; since there was an organization related with it; and in light of the fact that it ignited a significant blast. Nonetheless, the very first all-around penetrated anyplace on the planet, which delivered oil, was bored in 1857 to a profundity of 280 feet by the American Merrimac Company in La Brea (Spanish for "Pitch") in southeast Trinidad in the Caribbean.

Also, there was impressive action before Drake in different regions of the planet during the nineteenth century. In 1846, the main current oil well on the planet was bored in the South Caucasus locale of the Russian Empire, on the Absheron Peninsula north-east of Baku by Russian Major Alekseev in light of information of NikolayVoskoboynikov. A gathering coordinated by Major Alexeyev of the Bakinskii Corps of Mining Engineers hand-penetrated a well in the Baku area in 1846. There were motor penetrated wells in West Virginia around the same time as Drake's well. An early business very much was hand delved in Poland in 1853, and one more in neighboring Romania in 1857.

Refineries

At the around a similar time the world's first, however little, petroleum treatment facilities were opened at Jasło, in Poland, with a bigger one being opened at Ploieşti, in Romania. Worked in 1856 and introduced in 1857 by the siblings Teodor and Marin Mehedinţeanu, the Rafov Refinery, a processing plant worked at Ploiesti, had a surface area of four hectares, and the everyday creation came to more than seven tons, acquired in round and hollow iron and iron projects that were warmed by fire from wood; it was then called "the world's first precise oil refinery," establishing the standard for being the world's first petroleum treatment facility, as per the Academy of World Records.

This processing plant got, based on an agreement closed in October 1856 between TeodorMehedinţeanu and the City Hall of Bucharest, the selective right to supply the brightening of the Wallachian capital with oil light. The agreement started to be executed on April 1, 1857, while, by supplanting the abducted oil with the items provided by the Rafov processing plant, "Bucharest turned into the principal city on the planet enlightened completely with refined raw petroleum."

In 1857, the absolute creation of Romania was added up to 275 tons of raw petroleum. With this figure, Romania was enrolled as the main country in world oil creation insights, before other huge oil delivering states like the United States of America (1860), Russia (1863), Mexico (1901), or Persia (1913).

United States

In 1875, raw petroleum was found by David Beaty at his home in Warren, Pennsylvania. This prompted the launch of the Bradford oil field, which, by the 1880s, delivered 77% of the worldwide oil supply. Be that as it may, before the finish of the nineteenth century, the Russian Empire, especially the Branobel organization in Azerbaijan, had started to lead the pack underway.

Samuel Kier laid out America's first petroleum processing plant in Pittsburgh on Seventh road close to Grant Street, in 1853. Notwithstanding the movement in West Virginia and Pennsylvania, a significant early oil well in North America was in Oil Springs, Ontario, Canada in 1858, burrowed by James Miller Williams. The disclosure at Oil Springs ignited an oil blast that carried many examiners and laborers to the area. New oil fields were found close by all through the late nineteenth century and the region formed into a huge petrochemical refining focus and trade. The advanced US petrol industry is considered to have started with Edwin Drake's penetrating of a 69-foot (21 m) oil well in 1859, on Oil Creek close to Titusville, Pennsylvania, for the Seneca Oil Company (initially yielding 25 barrels each day (4.0 m3/d), before the years over yield was at the pace of 15 barrels each day (2.4 m3/d)). The business became through the 1800s, driven by the interest for lamp fuel and oil lights. It turned into a significant public worry in the early piece of the twentieth century; the presentation of the gas-powered motor gave an interest that has to a great extent supported the business right up 'til today. Early "neighborhood" observes like those in Pennsylvania and Ontario were immediately dominated by request, prompting "oil blasts" in Ohio, Texas, Oklahoma, and California.

The United States, which started to rule assets for oil, keeps on ruling today.

20th Century

By 1910, critical oil fields had been found in the Dutch East Indies (1885, in Sumatra), Persia (1908, in Masjed Soleiman), Peru (1863, in Zorritos District), Venezuela (1914, in Maracaibo Basin), and Mexico, and were being created at a modern level. Huge oil fields were taken advantage of in Alberta (Canada) from 1947. Seaward oil penetrating at Oil Rocks (NeftDashlari) in the Caspian Sea off Azerbaijan, in the end, brought about a city based on arches in 1949. Galician oilfields made the Austria-Hungary the third world's biggest oil maker country after the United States and the Russian Empire, with a 5 percent portion of the worldwide oil creation in 1908.

Accessibility of oil and admittance to it, was the fate of "cardinal significance" in military power when World War I, especially for naval forces as they changed from coal, yet in addition with the presentation of engine transport, tanks and planes. Such reasoning would go on in later contentions of the 20th century, including World War II, during which oil offices were a significant key resource and were widely bombarded. In 1938, immense stores of oil were found in the al-Ahsa district in the Eastern Part of the Kingdom of Saudi Arabia along the shoreline of the Arabian Gulf.

Until the mid-1950s coal was as yet the world's premier fuel, however after this time oil immediately dominated. Afterward, following the 1973 and 1979 energy emergencies, there was huge media inclusion regarding the matter of oil supply levels. This exposed the worry that oil is a restricted asset that will ultimately run out, basically as a monetarily reasonable energy source. In spite of the fact that at the time the most well-known and famous forecasts were very critical, a time of expanded creation and diminished interest before long caused an oil overabundance during the 1980s. This was not to endure, notwithstanding, and by the primary ten years of the 21st-century conversations about top oil had gotten back to the news.

Today, around 90% of vehicular fuel needs are met by oil. Oil likewise makes up 40% of absolute energy utilization in the United States, yet is answerable for just 2% of power age. Petrol's worth as a convenient, thick energy source controlling by far most of the vehicles and as the foundation of numerous modern synthetic compounds makes it one of the world's most significant wares.

The main three oil delivering nations are Saudi Arabia, Russia, and the United States. Around 80% of the world's promptly open stores are situated in the Middle East, with 62.5% coming from the Arab in Saudi Arabia (12.5%), UAE, Iraq, Qatar, and Kuwait. Nonetheless, with high oil costs (above $100/barrel), Venezuela has bigger stores than Saudi Arabia because of its rough saves got from bitumen. Austria-Hungary lose its primate on oil creation which had been at the base of the 1910 Petroleum War.

John D. Rockefeller

John Davison Rockefeller was an American business financier and giver. He is generally viewed as the most affluent American ever and the most extravagant individual in current history.

Rockefeller was naturally introduced to an enormous and helpless family in upstate New York that moved a few times before ultimately getting comfortable in Cleveland, Ohio. He turned into an associate accountant at age 16 and went into a few business organizations starting at age 20, focusing his business on oil refining. Rockefeller established the Standard Oil Company in 1870. He ran it until 1897, and remained its biggest investor.

Rockefeller's abundance took off as lamp fuel and gas filled insignificance, and he turned into the most extravagant individual in the nation, controlling 90% of all oil in the United States at his pinnacle. Oil was utilized all through the country as a light source until the presentation of power, and as a fuel after the development of the auto. Moreover, Rockefeller acquired a tremendous impact on the railroad business which shipped his oil around the country. Standard Oil was the principal incredible business trust in the United States. Rockefeller changed the oil business and, through corporate and mechanical advancements, was instrumental in both generally scattering and definitely diminishing the creation cost of oil. His organization and strategic policies went under analysis, especially in the compositions of creator Ida Tarbell.

The Supreme Court decided in 1911 that Standard Oil should be destroyed for infringement of government antitrust regulations. It was separated into 34 separate substances, which included organizations that became ExxonMobil, Chevron Corporation, others some of which actually have the most elevated level of income on the planet.

In the end, it worked out that the singular sections of the organization were worth more than the whole organization was the point at which it was one substance the amount of the parts were worth more than the entire as portions of these multiplied and significantly increased in esteem in their initial years. Therefore, Rockefeller turned into the country's first extremely rich person, with a fortune worth almost 2% of the public economy. His privately invested money was assessed in 1913 at $900 million, which was practically 3% of the US GDP of $39.1 billion that year. That was his pinnacle total assets, and sums to US$23.6 billion (in 2020 dollars; expansion changed).

Rockefeller spent a large part of the most recent 40 years of his life in retirement at Kykuit, his bequest in Westchester County, New York, characterizing the design of present-day altruism, alongside other key industrialists like steelhead honcho Andrew Carnegie. His fortune was for the most part used to make the advanced methodical methodology of designated magnanimity through the making of establishments that majorly affected medication, schooling, and logical examination. His establishments spearheaded improvements in clinical examination and were instrumental in the close annihilation of hookworm and yellow fever in the United States. He and Carnegie gave structure and driving force through their causes to crafted by Abraham Flexner, who in his paper "Clinical Education in America" decidedly invested experimentation as the reason for the US clinical arrangement of the twentieth century.

Rockefeller was additionally the author of the University of Chicago and Rockefeller University and subsidized the foundation of Central Philippine University in the Philippines. He was an ardent Northern Baptist and upheld many church-based establishments. He stuck to add up to restraint from liquor and tobacco all through his life. For counsel, he depended intently on his better half Laura Spelman Rockefeller with whom he had five kids. He was an unwavering gatherer of the Erie Street Baptist Mission Church, showed Sunday school, and filled in as a legal administrator, assistant, and intermittent janitor. Religion was a directing power all through his life and he trusted it to be the wellspring of his prosperity. Rockefeller was additionally viewed as an ally of private enterprise in light of a viewpoint of social Darwinism, and he was cited regularly as saying, "The development of an enormous business is just natural selection".

How Petrol Price Determined in India?

Fuel not set in stone by state-claimed Oil Marketing Companies, like Bharat Petroleum, Indian Oil and Hindustan Petroleum. There are four contributing variables to the cost of petroleum and diesel in the country. India imports Brent unrefined petroleum from the Organization of the Petroleum Exporting Countries (OPEC) nations. The unrefined petroleum is handled by bubbling and afterward refining to isolate different powers and gases. The base cost for these powers, for example, petroleum and diesel are set by the local government. The base cost for unrefined petroleum, for instance, on November 4 was Rupees 39.4 per litre, and the cost of petroleum subsequent to adding handling and cargo charges was at Rupees 48.28 per litre. Then, at that point, commission for the vendor at the petroleum siphon, focal government's extract obligation, and the express government's worth added charges are added to that add up to decide the last cost of the fuel in the particular state. Energizes are more costly in states with lower interests.

Why were Prices on the rise in recent times?

India's oil imports stand at 82%, while it has 618.95 million tons of unrefined petroleum holds. As indicated by a report by Scroll.in, the base cost of petroleum has diminished from where it was at 47 for each litre when the Modi government assumed responsibility in 2014, to 37 for every litre in June this year. Truth be told, worldwide raw petroleum costs dropped by 13% between 202-2021. In any case, focal extract obligation in India has just seen a lofty ascent from Rs 10 in May 2014 to Rs 32 in June this year. Recently, then, at that point, Petroleum Minister Dharmendra Pradhan asserted that the expenses were brought up in request to accommodate some post-COVID government assistance plans.

CHAPTER TWENTY-SEVEN

EXTRA FOR YOU

TEA POLITICS

Tea is the antidote to suffering, and honey is the drink of pleasure. In more detail, drinking water is more addictive than drinking alcohol. China was the first country in the world to introduce tea to the world. We cannot ignore tea because it came to China because tea has become an integral part of our lives. Did you know that the word Tea is derived from the Chinese words Teh and Cha? Not only that, but the word tea comes from the Chinese word. Teh means Tea changed, so it is called tea today and the water made from it is called tea. Similarly, the word Chai and Chaya are derived from the Chinese word Cha. Tea is said to have originated in Zhang Dynasty, which ruled China from the 1600s to the 1046s. That too was used as a medicinal drink. But the Chinese claim that tea contact with the Chinese has been around for a long time. Evidence of this can be found in the book Ben Cao Jing, which is said to have been written in the third century AD by Shen Nong, the ancient Chinese god of agriculture, and mentions the medicinal properties of tea.

The most important tea is from the Tang Dynasty, considered to be the golden age of China in the 7th century AD. It was during this period that tea became the drink of choice for everyone, not just for medical reasons. It was only after that that many tea gardens began to emerge throughout China. Lu Yu, a Chinese writer of the same century, wrote a book exclusively for tea, Cha Jing. In that book, it is clearly stated how to cultivate tea and how to make tea. To that extent, the Chinese held tea in the most important place and it continues to this day. Tea brought from China to Japan in the 8th century AD was also revered there as the most important place. The cultural tradition of making tea called Canoyu in Japan is still followed today. In the ninth century AD, tea from China to Tibet was used not only as a beverage but also as cash. How do I celebrate Pongal now as well as countries like China, Japan, Tibet are celebrating a separate festival for tea? Not only that but their tea making is a bit strange.

It describes them as "The Art of Tea". From ancient times the Chinese and Japanese used tea as a green tea in which they mixed milk and sugar. It was not until the fourteenth century AD that black tea began to form. Roy Moxham records in his book "A Brief History of Tea" that the practice of black tea originated in China, especially in the western part of China. Similarly, it was not until the fourteenth century that the Chinese began to develop the habit of drinking tea in ceramic jars without handles. Although we and the Chinese have a commercial habit from the Sanskrit era, we do not know why tea was not introduced. I think maybe we were unaware of the references. But no matter how much he defended; the Europeans sniffed right away. The Portuguese were the first to introduce tea to Europeans. Tea for Europeans was introduced to China by the Portuguese in the 1610s.

Tea was a very expensive commodity as it crossed the sea and joined Europe across many issues. Only kings and the rich used tea. As well as the French country tea is intoxicated. The British government was unfamiliar with tea at the time. Catherine of Braganza, the daughter of King John IV, married to King Charles II, who ruled England, and at that wedding, the Queen took a lot of wealth as a gift, one of which was a bundle of tea, which is how tea was introduced to the British. The English were very addicted to tea. The English were the first to drink tea with sugar, in which the enchanted English went to China in search of tea. The East Indian Company sent tons of tea from China to the British.

Tea was poorly bought and sold in the UK. At the same time, the British paid a lot of taxes on tea as it was in high demand. Thus, tea was sold at a higher price in the UK. Half a kilo of tea in the middle of the seventeenth century was sold for three hundred rupees in today's India. But at the same time, the average weekly income of a worker in the UK is three hundred rupees in India. After that tea was used not only as a beverage but also as a medicine and as a medium when it started to be prescribed by doctors. After that, the tea began to join the grassroots. Due to this, the use of tea began to increase. But at the same time, the price of tea did not go up and down. But due to high demand, it was adulterated and sold on the black market. This means that the blenders take the used discarded tea, dry it and mix it with fresh tea. Artificial colors were added to make it standard so there was a lot of physical abuse. To prevent this contamination the poor people of England made fantastic tea by adding low-priced milk tea and a little bit of high-priced sugar. It began to spread throughout the UK and thus the demand for tea in the UK was high. But prices have not just fallen in the UK. Due to that, the tea was smuggled and sold on the counterfeit market. In the middle of the eighteenth century, a gang of tea robbers called Hawkhurst smuggled their lives into the tea and sold it on the black market. So, the East India Company suffered a huge loss. At one point the rise in the tea market in the UK was due to the fact that the Seventy percentage of tea that came through the black market was high.

The East India Company then reduced the tax to just twelve percent on the 119percent tax levied on tea by the UK, after which tea became available to all. Exactly the same period when tons of tea, Ceramic Jars, and silks were being exported from China to the UK but no replacement came from the UK, China asked the UK government for a silver coin for that. But the government and the East India Company could not give China what they asked for because there was not enough silver coin and the Dutch were constantly at war with the British, so China did not export to the UK. So, the British cunningly sold opium to the Chinese people. From Seventh, Century Opium was used as a Medicine in China, but few people became addicted to it, and it was during this time that tobacco was discovered, and more and more people became addicted to it, claiming that the combination of the two would make it more addictive. This is what the East India Company used.

The British produced opium in the border areas of India and sold it to the poor in China and received silver coins. The silver coin was bought from China people and again given to the China Government by UK for tea. The Chinese government banned opium and ordered the death penalty for those who sold it, as more and more people became addicted to opium in China. But the British sold it to the people through Chinese intermediaries, and the British in exchange sold it to middlemen and through them sold it to the Chinese people. Concerned that the people were becoming overly addicted to drugs, the Chinese government appointed Lin Tse-Hsu, a commander-in-chief, who went to Beijing and Guangxi, now in China, found intermediaries, seized the opium they possessed, and dumped the opium worth around seventy-seven million rupees worth of opium into the sea. The British government openly went to war with China for dumping millions of opium into the sea. This war, known as the Opium War, lasted for double periods, when England finally won the war, and if the British won the war, opium was sold unrestricted in China, and an agreement was reached with the Chinese government that tea could be smuggled into the UK. But the British had a concern, thinking that war could break out again with China now and tea would not be available. The British began to search for it in other countries, such as Chinese tea.

It was revealed to the British that there was a kind of tea in India. As well as the Assamese lord Maniram Dewan who was very loyal to the East India Company in the year one thousand eight hundred and twenty-three, he told a man named Robert Press who had made the East India Company poor that there was a garden here like Chinese tea in the forests of Assam and that the Indians used tea like spinach in cooking. But at that time tons of tea was exported from China, and the East India Company did not see what Dewan was saying because China's tea was so delicious. But now that the situation has changed the East India Company has focused on Assam teas to break China's monopoly. After that, the researchers went to study the tea grown in Assam. This complete information was recorded in "A Taste of Time" by MohonaKanjilal. According to research conducted in Assam, the climate there is likely to produce not only Assam tea but also Chinese tea. So, they brought tea seeds from China and gave them to the forest of Assam and did research by sowing Chinese teas. Through that research, Assam tea developed better than Chinese tea. Thus, a ship sailed to England in the year one thousand seven hundred and thirty-nine, carrying the Indian teas produced in Assam.

The English people were very enthusiastic about those Indian teas that went to England. They celebrated that Indian tea is tastier than Chinese tea. Now the East India Company was very happy because there was no need to resort to China for tea now and they thought we could make our own tea now. But the East India Company invaded our seats for profit and used the people of India as slaves. But not only that, due to high demand, the British wanted to grow tea in places other than Assam. In the year 1839, Henry Mann, an Englishman, sowed and researched tea in Coonoor. The British used it only to export the tea made from such wild Deforestation. See that our forests have been given so much for their need. It is only when forests are destroyed in this way that various ecosystems are destroyed and the resulting climate change is wiped out and today, we are facing unparalleled rainy seasons and floods.

Moreover, India forced its people into slavery in its own country to work. Paul Harris Daniel, a doctor who worked there, described the atrocities and torture in his book "The Red Tea". R.R. Murugavel has translated the book into Tamil language as "Burning Ice Forest" in Tamil we say "எரியும்பனிக்காடு". People who were taken captive were brutally assaulted without knowing why, their wives were sexually abused, the officers who made it painful for only aspiring women to get income, the English who robbed the wives of those estate lords, the estate officials who used it to live in luxury, the people who died of diseases without adequate sanitation, about it in his book, Daniel sadly describes the embracing of whites who enjoyed a wine party without worry. Moreover, sad information was a movie "Paradesi" is the film that made Daniel ugly by writing like that.

Violence against tea workers took place not only during the British rule but also after India's independence. Sixteen people, including a one-year-old child, have been killed in police violence against mangrove plantation workers who demanded a pay rise of just thirty rupees in the nineteen nineties and demanded that they work only eight hours a day and during their maternity leave. He released a documentary, The Death of a River, based on the scenes. R. Srinivasan. In addition, Tamils were taken to Sri Lanka for tea plantation work during the British rule. They returned to India again after liberation. But the Tamil Nadu government came up with the law that they have to prove their citizenship, but the tea workers do not know what these workers will prove their citizenship and what to do. During the British rule, tea was only exported with cruelty, but during the time of The Great Depression in the United States, the tea was marketed to the Indian people due to the lack of people to buy it.

At first, the people of India did not see it as big, so they started the "Tea board of India" organization and advertised it in the off-limits in India. Only then did the Indians use tea. But it was only after it brought spices like ginger and cardamom into the hands of the Indians that tea quality tea began to spread rapidly in India. MohonaKanjilal mentions in his book "A Taste of Times" that masala tea originated in the state of Bengal in India for the first time. Due to the high demand for tea, estate employers sold the dust from the final processes of making tea. But the Indians also used to say that it was delicious too. We currently use powdered tea in India. They use quality tea from India only for export.This tea has undergone political changes in many countries. We first saw that tea was sold on the black market in England, so that the East India Company suffered a great loss, and to compensate for it the British government allowed the British colonial United States to sell it without any tax. But in the United States, the British government imposed excessive taxes on their daily necessities. History has it that the American people broke the entire tea ship brought by the East India Company because they favored the East India Company and paid too much tax for it, and it was called the "Boston Tea Party". So, the great revolutionary struggle took place in the United States, and the United States was got independence from the British colony. Think about it, the main reason for the liberation of the powerful nation of America we see now was a tea. In the nineteen nineties, Subramaniam gave a tea party for Ms. Sonia Gandhi and Ms. Jayalalitha to form an alliance. It is seen as the greatest diplomacy to date.

CHAPTER TWENTY-EIGHT

INDIA WAS DIVIDED BY WHITE

The happiness received by monthly wagers when they receive the "Salary credited" The message, nothing else satisfies them more but, we should be thanking Salt for our Salary (In Tamil we saySambalam) whenever we received it because both these words originated from Salt. Are you asking How? Come on let's see...!

Salt is praised as "White crystal nectar" in the Sangam period, it is also celebrated as "White gold in the Middle Ages, just like how oil politics is transcending the world today, in an earlier period, this Salt Politics has transcended this world, yes, the history of white salt in written with blood's red color, the history of Salt didn't start when man invented it. It started as early as the earth's origination, the current witness to that is the broad ocean on the earth, the salt's history, the salt's history is equivalent to the ocean's depth and width and I am going to say only a pinch of it.

Salt is filled all over the world because, salt is the key to vitality, confused? As for how breathing is essential for every living creature likewise, for every creature to function properly, salt is very important, we are thinking that salt is added just for our food's taste but, Salt is the basic reason for our body functioning for the tissues and fibers of our body need to function properly for we want to maintain the blood flow properly in our body, to make sure that we are not dehydrated, to digest our food properly for the nutrition from the food need to be separated properly salt is essential for all these activities to understand it, we will learn something about salt's chemical characteristics.

Salt is a mixture of sodium and chloride its chemical formula is NA-CL. Salt is very essential for our body's proper functioning. Sodium is the basic necessity for all our brain's communication to muscles through nerves likewise, chloride helps us to maintain the blood's PH value and pressure in our body both these chemicals are received through salt for us, we excrete salt, the essential thing for body functioning as sweat when we work to compensate it, we are in-taking salt. Salt is essential for not only humans but for all living creatures, Salt is essential for wild animals too, Herbivore animals like Deer, Bison take the necessary salt from the plants they eat. In case, if they didn't get the necessary salt from the plants they go to the salt mounds, which are formed naturally, they lick the salt from here and fulfill their salt needs. This is called Salt Licking. There is a salt cave in Kenya's Mount Elgon called as Kitum cave.

Do you know who carved that cave? – Elephants...!

When the salt necessary for them is not received through their food elephants have harvested the salt from these salt-rich caves for centuries, elephants break the cave wall into pieces using their tusks and then they eat them, the salt for non-vegetarian animals is obtained when they hunt and eat the vegetarian animals as to how non-vegetarian animals satisfy their salt necessity by hunting likewise, when man was behaving as a hunting community his salt necessity was easily received by him through his hunting but, When he started agriculture, he needed the salt separately that too when he started to cook the harvest from his agriculture the natural amount of salt in the harvest got decreased that's when he realized the necessity of salt and started to think as to how to manufacture it? That thinking was seen as the next stage of evolution, If the discovery of fire is the initial stage of human evolution, If the creation of agriculture is considered as the growth of human evolution, The thought of manufacturing salt was the next biggest progress likewise, after thinking from where can he take the salt and how to manufacture it like Kenyan elephants for his salt requirements the history between man and salt started after this thought.

Man has started to manufacture the salt even before thousands of years. In Romania around 6000 BC some Archaeological fossils have been discovered related to salt manufacturing Olivier Weller and GheorgheDumitroaia has started them in their research documents. The oldest record in the world related to salt was found in China. In that record, they were a demo as how was salt taken from a pond-shore The detail of the demonstration was started by Mark Kurlansky in his book "SALT".

Earlier Greek and Chinese people was salt as a divine thing, they even gave it as an offering to their gods. From those times, salt was seen as a very rare thing. This thought has continued till the end of the 20th Century that's why, there was a huge respect for Salt in the society. That's how, Salt got the name "White Gold", for the same reason, even during the period of commodity exchange salt has been kept at a very high position and respected heavily earlier Greeks and Romans have purchased slaves in exchange of salt likewise, they have even purchased costly items in exchange as an equivalent to salt. As for how the silt route was created based on the silk business likewise, many salt routes have been created based on the salt business. Many new roads have been created to carry salt for earlier Rome, those roads were named using the terms related to salt, that trend continues even today, for example, we can say about Italy's "VIA SALARIA". I remember this when saying as "SALARIA". I said the salary we receive came from salt, right? How it happened was, Romans gave salt as the salary for their warriors, they represented it using the Latin word "SALARIUM". That Latin work "SALARIUM" has converted to SALARY now. The desert country Egypt attained its prosperity by building extravagant Pyramids the reason for this is SALT. They cut the salt sediment at their borders and exported them to foreign countries the Egyptians harvested huge profits by this process. Not only do they harvest profits, they have also done research on salt. They have used salt in the Mummification process. As for how we added salt to fishes and created dry fish (In Tamil we say Karuvaadu). As for how we added salt to mutton and created dry mutton (In Tamil we say UppuKandam) Likewise, Egyptians have also added salt and created some meat varieties. Food preservation has started from this point, we can say that the main reason for natural food preservation is Salt. Actually, people would say that a fruit or vegetable will decay in 2 or 3 days Right? The reason as why the fruit or vegetable is not decaying for those 2 or 3 days is, the salt content in that fruit or vegetable Likewise, Egyptians who draw everything have drawn the procedure to manufacture salt in their Pyramids.

Okay, how is the salt actually manufactured? Salt is manufactured in 3 different types

One, they will leave the sea water or salt water through a channel into the Sea-Pan after that, when the water evaporates under the Sun, they take out the deposited salt from the process.

Second. From the natural salt beds and salt mountains, they create tunnels and extract salt just like they extract coal.

Third, People filter the mixture of salt water and salinity-rich soil then they heat the mixture and extract salt, in this method, the salt was manufactured in Bengal, using this the Britishers have created a huge fight.

One more place which is famous for the salt manufacturing is Timbuktu, as how paths were created for the incoming salt of Rome Likewise, for this African town Timbuktu's salt market multiple paths has been created for various people who come from all over the world. Do you think that you have heard about this Timbuktu earlier, this city was constructed by the world's richest man Mansa Musa.

Not only in the commodity exchange process, but Salt was also used as Money, In Tibet around the 13th Century they were salt coins that had the king's picture in them by Marco Polo has mentioned it in his travel notes. In the same period, the Arabians had used salt rocks as money, to check whether the money is fake or real we will expose the money under the light, right? Likewise, People will take and lick it to check whether it is real or not if the sanity is there, then they will accept it as salt and use it, think once, if Corona was there during that time, what would have happened? Salt was also seen as a very expensive material even in Tamil Nādu.

"The measurement of salt is equal to the measurement of paddy to exchange, people equal measure of white grainy salt for rice paddy"

People have seen paddy as an equivalent to salt there were mentions in Sangam literature songs proving it, what we can know from this Sangam literature songs is, in olden days of Tamil Nadu the salt was manufactured by the people of maritime regime especially fishers among them, After cutting the tunnels for salt water and building the salt-bed the salt was manufactured using this method and it was brought in exchange of paddy after that, the salt traders have carried it using donkeys and bullock carts and transported it to multiple places and sold the salt via commodity exchange these salt traders are called "UMANARGAL" in Sangam literature. Earlier, the fisherman had the salt manufacturing as a business but today, they have forgotten the business completely and run to stores to get salt. This position change is said to be happened in the period of Pallavas and Britishers, that too the Pallavas realized the high income in salt manufacturing and made all the salt-begs as government aided organizations then, they announced that the salt-beds can be taken for lease by people. Fishermen didn't have such wealth. But salt sellers had earned well by selling salt. so, they gave the lease amount asked by the government and leased the sea-beds employed other community people as labourers and started the salt manufacturing. This is how, Salt sellers became salt manufactures in parallel, fisherman forgot the business of salt manufacturing, this has been mentioned in "UPPITTAVARAI" book by A. Sivasubramanian, A social researcher who wrote many important books on salt.

Salt has one more important in Tamil as how the word salary originated from Salt Likewise, people say that the word "SAMBALAM" originated based on the salt manufacturing. How means, the salt manufacturing field is called as "ALAM". That's why, it is called as "UPPALAM" (Salt field). They used to give "SAMBA RICE" as a wage to the workers of salt-field. People started to say it as "SAMBA-ALAM", which later turned into "SAMBALAM". Every time when you got your salary, take a moment and think of salt Likewise, Tamilians have named the places or large salt-field after their kings that's how, "PERALAM and KOVALAM" have originated. Even in food, salt has been placed in a prime position in the Tamil custom, after placing a banana leaf to eat the first item served is Salt in the left corner but, even in this custom, there is a small social politics it has been documented by Mr. Tho. Paramasivan (Tamil Author). He is stating that, only the high caste people had the habit of eating salt separately whereas the oppressed working community people had the habit of adding salt when the food is being cooked also, they were permitted only to do so he has documented their salt is seen as the destroyer of an evil power that's why removing the cast evil eyes using salt has been a tradition Likewise, Hindu's sea salt as goddess Lakshmi. It has been a tradition to light salt lamps on certain days.

There is a huge connection between Jews and Salt. Jews see the salt as an agreement made with God. Salt is considered as a very pure thing in Christianity, just like holy water, some churches offer pure salt to the followers even in the Muslim community, salt is seen as a token of agreement, even Buddhism places salt in a very superior position Likewise, in all the religions around the world salt is placed in a superior position. There have been multiple wars for salt trading, many countries fought wars for their ownership of salt Likewise, in earlier days, many ships have transported salt via oceans. People have revolutionized many times opposing the taxes imposed on salt. The important reason for the French Revolution is the taxes imposed on Salt. When we are discussing about the salt taxes, we should also discuss about the taxes imposed on us by the Britishers. Even in the Mughal Period, salt was taxed, Mughals have collected 5 percent tax from Hindus and 2.5 percent from Muslims. But no government has tried to overtake the salt business in India except the British. What did they do? You would have heard about the Great Wall of China but, have you heard about a Great Wall built by the Britishers in India for Salt? "Starting from Maharashtra's Burhanpur through the route of Madhya Pradesh, Uttar Pradesh, Haryana and Sind of Pakistan there was a Wall which has extended till the borders of Kashmir. Actually, it was not a wall, it was a fence for salt. It was a fence built by the British to get the salt tax mercilessly from the people, initially the fence was constructed by the "East Indian Company" then the wall continued to exist even after the regime was taken by England Monarchy. In earlier Bengal, 3 paise was collected as tax for one bundle of salt but, Britishers changed it to 3.25 rupees after their victory. In simple words to understand, to earn salt for a family for one year, they need to pay 2 months' salary as tax. Such a huge tax was collected there, People started to manufacture salt in small quantities to handle the huge taxes imposed but the British government has banned this initiative. Then, they tried to smuggle & use salt from eastern parts of the country like Gujarat but the Britishers tried to stop this process too that's why, they created this fence.

The construction of this fence started in 1803 and ended in 1869, initially this fence was constructed shortly using palings later it was constructed with huge walls with a height of 12 feet. This fence wall was 2500 miles long, if the British government has employed 14000people to guard this wall think, how much would the government have earned through this salt tax? But, after a common salt tax was established all over the India, **everyone has forgotten about such a wall just like Athipatti village gone, there is no trace of this wall anywhere, not in any government gazettes, none of the Indian writers have documented about this wall.** But there was a wall like this and people suffered heavily because of the wall also, there were severe punishments for those who tried to cross the wall these are all well searched and documented by a Britisher **His name is Roy Moxham.** In 1995, in an old bookstore in England Roy Moxham got a dairy note of a British officer who worked in India in 1800s, in which, how a large wall like this was constructed in India based on that, how salt taxes are charged he has mentioned all these in his notes. After reading that, Roy Moxham was truly surprised, is there a wall constructed like this truly? Why there are no notes on it? He started to search for them but there were no notes on it anywhere. He came to India and he searched for the wall for 3 years in every village and every street later, he found a small part of the wall, which is remaining now, and released a book as his travel document. The book called as **"THE GREAT HEDGE OF INDIA"** has showcased the tortures done by the British to extract the tax from the people, it also documents as how the British looted us in more painful words. The author "CYRIL ALEX" has translated the book as "UPPU VELI" in Tamil.

The common salt tax established by the British government later was very terrible even a small amount of salt needed by people for themselves cannot be boiled, cut down, manufactured. This was the new salt tax if violated, severe punishments were given also, all the manufactured salt should be sold only to the government and the government will decide the price of it. It should not be sold to anyone else British government has announced these rules. Due to this, the price of salt increased abundantly, people were forced to spent 25 percent of their earnings to purchase salt.

At that time, by opposing it, Mahatma Gandhi took salt as a great weapon, as an extension of the non-cooperation movement, He start Salt Satyagraha as an opposition for the law which started salt cannot be manufactured without license Gandhi has announced that Indians will manufacture the salt needed for them also, as a symbol of implementing that Gandhi marched to Dandi and took salt on April 06, 1930. The vibration made by him echoed all over India. Then, the British government bowed down to the people's Revolution later, the British announced that people can manufacture the salt by themselves but, the manufactured salt should be carried only over the heads by the British government allowed salt manufacturing with the above restriction. Like this, we were tortured by imposing taxes on normal salt by the British government. But today, the same Britishers Company "British salt" is owned by "TATA Group". When I say TATA, we may remember "TATA SALT" even though it is TATA Salt, it is a corporate company, by being a corporate company, what is the impact on salt? This is Pin-Pointed to us by new world politics. As there are many Americans with Iodine deficiency American government thought about how to add Iodine in people's daily food so they chose Salt to do that. That's why America created Iodized-Salt, they even broadcast it all over the world by saying it as the right way. It is also broadcast in India too. That's how, the Iodized salt came into existence. The main reason for the creation of Iodized salt is the ideology of bringing in big corporate companies into the salt manufacturing. After this, many grand-dads and grand-moms have disappeared from the sea fields and these sea-fields were handed over to big corporate companies.

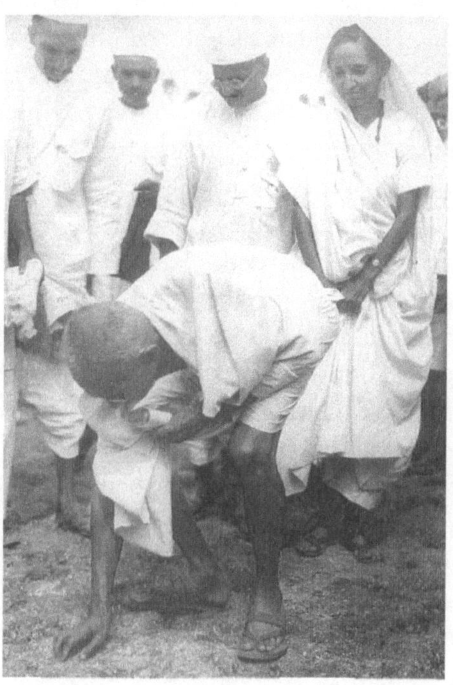

In earlier days consumption of Iodized salt was promoted heavily as too good Likewise, in recent times they are promoting this salt. It is called as Himalayan salt as the salt is found in the Himalayas. That is called as Indu Salt in Tamil, consumption of Indu Salt is very good for our body, it gives good strength to us, they say all these things but none of these statements have proven records. It is seen as a marketing strategy, why is it seen as a strategy? It is because of the 2 countries' politics behind this even if it is named as "INDU SALT" even if it is promoted as India's Salt or salt generated from the Indian Himalayas, the actual place of "INDU SALT" generated in Pakistan. We are getting this Indu salt in large quantities from

Pakistan Himalayas, it is cut through tunnels and it is exported to India by Pakistan. India creates many products like table salt from it. They label it as "MADE IN INDIA" and sell them all over the world. In this process, the profits are very less for Pakistan. The profit for Pakistan for exporting 1 ton of Indu salt is 40 American dollars only but, if they export it to Europe, they will get a profit of 300 American Dollars. As they don't have proper facilities to process the salt in Pakistan, they are completely dependent on India. But, in 2020, after Imran Khan became the Prime Minister, he banned the export of Indu salt to India. He decided that all the operations should run from Pakistan. But the problem is, there were no companies in Pakistan that can generate the products in the standard quality which the Europeans expect. Therefore, the Indu salt business became stagnant in Pakistan. There are so many types of salt today all over the world.

In 2020 alone, 270 million tonnes of salt have been manufactured all over the world. That too, China is the largest manufacturer of salt, next comes America and India is in the third position. The state which manufactures a large amount of salt is Gujarat, Tamil Nadu is in the second position after Gujarat. Tuticorin is the place where the highest amount of salt is manufactured in Tamil Nadu. When people had more physical work, salt became very essential for us, that's why, in the 18th and 19th Centuries when they extracted the work from slaves to compensate them, they served foods that had more salt in them. But today, the physical work has come down to a maximum extent. so, the doctors are suggesting we reduce the consumption of salt because in-taking large quantities of salt will cause kidney-related problems and blood pressure will increase they are stating this as the reason. Even WHO recommends us to in-take at least 5 grams of salt daily. Like this, salt has started from the evolution of humans but, today it became a part of our normal life. Even today, salt has become a common term in many cultures & languages of the world.

"Salt has a solution to all types of problems

It may be in the tears that roll down or

In our sweat or in the waves which caress our legs"

Suppose, if you are worried, Go to the Salt...!

CHAPTER TWENTY-NINE

BLACK GOLD

A lot of people would say, the smaller the anchor, the bigger the ship stops. Similarly, she is the little pepper that turned this world upside down. The black gold is an object that this world has been searching for, it is pepper. Just as petrol is what determines the economy today, it was once determined by the pepper. For hundreds of years, thousands of ships sailed along the shores of the Indian subcontinent in search of this black gold mine. Because India is the only mine that can produce that black gold.

Yes, pepper is the summer that India gave to this world. Especially the summer gave by South India. This pepper had a huge impact on the world. The pride, specialty, and history of the Tamils, especially the Tamils, are intertwined in this pepper politics.

This pepper is a contemporary witness to the fact that this South Indian land was once ruled by the Cheras, Cholas, and Pandyas as the focal point of the world economy. The climate in southern India, especially in Kerala, was favourable for growing pepper, so it was here that pepper was most abundant. The port of Musiri, which was under the rule of the Cheras, was the gateway to Pepper in ancient times. Ships were coming in to take tons of pepper from that gate. The beginnings of such ships date back to before the time of the Greeks. Before the introduction of our pepper to the Greeks, or about the same time, there was the introduction of the pepper called Pippali, which may have been present in North India. Pippali is Thippili. The Greek people generally thought that this Thippili and pepper were one and the same. In fact, the Greeks called it Pippali (Thippili) in Sanskrit, and over time it became known as Pepper.

The Greek philosopher Strabo, who lived in 64 BC, records that more than 120 ships sailed each year to bring pepper to Greece from India. The book Periplus of the Eritrean Sea, which is believed to have been written in AD 40, contains references to pepper being taken from Malabar to Greece and Romans. When the Greeks fell and the Romanian Empire came to power this pepper trade was going on for them too. The Romanian philosopher Pliny the Elder, who lived in 70 CE, recorded in his writings how much tipple and pepper were sold in Greece and Rome. It says that Thippili was sold for 15 silver coins and pepper for 7 silver coins. Although the Alkali of Thippili was higher than that of pepper, the demand for Pepper in the ancient world was higher than that of Thippili at a cheaper price. Due to this, more and more ships came to the coastal areas of South India in search of peppers.

Do not underestimate the quality of pepper just because its price is low. The selling price of pepper in those days was viewed in exchange for gold. That is why it is called black gold. Pepper was used as a medicine in Greece and Rome. After that pepper became an important part of their main course. Seventy percent of the dishes mentioned in the Roman cookbook name"Apicius", written in the first century CE, contain pepper. Similarly, the Greeks and Romans used this pepper to mixed in Wine. This pepper was seen as a very expensive commodity. So, there was a situation where only the rich and kings could buy this pepper.

This is why the pepper trade was one of the most lucrative businesses of that time. Pepper imported from India was stored in a warehouse built for this purpose in Alexandria (Egypt) and put in a multi-layer security. In those days pepper was consider equal to gold value used as cash in exchange goods. There is a reference in the Sanskrit literature that pepper, which was such a valuable commodity, was mostly taken by the Greeks and Romans from the town of Musiri. In ancient Tamil the name of the pepper was karungari (கரூங்கரி) was mentioned in the book "Cultural Movements" in Tamil (பண்பாட்ட்ᴗஅசவைᴗகள்) written by Tho.Paramasivan. The Ancient Tamil people used the name Yamanargal in Tamil (எமனர்கள்) for the outer nut peoples like the Romans and Greeks. In fact, the ancient Tamils called this pepper Yamanapriyain Tamil (எமனப்பிரிய) as it was a favorite food of foreigners. An Ancient literacy called in Tamil (எட்டᴗத்தொகைபாடல்) depicting the town of Musiri Town, where huge ships come and go to buy pepper with gold.

A Pattinapalai song describes the Kaveri boompattinam as a port where piles of pepper bundles could come and go for export from the Chera country. In fact, researchers have found fossils of pepper from the nose of a processed mummy of Pharoah Ramses II, who died in the year 1213 BCE, long before the Greeks.

So, just think about the Tamil Peoples, how long before had a trading relationship with many countries.

An excavation of a manuscript dating to the 2nd century AD has uncovered a treaty between two merchants. The agreement stated that 250 tons of pepper, ivory, and clothing would be shipped from India to Alexandria. Foreign traders have been pouring gold in exchange for the pepper taken from here. That is why ancient Tamil Nadu became a prosperous place in the world. Another thing to note is that another place where pepper is grown in large quantities is the Indonesian islands like Sumatra and Java. It is said to have bordered those islands during the Chola period. Like the Greeks, the Chinese bought more pepper from us. Pepper was also used medicinally in China, after which they used pepper as their staple food. The recipe for cooking peppers taken from here as early as the 6th century AD is mentioned in the book Chi Min Yao Shu. Similarly, there are references to the importation of pepper in the Tang Dynasty. Pepper prices have been high in China as well as in Greece and Roman times. Like Marco polo, who travelled to India and China in the 16th century AD, he mentions in all reference books that pepper was imported from China by ship in bundles. Although pepper is an expensive commodity in other countries, it was seen as a part of our lives in India, especially in Tamil Nadu. Sprinkle pepper on the meat available on the hunt and eat shot in the fire. The British, who came to India in search of pepper and then ruled India, became adamant that this pepper's water.

Did the British come to India in search of Pepper?

Yes, pepper is the main reason why the British come here.

Beginning with this, the pepper trade went into the story of the Arabs after the Roman period. The pepper trade route to countries such as the Greeks, Romans, and Arabs is historically referred to as the Spice Route. This spice route contained not only pepper but also salmon and bark. But the value of chillywas high compared with other ingredients. Two things were bigger with the Romans as they expanded their dominance throughout Europe, one was Christianity and the other was this pepper-based cuisine. As the Greeks, Romans, and Europeans also became addicted to this pepper, the spice route trade went to its peak. Those who were in control of the pepper trade at that time were magnified among other nations. It was the Arabs at that time who traded most of the pepper from Malabar. It spread from the Arabs to other European countries through Italy. It was at that time that the crusades to keep Christianity took place. Wars broke out between the Arab countries that followed Islam and the European countries that could follow Christianity. Due to this war, other European countries continued to seek to provide trade routes for the Arabs and to reduce Italy's dominance in the pepper trade. Some of the most important of these were the Europeans' search for an alternative route to India. The fuel for that search was their love for pepper. Vasco da Gama was the first European to arrive in India by conquering and converting in an effort beyond that. When he arrived at the port of Calicut in Kerala, he was greeted enthusiastically by the King samoothiri.

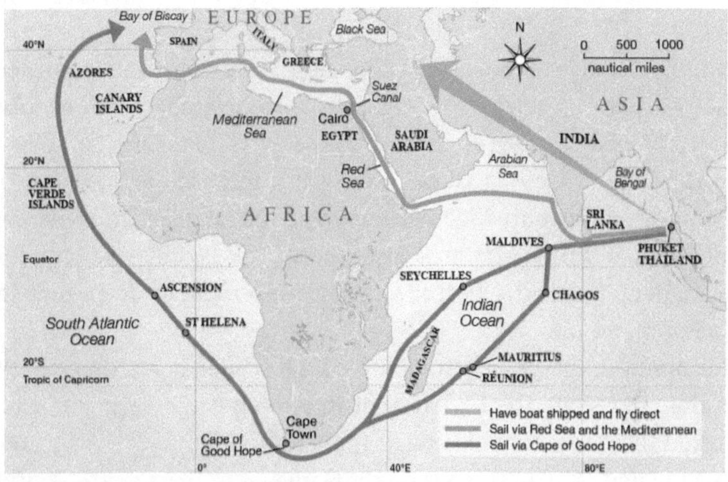

King Samoothiri would ask why you came to India, and Vasco da Gama said that I had come here in search of Christians and pepper. This is how the Europeans came to India out of commercial greed under the guise of protecting Christianity and Christians. Vasco da Gama told King Samudri that the boards should make an agreement with the government to trade pepper. But the gifts he took for the king were never so great. Vasco da Gama brought only a few garments and a few hats, but Vasco da Gama did not bring any material for the king. So, everyone there laughed at Vasco da Gama. The king said to Vasco da Gama that if we buy as a gift, we will buy only gold or silver and will not buy anything else. He also said that if you want pepper, give gold like the others and worship it. But Vasco da Gama Boards returned to the country, where he was given a rousing his. Later, under the guidance of Vasco da Gama, the Portuguese led by Pedro Alvares Cabral came to India and traded. But the sectarian conflict that already existed between the Portuguese and the Arabs began to provoke great unrest in India as well.

The Portuguese camp was crushed by the Arabs. Pedro Alvarez Cabral writes to her government that the reason for this is the king in India. In retaliation for that attack, 15 ships led by Vasco da Gama left the boards and camped at Calicut. At the same time, a ship set sail from Calicut carrying passengers on a pilgrimage to Mecca. Vasco da Gama turned the ship around and abducted all the passengers on board, including the women and children, and tied up the ship's owner and the Egyptian ambassador on their board.

As the problem worsened, the king sent an envoy to make peace with the Vasco da Gama. But Vasco da Gama cut off the ambassador's mouth and hand and stitched the dog's ear and Vasco da Gama sent the ambassador back to the king. Vasco da Gama also sent a message to the king that he would stop the attack only if he massacred all the Islamists in the slums. The king denied it, and then war broke out there. The Portuguese plundered all parts of Calicut. Thus, the Portuguese began to plunder and exercise their complete domination.

Think about it, the pepper trade in India has been going on smoothly for generations. But since the first European person came here, riots and war have kicked the peace that existed in India until then.

This violence, started by Vasco da Gama, was the footsteps of all the colonial domination that began here after him. The Portuguese began too high. After that, they became the benefactors of the whole world. Other European nations began to try to capture India by handing over those Portuguese. The East India Company was started by some employers in India. At that time there were rivalries between the East India Company and the Dutch Company called VOC. Britain's boom in this war that claimed many lives. It also made them a superpower. Columbus came to discover India because of this kind of wealth in India and Columbus discovered America by Accidentally some confusion.

Just think, some of the countries that dominate India are for some goods that are within our figure size.

Summary

PART I: EXTRA ADDED ILLUMINATI FAMILIES
The dominance of cash crocodiles is increasing.
PART II: WORLD WAR'S
1. WORLD WAR 1
The First World War, a war that set world history apart, A war that has ruthlessly massacred more lives in the world, the war that ended the British rule that turned the world into its own colony.
2. WORLD WAR II
World War II taught the people of the world the lesson that an atomic bomb could have an impact on people's lives. The power map of the world was turned upside down. The world's ruling powers are the nations that emerged as power at the end of World War II.
3. COLD WAR
The indirect war between America and Russia after the end of World War II.
PART III: THE NEW WORLD
1. OVERVIEW
America is known as the new world. America is the powerful country between the other countries in the world. And also called the Modern Illuminati Nation.
2. ARRIVAL OF COLUMBUS
In the 15th and 16th centuries, Europeans wanted to find sea routes to the Far East. Columbus wanted to find a new route to India, China, Japan, and the Spice Islands. If he could reach these lands, he would be able to bring back rich cargoes of silks and spices. He accidentally found the new world.
3. SLAVERY
Throughout the 17th and 18th centuries, people were kidnapped from the continent of Africa, forced into slavery in the American colonies, and exploited to work as indentured servants and labor in the production of crops such as tobacco and cotton.
4. CORPORATE PLAN (THE GREAT DEPRESSION)
It began after the stock market crash of October 1929, which sent Wall Street into a panic and wiped-out millions of investors. Over the next several years, consumer spending and investment dropped, causing steep declines in industrial output and employment as failing companies laid-off

workers.

5. MONEY CONTROL

The U.S. dollar remains the strongest world currency. It may continue to be the top global currency in the years to come.

6. FIRST BANK OF ENGLAND

Bank of England was the first bank of showing their politics to control and enslaved the people.

7. FEDERAL RESERVE BANK (BEHIND POLITICS)

The Fed can influence the money supply by modifying reserve requirements, which generally refers to the amount of funds banks must hold against deposits in bank accounts. By lowering the reserve requirements, banks are able to loan more money, which increases the overall supply of money in the economy.

8. ABRAHAM LINCOLN DEATH

Some money bosses enslave people for money, and death is more than enough for a person who thinks he should oppose it and make people live freely.

9. 2008 PREDICTION

The world was affected by the greed of some banks in the United States. We do not respect a genius who predicted it in 2005. This is just an average thing that happens in our world. We do not listen to a nerd, but we keep celebrating after what he said has happened. This has become our routine. If only we had listened to what he had to say, maybe our India would have survived this accident.

10. OSAMA BIN LADEN (BEHIND POLITICS)

They reject that the CIA or other American authorities had contact with Bin Laden, not to mention outfitted, prepared, trained, or influenced him. American researchers and correspondents have called the possibility of a CIA-upheld Al Qaeda "garbage", "sheer dream", and a "typical legend". U.S. government authorities and various different gatherings keep up with that the U.S. upheld just the native Afghan mujahideen. Canister Laden himself once said "The breakdown of the Soviet Union goes to God and the mujahideen in Afghanistan. The US played no mentionable part," however "breakdown made the US haughtier and more presumptuous."

11. CORONAVIRUS AND EVENT 201

Event 201 simulates an outbreak of a novel zoonotic coronavirus transmitted from bats to pigs to people that eventually become efficiently transmissible from person to person, leading to a severe pandemic. The pathogen and the disease it cause are modelled largely on SARS, but it is more transmissible in the community setting by people with mild symptoms.

The disease starts in pig farms in Brazil, quietly and slowly at first, but then it starts to spread more rapidly in healthcare settings. When it starts to spread efficiently from person to person in the low-income, densely packed neighbourhoods of some of the megacities in South America, the epidemic explodes. It is first exported by air travel to Portugal, the United States, and China and then to many other countries. Although at first some countries are able to control it, it continues to spread and be reintroduced, and eventually no country can maintain control.

There is no possibility of a vaccine being available in the first year. There is a fictional antiviral drug that can help the sick but not significantly limit spread of the disease.

Since the whole human population is susceptible, during the initial months of the pandemic, the cumulative number of cases increases exponentially, doubling every week. And as the cases and deaths accumulate, the economic and societal consequences become increasingly severe.

The scenario ends at the 18-month point, with 65 million deaths. The pandemic is beginning to slow due to the decreasing number of susceptible people. The pandemic will continue at some rate until there is an effective vaccine or until 80-90 % of the global population has been exposed. From that point on, it is likely to be an endemic childhood disease.

Note the Point: This Event conducted in October 2019, and the first Coronavirus case was filed in December 2019. How is this possible? How they conduct this Event before knowing Coronavirus in the World? Think yourself and search for Yourself...!

PART IV: COMMUNISM

1. ABOUT

Communism, which was started with a good intention, has now changed its purpose. Communism is supposed to make everything equally available to all, but communism has not been able to succeed in opposing world politics. The very purpose for which communism was started changed and we became addicted to money.

2. KARL MARX

Marx's most famous hypothesis was 'recorded realism', contending that a set of experiences is the consequence of material circumstances, rather than thoughts. He accepted that religion, profound quality, social designs, and different things are completely established in financial matters. In his later life, he was more open-minded toward religion.

3. VLADIMIR LENIN

Vladimir Lenin thought that communist political views should be spread all over the world. But his intention did not last. He died within a year of taking office. And even the leaders who came after him could not spread it all over the world. Because at that time the dominance of the Capitalism was high.

4. JOSEPH STALIN

Joseph Stalin was the main reason for Russia's victory over the nations of the world in World War II. Although portrayed as a protagonist in the worldview, he portrayed himself as a beast among the people of his own country. Because he killed his own people.From 1928 until his passing in 1953, Joseph Stalin controlled the Soviet Union as a despot, changing the country from an agrarian laborer society into a worldwide superpower.

PART V: AFRICAN RESOURCES

This world is earning by keeping the country of Africa as if stealing traps from the homes of others for our hunger. Some of the richest countries in the world are living happily using the country of Africa. Imagine for a second, how wealthy is Africa. But all this is unknown to the political leaders in Africa. Because there is no proper scholarship yet.

1. BLACK PANTHER

If we close our eyes thinking of the country of Africa, we will remember the people who live with hunger and starvation. But at one time the people of Africa lived in affluence. In particular, Africa's economic growth was at its peak during the reign of the wealthy king Mansa Musa. But even I don't know that, now African People still remember that great King?

2. EXPLOITATION OF AFRICA

Just as the European nations at that time saw the abundance of wealth in the country of India and competed to turn India into a colonial country and exploited the wealth here, just as the nations of the world are now exploiting the wealth there in the name of business, they indirectly destroying the Africa by richest countries like China, America.

3. CRUDE OIL RESOURCES

War has been raging between many countries based on this petrol since 1950 till now.

PART VI: EXTRA FOR YOU

1. TEA POLITICS

It is said that the butterfly effect and this tea were the main reason for the liberation of the United States, which is now ruling the world.

2. INDIA WAS DIVIDED BY WHITE

In the wonderful film Jai Bheem, actor Surya would say that we are still living in slavery because we do not know the history, and this salt was the reason why the wall in India split this country into two, just as a wall here in Berlin halved that country. Even more shocking is the fact that the first person to tell the world that this incident took place in India was a foreign writer.

3. BLACK GOLD

This pepper, which is not even on our finger size, has caused political turmoil in many countries around the world.

Reference

ILLUMINATI
Bloodlines of the Illuminati book by Fritz Spring Meier Volume 3
https://citeseerx.ist.psu.edu/viewdoc/
download?doi=10.1.1.475.3562&rep=rep1&type=pdf
WORLD WAR 1
https://en.wikipedia.org/wiki/World_War_I
https://www.sparknotes.com/history/european/ww1/summary/
https://history.state.gov/milestones/1914-1920/wwi
https://www.pacificatrocities.org/forgotten-history-of-pacific-asia-war-podcast.html
WORLD WAR II
https://en.wikipedia.org/wiki/World_War_II
https://www.kards.com/ww2?
gclid=EAIaIQobChMIyb7WqYf99QIVMZJmAh1AkAj5EAMYAyAAEgLMbvDBwE
https://www.beachesofnormandy.com/articles/Americas   politics
before -
World War II?id=17d8cc6709
https://www.thoughtco.com/overview-of-world-war-ii-105520
COLD WAR
https://www.jfklibrary.org/learn/about-jfk/jfk-in-history/the-cold-war
https://www.nationalgeographic.com/culture/article/cold-war
https://www.cvce.eu/content/publication/2011/11/21/
6dfe06ed-4790-48a4-8968-855e90593185/publishable_en.pdf
https://www.linkedin.com/pulse/chhatrapati-shivaji-maharaj-vietnam-raj-sharma
https://www.quora.com/What-is-the-true-link-between-Shivaji-Maharaj-and-the-US-
Vietnam-war-Was-there-a-similarity-in-their-guerrilla-tactics
https://en.wikipedia.org/wiki/Vietnam_War
https://www.space.com/space-race.html
https://www.jfklibrary.org/learn/about-jfk/jfk-in-history/cuban-missile-crisis
https://www.archives.gov/publications/prologue/2011/fall/berlin

THE NEW WORLD: OVERVIEW
https://www.quora.com/What-made-the-United-States-of-America-the-strongest-country
https://en.wikipedia.org/wiki/Potential_superpowers
ARRIVAL OF COLUMBUS
https://www.biography.com/news/christopher-columbus-day-facts
https://www.smithsonianmag.com/history/meet-the-indigenous-activist-who-toppled-minnesotas-christopher-columbus-statue-180979488/
https://gulfnews.com/games/play/word-search-see-how-trade-was-done-in-ancient-times-from-the-silk-road-to-the-spice-routes
https://www.premiumtimesng.com/opinion/505860-the-unraveling-of-the-portuguese-empire-a-historical-imperative-by-osmund-agbo.html
https://en.wikipedia.org/wiki/Christopher_Columbus
How The US Became One of the World's Superpower book by Baby Professor
SLAVERY
The History of Slavery in America Documentary
https://www.theguardian.com/news/2019/aug/15/400-years-since-slavery-timeline
How The US Became One of the World's Superpower book by Baby Professor
CORPORATE PLAN (THE GREAT DEPRESSION)
https://www.federalreservehistory.org/essays/great-depression
https://www.stlouisfed.org/-/media/project/frbstl/stlouisfed/files/pdfs/great-depression/the-great-depression-wheelock-overview.pdf
https://en.wikipedia.org/wiki/Great_Depression_in_the_United_States
How The US Became One of the World's Superpower book by Baby Professor
MONEY CONTROL
https://www.investopedia.com/articles/forex-currencies/092316/how-us-dollar-became-worlds-reserve-currency.asp
https://www.cfr.org/backgrounder/dollar-worlds-currency
https://en.wikipedia.org/wiki/Dollar

https://projects.exeter.ac.uk/RDavies/arian/dollar.html

How The US Became One of the World's Superpower book by Baby Professor

FIRST BANK OF ENGLAND

https://en.wikipedia.org/wiki/Bank_of_England

https://www.chicagofed.org/publications/economic-perspectives/1981/ep-

mar-apr1981-part4-wood

https://www.mindcontagion.org/banking/hb1763.html

https://founders.archives.gov/documents/Franklin/01-01-02-0041

FEDERAL RESERVE BANK (BEHIND POLITICS)

https://www.frbsf.org/education/teacher-resources/what-is-the-fed/history/

https://www.donaldwatkins.com/post/the-rothschilds-controlling-the-world-s-money-supply-for-more-than-two-centuries

https://www.forbes.com/sites/williammeehan/2020/10/21/can-the-federal-reserve-print-money-forever-or-how-continuing-to-print-

money-to-support-deficit-spending-may-end-badly-with-chinas-help/?sh=6ac47af458d4

https://www.investopedia.com/articles/investing/081415/understanding-how-federal-reserve-creates-money.asp

ABRAHAM LINCOLN DEATH

http://www.heritech.com/pridger/lincoln/lin-ken.htm

https://en.wikipedia.org/wiki/Greenback_(1860s_money)

https://www.mentalfloss.com/article/26624/abraham-lincoln-created-secret-service-day-he-was-shot

https://en.wikipedia.org/wiki/Abraham_Lincoln

2008 PREDICTION

https://economictimes.indiatimes.com/news/economy/indicators/ignoring-raghuram-rajans-2005-prediction-was-a-big-mistake-imf-chief-christine-lagarde/articleshow/46600576.cms?from=mdr

https://cleartax.in/s/why-economy-crashed-in-2008

OSAMA BIN LADEN (BEHIND POLITICS)

Confessions of an Economic Hit Man book by John Perkins

https://www.cfr.org/timeline/us-war-afghanistan

https://en.wikipedia.org/wiki/Allegations_of_CIA_assistance_to_Osama_bin_Laden

https://www.theatlantic.com/international/archive/2016/08/twenty-years-war/496736/

https://economictimes.indiatimes.com/topic/cia-osama-bin-laden-controversy

CORONAVIRUS AND EVENT 201

https://www.webmd.com/lung/coronavirus-history

https://www.insider.com/china-conspiracy-theory-claims-us-created-coronavirus-2021-1

https://www.nytimes.com/2020/03/13/world/asia/coronavirus-china-conspiracy-theory.html

https://www.centerforhealthsecurity.org/news/center-news/2020/2020-01-24-Statement-of-Clarification-Event201.html

https://www.centerforhealthsecurity.org/event201/scenario.html

https://www.centerforhealthsecurity.org/event201/

COMMUNISM: ABOUT

https://en.wikipedia.org/wiki/Communism

https://www.nationalgeographic.org/encyclopedia/communism/

KARL MARX

https://www.bbc.co.uk/history/historic_figures/marx_karl.shtml

https://www.investopedia.com/terms/k/karl-marx.asp

https://en.wikipedia.org/wiki/Karl_Marx

http://news.bbc.co.uk/2/hi/461545.stm

VLADIMIR LENIN

https://www.britannica.com/biography/Vladimir-Lenin

https://www.newworldencyclopedia.org/entry/Vladimir_Lenin

JOSEPH STALIN

https://en.wikipedia.org/wiki/Joseph_Stalin

https://www.bbc.co.uk/teach/joseph-stalin-national-hero-or-cold-blooded-murderer/zhv747h

AFRICA RESOURCES

https://www.nationalgeographic.org/encyclopedia/africa-resources/

https://en.wikipedia.org/wiki/Natural_resources_of_Africa

BLACK PANTHER

https://www.bbc.com/news/world-europe-46538253

https://www.nationalgeographic.org/encyclopedia/mansa-musa-musa-i-mali

https://en.wikipedia.org/wiki/Mansa_Musa

EXPLOITATION OF AFRICA

https://edition.cnn.com/2016/04/18/africa/looting-machine-tom-burgis-africa/index.html

https://www.forbes.com/sites/wadeshepard/2019/10/03/what-china-is-really-up-to-in-africa/?sh=299961dd5930

https://www.orfonline.org/research/china-in-africa/

https://en.wikipedia.org/wiki/United_States_Africa_Command

CRUDE OIL RESOURCES

https://en.wikipedia.org/wiki/Petroleum

https://en.wikipedia.org/wiki/History_of_the_petroleum_industry

https://en.wikipedia.org/wiki/History_of_the_oil_industry_in_India

TEA POLITICS

The Brief History of Tea book by Roy Moxham

A Taste of Time book by MohonaKanjilal

https://twitter.com/knowthenation/status/1301825358455422977?lang=en

Red Tea book by Paul Harris Daniel

Death of a River Documentary by R.R Srinivasan

https://en.wikipedia.org/wiki/History_of_tea_in_India

http://www.coffeeteawarehouse.com/tea-history.html

https://www.bostonteapartyship.com/boston-tea-party-history

https://www.bbc.co.uk/bitesize/articles/zm2txyc#:~:text=The%20world%20began%20to%20learn,drink%20that%20very%20few%20consumed.

INDIA WAS DIVIDED BY WHITE

The Great Hedge of India book by Roy Moxham

https://en.wikipedia.org/wiki/History_of_salt

https://en.wikipedia.org/wiki/Salt_March

https://www.erih.net/how-it-started/history-of-industries/salt

BLACK GOLD

Cultural Movements (பண்பாட்டு அசைவுகள்) book by Tho. Paramasivan

https://en.wikipedia.org/wiki/Black_pepper#Ancient_times

https://www.news18.com/news/lifestyle/on-this-day-portuguese-explorer-vasco-da-gama-set-foot-in-india-via-sea-in-1498-3756026.html

https://www.timesnownews.com/mirror-now/in-focus/article/over-520-yrs-ago-today-vasco-da-gama-landed-in-india-heres-how-he-discovered-the-country/759204

https://www.bbc.co.uk/history/british/tudors/
vasco_da_gama_01.shtml
https://www.atlasobscura.com/articles/long-pepper-better-than-black-
pepper#:~:text=With%20trade%20routes%20by%20sea,
cost%20a%20third%20as%20much.